The Marriage Bureau

PENROSE HALSON

The Marriage Bureau

The True Story of How Two Matchmakers Arranged
Love in Wartime London

WILLIAM MORROW

An Imprint of HarperCollins*Publishers*

HarperCollins books may be purchased for educational, business, or sales promotional use. For information, please email the Special Markets Department at SPsales@harpercollins.com.

Originally published as *Marriages Are Made in Bond Street* in the United Kingdom in 2016 by Macmillan, an imprint of Pan Macmillan.

FIRST WILLIAM MORROW EDITION

Library of Congress Cataloging-in-Publication Data has been applied for.

ISBN 978-0-062562661

17 18 19 20 21   DIX/RRD   10 9 8 7 6 5 4 3 2 1

For Bill, and in memory of Heather Jenner

CONTENTS

The Marriage Bureau

Prologue

"Buy a marriage bureau? You and me? You must be joking!"

"No," said Bill, "I'm totally serious. You can interview the clients and do the matchmaking—you're very good at that, I know—and I'll do the finances and the advertising. Come on, let's do it!"

So we did. In 1986, after a motley career in writing, editing and teaching, I found myself, aged forty-six, sitting in a cramped little office in a seedy alley off Oxford Street, nervously awaiting my first client as proprietress of the Katharine Allen Marriage & Advice Bureau.

"KA" had been founded in 1960, modeled closely on the Marriage Bureau established by Heather Jenner and Mary Oliver in 1939. In 1992, faced with a 700 percent rent increase, Heather Jenner's daughter asked me to take over her clients. So two small, eccentric, individualistic institutions became one. Their story begins in Assam, Northeast India, in 1938 . . .

I

Audrey's Uncle Has a Brain Wave

In 1938, farmer's daughter Audrey Parsons was staying with her uncle, a tea planter who managed a remote plantation in the hills of Assam. Audrey was twenty-four, pretty, petite and fragile-looking, with a pink and white complexion, dark hair, big brown eyes and an infectious laugh.

Six years earlier, after a whirlwind romance in England, she had sailed out to India to marry a young man who worked for her uncle. When she had first met him in England, Peter had seemed as exciting as Audrey could desire in a husband, and she had been in raptures as they went from ball to party in a dizzying round of gaiety. But in India she found him passionately (for him) and tediously (for her) absorbed in his work, and juvenile, dull and vapid when not busily engaged in planting tea.

"I am sorry, Uncle George," she had apologized, "but I simply cannot marry Peter. I shall go home and think what to do next."

Uncle George was exceedingly fond of his vivacious niece, and sympathized since, much as he liked Peter, who was an ideal employee, he could see that she was not cut out for a conventional marriage to a pleasant, straightforward but unoriginal man in a remote and lonely place. Sorrowfully he waved her goodbye, begging her to come back soon to add sparkle to his solitary life. Most of the time he was content, but the isolation of his plantation, miles from any of his handful of European neighbors, sometimes threatened to overwhelm him.

So Audrey had returned to her parents in Cambridgeshire. Her father, a down-to-earth farmer, was dismayed by her attitude: "I liked Peter. He's not a chinless wonder with a one-track mind, like you say he is, my girl—he's a decent fellow with a good future. You're being too picky, like you always have been, always wanting something else. What do you think you're going to do now? You can't stay here forever; I can't keep you. You don't like our farm anyway—you're always off to London whenever you can. Find yourself a husband and get out!"

Audrey's mother was a bit more lenient, but nevertheless insistent that Audrey had to marry. One of her two brothers would eventually take over the farm, which had been in the family for generations, and there would be no place for Audrey in the farmhouse.

But Audrey's brush with possible matrimony had made her long to try some other way of life. In a local newspaper she spotted an advertisement for a job in a factory, packing and labeling papers for dispatch. Determined to be independent and to earn some money, she applied and had a short interview with the factory manager, who was so startled that a girl so well-spoken and smartly dressed should want such a menial job that he bowed to her enthusiasm and said she could start next week.

Audrey found the work physically exhausting and mind-blowingly boring, but she earned £1 a week, which was just enough for her to live in factory girls' lodgings. By the end of the day she was weary, but not too tired to want some entertainment, of which there was none apart from the local cinema. The other girls regarded her with deep suspicion. Audrey did not dress like them, she did not talk like them, she was patently not one of them. They largely ignored her, excluding her from their interminable heart-to-hearts about makeup and boyfriends.

It did not take many weeks before Audrey quailed at the dismal prospect of confronting another mountain of parcels, and of turning a deaf ear to yet another animated description of the relative merits of Ted and Fred. However, she had proved herself to be an independent woman with a spirit of adventure. She continued to demonstrate her success by getting a job as a dentist's receptionist, making appointments and soothing fearful patients.

On her first day, the dentist instructed her to leave her desk to assist him with an extraction, during which she was to observe where the torn-out teeth landed, pick them up, and wipe the blood off the floor. She promptly handed in her notice, marched out banging the door behind her, and walked up the street, until a card in an office window caught her eye: a photographer's assistant was required.

Once again Audrey found it easy to get the job, but hard to like it enough to stay. The negatives were developed in a darkroom, which she found oppressive and almost frightening. Her employer added to her discomfort by reprimanding her sharply when, in the unaccustomed darkness, she dropped a vital roll of film, or bumped into a tank of precious developing liquid. Late every afternoon she stumbled blinking into the daylight, until she admitted defeat and handed in her notice before, she feared, she was told to go.

As the years passed, the thrill of being independent began to wear thin. Audrey yearned to travel, but could not afford to; and without qualifications, only menial work was open to her. She got a job delivering for a cake shop, but it ended when she was caught eating the tastiest cakes. Her final act of defiance was a job as a riding instructor. She was an excellent horsewoman, having been in the saddle since she was two, and a good teacher; but once again the job description had not been precise, and she jibbed when instructed to muck out the stables.

Audrey walked home from the riding school wondering what on earth to do next. In the hall of the farmhouse she found an air letter: Uncle George would gladly pay her fare if she would come and lighten his life again (and there would be no embarrassing meetings with Peter, since he now had his own tea plantation, many miles away).

Desperate to escape the recriminations of her father and the tight-lipped reproach of her mother, Audrey accepted this generous offer and once again took ship for Assam. Her uncle was delighted to have her company, and took her around to meet his neighbors, often half a day's ride away. Social occasions were few and far between, but Uncle George made an effort to entertain his favorite niece, introducing her to several single men. After her unsociable life in search of independence, Audrey got a kick out of flirting with the men, who were all itching to get married, but for whom there were scarcely any potential wives in Assam. At night, though, she lay in bed disconsolately considering her future: "I can't stay here for ever, and I can't go back home and flit from job to job. Perhaps I shall have to give up and get married after all."

So, in an uncharacteristically low moment, Audrey accepted the proposal of a most eligible man. However, as with her jobs, she found it easy to get engaged but hard to carry the engagement through to its logical conclusion: marriage. Her much older fiancé constantly lectured her about the wifely duties he expected. In return for his protection, she was to defer to her lord and master in an appropriately servile manner. Obeying would be the order of the day, not laughing and having fun and doing interesting things together. Growing more and more apprehensive, with a lavish and expensive wedding imminent, Audrey handed back her engagement ring.

Once again, Uncle George was sympathetic. His own hasty, superficially suitable marriage had brought misery to both him and his wife, who for many years had lived in England. Before his niece left, he made a suggestion that was to change life not only for Audrey but also for countless others: "When you get back to England, why not do something about introducing the single young men you've met here—and, you know, there are thousands more like them—to marriage-minded young women, during their leave in England? As you've observed, marriageable girls are like gold dust here, and when the men are back on leave it's hard for them to get to know the right sort of girls after being abroad for so long, and falling out of touch with their old friends. Think about it, my dear."

During the voyage back to England, Audrey pondered on this suggestion. It piqued her imagination. But what on earth could she do about it?

Back at her parents' farmhouse Audrey was greeted coldly. Mr. Parsons could scarcely conceal his anger at her failure to get off his hands by doing what every normal young woman did: get married. His wife too was becoming intolerant of Audrey's bizarre behavior. Why could not her only daughter behave like other girls?

Audrey sought escape, any escape, preferably to somewhere far, far away. She answered an advertisement for a lady's maid in the "Governesses, Companions, and Lady Helps" classified column of the *Lady* magazine, as the advertiser, an autocratic widow, said she was about to embark for the Far East. Audrey was paid twelve shillings and sixpence a week, plus her board and lodging. Preparing her extensive wardrobe for the voyage, the widow instructed Audrey to sew in old-fashioned dress preservers, designed to protect clothes from underarm perspiration. Thinking these strange objects were padding, Audrey sewed them neatly and firmly into the shoulders of all her employer's dresses. She was promptly dismissed.

Not finding another job abroad, Audrey settled for becoming a games mistress, which she loathed, and then a chauffeuse. Her parents had refused to let her learn to drive in their car, for in any case why did she need to drive? Her husband would do any necessary driving. Fortunately her employer, a neurotic old woman who took drugs to calm her nerves, was so sedated that she did not notice that, driving up Ludgate Hill, Audrey sped along the pavement.

Audrey's final employer, an equally elderly but iron-nerved lady, took her on as skipper on her private yacht. Audrey could scarcely tell a yacht from a canoe, but in the train on her way down to the east coast she read some informative books, picked up the basics, and took to running the forty-five-foot sloop-rigged sailing yacht like a duck to water. Fortunately the very nice old lady went to bed early, so every evening Audrey picked the brains of the skippers in the pubs by the harbor, and soon managed as if she had been born at sea.

The old lady pulled the plug on the only job Audrey had thoroughly enjoyed when she decided her sailing days were over, and retired to a comfortable flat in Kensington. Audrey had no choice but to go back to the unwelcoming farm, and accepted with alacrity the invitation of a girlfriend to go and stay in London.

• • •

At a Chelsea party, Audrey met Heather Lyon.

Ex-debutante Heather was twenty-four, strikingly handsome, party loving, strong-minded, six foot tall, with heavy blond hair, a throaty, sexy voice, and a commanding presence. After being presented at Court and "doing the Season" in London, she had sailed out to join her father, a British Army brigadier, in Ceylon. One of a tiny handful of young white women, surrounded by hordes of young and not-so-young British Army officers, colonial servants, businessmen, tea planters and missionaries—all males starved of female company—Heather was feted and flattered, wined, dined and worshipped. Dizzied by her popularity, lulled by the luxurious comfort provided by umpteen servants, warmed by the exotic sunshine, she was wooed so assiduously that at nineteen she was married.

A suitable marriage at nineteen was the natural first step along the conventional path for a young woman of Heather's background, to be followed as night succeeds day by children, housekeeping, and entertaining in furtherance of her husband's career. But Heather was feeling her way toward a less subservient, more independent existence. Her husband was nonplussed. The marriage quickly foundered, and Heather sailed back to England as a single woman.

Heather with a broken marriage and Audrey with two broken engagements had failed to comply with the unwritten rules of their sex, age and class. Lacking husbands, what were they to do next? They were both in the same boat, and their common determination to find a future drew them together.

"Listen, Heather," urged Audrey, "my Uncle George gave me an idea. In fact, I think it's a brain wave. Remember what it was like on the ship you came back on? Hardly any girls among masses of men, most of them going back home to find a wife, lonely and sex-starved and forlorn, poor lambs. On my ship they kept giving me the glad eye—I could have been engaged half a dozen times before we even got into port! They visit their families in England, but every second of the day they're on the prowl for a girl to marry. If they don't find one, in a couple of months they have to go back to Ceylon or India or wherever, and they won't have leave again for years and years. And you know what it's like in Ceylon: there are so few girls that most of those chaps haven't got a hope in hell of finding a wife, or they marry the first halfway presentable one who comes along—and we both know how dire that can be! So while they're on leave in England, we could help them. We could introduce them to suitable girls, starting with our girlfriends. I've got plenty who can't find a decent man in England, and I'm sure you have too. What a waste. The men come over here, the girls are already here, they all want to get together but they never meet! Let's introduce them—let's start a marriage agency!"

Heather was intrigued, but thought the idea was a joke, not a serious proposition. She had only just arrived back in London, where an allowance from her father paid for a small flat so she could enjoy a gay life of parties, gossip and flirtations, interspersed with bits of work as an actress and model. She said she would think about it, but did not mean to. The two girls exchanged addresses and parted.

Audrey returned to the farm, her mind buzzing. She had often worried away at Uncle George's idea like a dog with a particularly meaty bone, convinced that it had a future; but had thought it too difficult to undertake by herself. Now, Heather struck her as exactly the right partner: she had a real understanding of the problem, the impressive poise and self-confidence of her class, a good brain and stunning looks. Audrey determined to keep in touch with Heather, and to do some research.

Fobbing off her parents by saying that she was visiting a London friend who socialized with a crowd of nice young men, Audrey went along to Scotland Yard. In a small bare room she inquired of a startled policeman whether a marriage agency, introducing single people in search of a matrimonial partner, would be breaking the law in any way. The astonished copper scratched his head in puzzlement over this unusual request, but could find no objection, nor any record of any existing marriage agency. So Audrey returned home, refusing to explain the enigmatic smile that baffled and irked her parents.

Audrey bought one of the weekly matrimonial newspapers that carried seductive advertisements, placed by people seeking or offering themselves as spouses. But such advertisements, extolling the virtues of potential wealthy husbands and beautiful wives, were often invented by the newspapers themselves or by agencies advertising under box numbers, and could not be trusted: Audrey had heard of a swindle operated by a cynical pair, a Frenchwoman who had introduced her lover to three single ladies looking for a husband, charging each one about £70. When arrested, she had been sentenced to eighteen months in prison, and the lover to two years. Determined to investigate this shady world, Audrey invested £5 of her £15 capital in advertising for a husband.

To her amazement and mounting alarm, letter after letter was forwarded to the farm by the matrimonial paper. Her parents suspected something was afoot but, seeing the uncompromising look in Audrey's eye and the mulish set of her lips, they shrugged their shoulders and asked no questions. She took to intercepting the postman before he reached the farmhouse, and hurrying up to her bedroom, where she read the often illiterate but flattering self-portraits of wife-seekers, mostly unsuitable: railway porters, bus drivers, commercial travelers, bank clerks, farm laborers, tailors, rat catchers, postmen, plowmen, salesmen, doormen.

Plucking up her courage, Audrey replied to a pleasant-sounding teacher, whose letter, on headed writing paper, correctly spelled, stood out from the rest. She met him one afternoon in Cambridge, where for an awkward hour they made stilted conversation before saying a formal, relieved farewell.

The next day Audrey was walking to the village bakery when a little man outfitted in a black suit, high-collared white shirt, maroon tie and highly polished black shoes, carrying a neatly furled umbrella and an incongruous string shopping bag, tipped his bowler hat to her, as in a reedy voice he inquired, "Excuse me, Miss, I beg your pardon, but I should be grateful if you could assist me. I am looking for Hall Farm, the residence of Miss Audrey Parsons. If you are cognizant of the whereabouts of that establishment, would you be so kind as to direct me?"

Comprehending in a flash that the matrimonial paper had mistakenly parted with her name and address instead of forwarding a reply to her, Audrey lied like a trooper: "Oh, certainly. But I fear that you are not in luck, since my friend Miss Parsons is in London today."

His face registered such disappointment that Audrey felt a momentary twinge of guilt, and asked solicitously: "Have you come far? Was she expecting you today?"

"No, my presence was not anticipated by the young lady. Notwithstanding, it is with great regret that I shall not have the pleasure of making her acquaintance today. However, I shall return on another occasion. It is my good fortune to live but a few miles from this charming village, and to be in possession of a car." Transferring the shopping bag to the same hand as that clutching the umbrella, he pointed at a dark green Austin 7 parked in the road. His chest swelled with ineffable pride. "I purchased this vehicle with the profit from my shop. Alas, there were naysayers in the village who expressed their opinion that the proceeds of trade should not be expended on earthly pleasures, in particular not by a follower of Christ. However, I am persuaded that Our

Lord would not have gainsaid my action, which was taken not simply for the gratification of myself, but also for the delectation of my future wife. You see, Miss, I anticipate entering the state of holy matrimony in the very near future. I am desirous of acquiring a suitable wife—that is to say, a young lady in my station of life."

Audrey was mesmerized by the little man's high, singsong voice, his fulsome language, and visions of a forgiving Jesus standing at his shoulder—or perhaps driving the Austin 7, pictured Audrey irreverently. Driving to a station? Unable to resist, forcing herself not to laugh, she asked, "And what is your station in life?"

The little man drew himself up to his full five feet four inches as he proclaimed, "I am a butcher, Miss. I own my own butcher's shop. I work hard, and on Sundays I have the honor to serve Our Lord as sidesman in our church."

As he paused for Audrey's admiration and approbation, the postman, looking hot and flustered, approached on his bicycle. Seeing Audrey, he drew up and, panting, handed her some letters. "I'm glad to see you, Miss Parsons. I'm on the late side, so I'd be grateful if you would take these back to the farm—they're for you and your father."

Audrey seized the letters, mumbling and blushing, fully aware that the little man was wearing a puzzled expression

"Miss Parsons?" he queried, more uncertain than accusatory. "A farm? Are there two Miss Parsons living on a farm in this village?"

Audrey could stand her own deceitfulness no longer. "No!" she confessed, screwing up her eyes as if to blind herself to her own wickedness. "No, there is only one, and I am she. I am most dreadfully sorry."

"But why did you not enlighten me at the outset?"

Despite her distress Audrey's mind was functioning at top speed. She simply could not tell him that one look at him had been enough to make her lie. Now she took refuge in a second glib untruth. "Because I am already suited. I did not want to mislead you. I am so sorry."

"Ah, Miss, you misjudged me. I should have delighted in felicitating you on your future happiness, as indeed I do now. May the Lord bless you. And before I take my leave may I offer you this small gift." The little man reached into the string bag and withdrew a large and lumpy parcel, wrapped up in brown paper and securely tied with thick string. He handed it to Audrey, tipped his hat, bowed slightly, turned on his heel, got into his car, and drove off.

Audrey walked back to the farm in a state of pure misery. How well the little butcher had behaved, and how badly had she. That he had brought her a present was salt in her wound.

Before going into the farmyard she sat on a stile, opened the parcel, and dropped it with a piercing shriek. There on the grass lay the cleaned but still bloody carcass of a large rabbit, no doubt the finest from the butcher's shop.

For several days Audrey was cowed by her encounter. But as she recovered, she saw it as simply reinforcing the need for a marriage agency. She felt that young men vaguely expect that in some miraculous but unspecified way they will meet their dream girl. In reality this mythical female is sitting patiently in her parents' home waiting for "Mr. Right," but as he does not know she is there, so does not materialize, she grows increasingly forlorn and morose. How sad. How unnecessarily sad. How preventable.

Audrey persevered with Uncle George's idea. She wanted to start the marriage agency in London, which would be particularly convenient for clients coming on leave from abroad. She arranged to meet Heather, who was living a hectic, glamorous urban life of parties, nightclubs, and dinners with beaux, and still did not quite believe that her friend was serious, nor that such an extraordinary, dotty idea might work.

Audrey persisted, and gradually if reluctantly Heather yielded to the enthusiasm and conviction radiating from her friend (who kept mum about her matrimonial advertisement).

"All right," she said, "it's lunatic, batty, but I'll join you and give it a whirl. But I don't like the word 'agency.' Let's call it a Marriage Bureau."

The Marriage Bureau was born.

2

No, It's Not a Brothel

Heather was working off and on as a mannequin and a film extra—her last appearance was in a ballroom scene in *Goodbye, Mr. Chips* in 1939. But she did not envisage life as a professional model or actress, and, much though she loved glamour and parties, she was too intelligent and capable to find her current way of life permanently satisfying. Still a shade hesitant, she found herself being drawn ever deeper into Audrey's mad scheme.

In all strata of society, Heather knew, parents worried if their daughters remained single after the age of about twenty. However, even in the aristocratic set girls were starting to rebel against such expectations. They were refusing to be sent out to India in what was known as the "Fishing Fleet": gaggles of scarcely educated girls who had failed to find a husband and so were dispatched by ship with the express purpose of finding one among the lonely men serving the British Empire in India. Such young women were beginning to demand as good an education as a boy, and the right to leave home, take a job, and choose their own friends. After all, many of their mothers had worked, either in paid jobs or in the voluntary services, during the Great War, and had felt frustrated at having to return to domesticity in peacetime.

However, Britain was still enduring a severe economic crisis with terrible unemployment, and any girl with visible means of support who could live with her family was therefore castigated as immoral and unpatriotic if she took a job that a man could do, because if he was out of work his wife and family would starve.

Audrey and Heather had observed this state of affairs from the Far East, and they both had girlfriends in England who were living at home, leading very dull lives—being dutiful and walking the dogs, doing good works, helping in the house, going to church, arranging the flowers, and meeting virtually no eligible men.

"But you can see as well as I can, Heather," insisted Audrey, "out in the Far East there are twenty eligible men to one woman, and all of them want a wife. They always say, 'When I go home on leave I'm going to be married.' When you say, 'Congratulations! Who's the lucky girl?' they look a bit shuffly, poor lambs, and mutter, 'I don't know, but I hope to meet somebody.' They have only a few months' leave in England, which is hardly long enough to meet, woo, and wed, so they are often still sad and lonely bachelors when they return. My heart bleeds for them."

Heather's heart did not bleed, but slowly she became thoroughly infected with Audrey's enthusiasm, and began to see in Uncle George's brain wave not only a different and ingenious occupation but also one that would earn her some money. Unlike Audrey, Heather had a shrewd business head; and now convinced of the need for the Marriage Bureau, bent her mind to the practicalities of establishing it. "Audrey was imaginative and romantic and I was practical and logical," recalled Heather, "and we were both serious about the Bureau, so the partnership worked well from the start."

As their plans progressed, Audrey spent more and more time in London. She dropped little hints to her parents that, without telling a complete fib, implied that she was being wooed by a suitor on leave from Ceylon whom she had met through her good friend Heather. In her anxiety to avoid the wrath of her parents should they discover what she was really up to, Audrey decided to use a different name in the Marriage Bureau. "My second Christian name is Mary," she announced to Heather, "so I shall transfer it to my first name. I never liked 'Audrey' much anyway, and I used to get called 'Tawdry Audrey.' My mother's maiden name is Oliver, so I shall call myself 'Mary Oliver.' And I don't want people to find out who I am, and tell my parents, so I shall stop being a farmer's daughter, and become a parson's daughter. That's near enough the truth, as he's Mr. Parsons! I'll stick to Cambridgeshire—I can't see any reason for changing it. So from now on I am Miss Mary Oliver, daughter of a Cambridgeshire parson. That sounds very nice and respectable, a person the clients can trust. And I'll say I was a deb, like you, don't you think?"

Heather agreed. She was not unconcerned about her own

parents' reaction to their daughter's extraordinary new departure, which they were bound to hear about since they lived in London. But she was confident she could twist her father around her little finger, and eventually convince them both.

Heather and the newly christened Mary wrote to their girl-friends, and to several of their male friends and acquaintances in India, informing them that they would be the Marriage Bureau's first clients. "We wanted a nucleus of clients," explained Heather, "so that we had enough possible introductions, and we also wanted to practice interviewing. Some of the friends we wrote to were annoyed, as people often are if you produce a really practical solution to their problems—and far more annoyed later when we did not use them!"

They resolved that Bureau marriages should be solidly grounded. The matchmakers would ensure that a man and a woman came from the same social background, and had a similar income and attitude to finances (though of course most women would have less money). They would have shared tastes and aspirations, and probably be of the same religion. The Bureau would interview all prospective husbands and wives, asking them for details about themselves and the kind of person they wanted to marry. Clients would fill in a registration form, the interviewer would add her own comments, and then she would select a suitable introduction. The Bureau would give the woman basic information about the man, and no introduction would proceed unless she agreed (she might throw up her hands in horror on being presented with details of a former boyfriend, or even an ex-husband). If the woman was happy, she would write to the man and they would arrange to meet. They would then inform Heather and Mary as to how the meeting had gone, and whether they proposed to get to know each other better, or would like a new introduction. The Bureau would charge a modest registration fee for a year's introductions, and when a couple married, they would pay the After Marriage Fee, so that the Bureau could prosper. Everything would be conducted in confidence and with the utmost carefulness.

Their tentative beginnings remained enshrined in Heather's memory. "We had nobody to copy, no reference books to help us. We just had to rely on common sense, good taste, and our certainty that we were doing something which was needed. We had to really think it out. The legal part took a long time."

Mary and Heather decided to take advice, so they consulted a firm of well-known and established solicitors. "We saw the junior partner," Heather recalled, "a fearsomely correct and conventional man dressed in a funereally sober suit—he only needed a black silk top hat with ribbons flowing down it to be the perfect undertaker. He was all fawning smiles and unctuous solicitude as we sat down and faced him across his huge polished desk. He knew my father (and thought him far richer than he in fact was) and was hoping for some good business from me. But the sunshine vanished behind the blackest of storm clouds when he heard our proposals. He clearly thought we were wanting to set up some kind of superior West End brothel, providing high-class prostitutes, no doubt glamorous but impoverished ex-debs like me, for wealthy men who would get an extra kick out of having well-born girls like us as madams. He was so overcome that his face turned bright red and his breath (nasty) came in quick gasps. He couldn't get a word out, and I feared he might have a heart attack.

"With a huge effort of self-control he calmed down. It was obvious that we were getting nowhere, but really for something to say more than anything else, I think, he managed to suppress his revulsion just enough to ask us how much capital we had. Mary, who was by this time thoroughly bored with him, gave me a gloriously innocent glance with her big brown eyes, looked demure, and murmured, 'I don't know, but I don't think my beat's worth much. What about yours, Heather? Is it worth more than mine, do you think?' That effectively finished the interview: the solicitor clearly thought we really were ladies of ill fame, turned purple, and spluttered inarticulately, so we waltzed out without any fond farewell, and went to look for somebody more helpful and less stodgy."

Heather's address book was full of useful names and numbers. She and Mary pored over the pages, which took time as Heather's handwriting, all loops and flourishes, was scarcely legible even to her. Luckily a name caught her eye: Humphrey, a friend who had recently qualified as a solicitor. He would be much less old-fashioned than the apoplectic one, Heather thought, and certainly much more intelligent.

Humphrey, young, keen and open-minded, immediately got the point. He advised the two matchmakers that their idea was startlingly novel but basically very sound, and that if they did

things properly and efficiently they stood a good chance of suc-
ceeding. He himself might even become one of their first clients!
However, his considered advice was that they seek Counsel's
opinion on how to protect both their clients and themselves.
They needed some basic, formal rules, and some terms and conditions to be printed on the registration forms. Humphrey knew
just the man, and took the two matchmakers to see him.

The Bureau never had to alter Counsel's excellent rules. The
first was that all clients would be interviewed, and that the interviews would be free. Nobody would be taken on unless they were
free to marry, so anyone getting a divorce had to have the Decree
Absolute. The Bureau would register clients only if there was a
reasonable number of people to whom they could be introduced.
The registration fee was the same for everybody, with the After
Marriage Fee greater than the registration fee. The initial fee en-
titled the client to introductions one at a time, as and when there
was a suitable candidate, unless the Bureau heard nothing from
him or her for one year. The Bureau would never send out lists or
photographs of clients, nor would it take up references.

Counsel's wording on the Bureau's registration form also remained unchanged for decades:

The purpose of the Marriage Bureau is to introduce with
a view to marriage persons who desire to find matrimonial partners. Applicants are required to give full particulars of themselves and those particulars are then placed
on the Register of the Bureau. The more difficult the

applicant's case the more limited the introductions will naturally be. The Bureau of course cannot do more than effect introductions nor hold themselves responsible for the results and does not vouch for the correctness of the particulars passed on. These particulars should be verified by you. In the opinion of the Bureau it is essential for the applicant to meet the relatives and friends of a potential husband or wife before they commit themselves to an engagement or marriage. If the applicant has any cause for suspicion or complaint they are asked to inform the Bureau immediately. The matter will of course be dealt with confidentially.

Mary and Heather were both in their midtwenties, young and inexperienced, spirited and lighthearted, but with each step they completed they became more serious about what they wanted to do, and more determined than ever to do it thoroughly and properly. Heather's misgivings had completely disappeared, and off she went to the London County Council, where an astonished official, awed by the sight of the svelte, elegant blonde sitting opposite him, listened openmouthed to her plummy-voiced request for a license to open a marriage bureau.

"The LCC man was full of his own importance and quite stupid," reported Heather to Mary, "and I was longing to tell him to shut his mouth when he wasn't speaking so I did not have all his dental cavities and fillings in my line of vision. So unattractive. He simply could not grasp the idea of a marriage bureau, and his Adam's apple, which was rather prominent, kept jiggling up and down as he gulped and gawped and almost choked. I was very patient, I spelled it all out in simple words, but all he did was keep looking things up in big fat rulebooks, running his grubby finger up and down the pages, and mumbling to himself. He had a stab at exercising his authority: he put his fingertips together and leaned forward over the desk (so I leaned back) and pronounced his decision. He concluded that while there were no specific LCC rules governing marriage bureaus, he could see no impediment to our opening such an establishment on a trial basis of a year. In other words, he couldn't find anything at all which fitted our case, but he would graciously put us on probation! So that will have to do. At least we tried!"

Now the Bureau needed an office. Heather wanted to be in Mayfair, somewhere like Bond Street. Everybody knew Bond Street, she reasoned, and its shops attracted wealthy people, who were more likely to become clients than poor ones, who would not be able to afford the Bureau's fees. Mayfair was the most glamorous and sought-after part of London, largely residential with gracious family houses, many of them home to rich debs in search of a husband. Heather remembered two who had had a bet as to which of them would sleep with their hundredth man first. The competition ended in a draw, but both contestants married well and wearing virginal white, which was the end product of the very expensive business of being presented at Court and doing the Season. "It was a very costly and commercial marriage market," commented Heather. "Our Bureau will be much cheaper and much more effective!"

Mary agreed that Bond Street or nearby was a desirable location, easy to find and highly convenient for the clients who had inspired Uncle George's idea: men living abroad, with only a limited time in England to find a wife.

In a newspaper advertisement, Mary found premises that sounded perfect: "Comfortable office facilities near Piccadilly Circus, twelve shillings and sixpence per week." The address was ideal, and they still had £10 of her original capital, enough to pay the rent at least for long enough to find out if the Bureau could work.

Mary hesitated at the office door, staring into a gloomy, ill-lit, freezing room heaving with men huddled in gray raincoats or ill-fitting overcoats. Some sprawled in their swivel chairs with their feet on their desk; others drifted around, laughing and chatting, puffing on malodorous pipes and cigarettes whose smoke intensified the grayness of the atmosphere. They paused only to stare in amazement as Mary picked her way around, carefully skirting the desks and overflowing wastepaper baskets, a diminutive figure in a long coat of scarlet hunting cloth with a black velvet collar, totally out of place in the mob of traveling salesmen.

It rapidly dawned on Mary that the sole empty desk, sandwiched in the middle of rows of brown-varnished, grimy old wooden wrecks, was where she and Heather would have to sit and listen as the clients poured out their secrets and longings, while the men pricked up their ears and leered and winked. Ignoring the admiring and suggestive remarks assailing her from all sides, she beat a swift retreat, emerging into the street like a soul released, longing for a scented bath to eliminate the stale smoky stench clinging to her.

Heather listened to Mary's tale of woe but did not shrink. "We'll try another route. Never mind advertisements—let's consult a house agent."

Together Heather and Mary visited agencies where a warm welcome greeted the two disarming, well-spoken young women, the one statuesque, blond and cool, the other petite, dark-haired and friendly. But the minute they said they were looking for an office to start a marriage bureau the agent stopped smiling, gave an embarrassed cough, shuffled the papers on his desk, regretted (unconvincingly) that he had nothing suitable nor was likely to, and ushered the hopefuls out with positively indecent haste.

"They have no vision, no imagination—not even common sense!" grumbled Mary. "We have good money to pay, but they jumped like March hares when we uttered the fearsome words 'marriage bureau.' Anyone would think we are intending to open a backstreet gambling den or white-slave bureau!"

At this low point, there stole into Mary's mind an image of a small office in Bond Street. She had come across it on an earlier visit to London, when she had inspected several small flats and offices, wistfully imagining herself living and working in the city. She had passed the building one Sunday, seen the agent's board, and dreamily visualized herself installed in such a hideaway, far from the farm, busily engaged in some as yet unimagined work. She had never revealed this dream to a soul. Whenever she

looked contemplative, her mother assumed that she was picturing the knight in shining armor who would surely win her heart.
Poor Mrs. Parsons would have been stricken had she known her
daughter was staring up at a house agent's board fixed to the
wall of a Bond Street building. Much of the painted lettering
had flaked off, making the wording hard to read, but Mary and
Heather could just make out SMALL OFFICE TO LET.

The hairdresser on the ground floor remarked despondently
that nobody wanted the pesky office: he'd shown it to a few possible takers last year but not a soul had turned up to see it for a
good six months. It was too small—you could hardly swing a
cat in it—and too dusty and dirty, and up too many stairs. The
lavatory was even farther up, in the attic, and the drains were
none too reliable. The room wasn't a ha'penny-worth of good to a
smart West End business. And it wouldn't be long before Hitler
dropped a bomb or two on Bond Street, which wouldn't do his
hairdressing business any good, so he didn't rightly know what
he himself would do, but he'd probably get out of the West End,
Lord love you, he didn't want to be a sitting duck, were the two
young ladies in their right minds?

Mary and Heather were well aware of the grim black cloud
of impending war darkening the country and disrupting plans of
all kinds, but both remained optimistic, philosophical, and unflinchingly dedicated to Uncle George's brainchild. They assured
the melancholy hairdresser that they did know what they were
doing, and would be most interested to view the office. Shrugging his shoulders in resignation he foraged in a drawer, found

the key, and handed it over with dire warnings about the dangers of the unlit stairs. Impatiently, Mary and Heather bounded up five narrow flights and unlocked a rickety door that creaked open as they gazed inside.

The room was small and shabby, the brown linoleum on the floor blotched with ink stains, the white paint faded to a dirty, jaundiced yellowy-brown. It was furnished with two battered old desks (one of them three-legged, propped up against the wall), two dilapidated swivel chairs that had long since lost their ability to revolve, and a bookcase fixed to the wall at a strange angle, apparently about to fall to the floor. A grubby and cracked telephone trailed a frayed cord. The lighting was a single bulb dimmed by a scorched and torn lampshade, dangling from a disintegrating plaster ceiling rose. Heating was a two-bar electric fire (of which, they discovered later, only one bar ever lit up, however often a chilly person tried to kick it into life).

A dirty slip of paper pinned to the wall gave the rent for this urban rabbit hutch as twenty-five shillings per week, by the week. Included were a poky and squalid lavatory, plus all fixtures (what fixtures? wondered the two matchmakers), fittings (though nothing fits, they observed), and rates.

Mary was sure that destiny had struck. Heather was ecstatic.

"We'll take it!"

"We'll paint it!"

"The clients will love it!"

"So shall we!"

The Marriage Bureau had found its home.

3

Open for Matrimonial Business

The two matchmakers set about cheering up their scruffy little office. Heather bought buckets of sunshine-yellow paint, and for several days they clanked up and down Bond Street wearing slacks and old clothes, hoping nobody they knew would spot them among the smartly dressed shoppers. While they were painting, their friends visited the office, full of curiosity and fascination, but usually disapproving: "You're young and not obviously criminal, so people will think you mad rather than bad, but even so you'll probably end up behind bars for white-slave trafficking or prostitution. We'll come and visit you, and bring you some decent food to supplement the prison muck, so you won't starve!"

A practical-minded friend asked how people were going to hear about the Marriage Bureau.

"We'll advertise," Mary cheerfully asserted, unaware that

the prestige papers would not take advertisements from such a suspicious-sounding organization for another fifty years.

The week before the Bureau opened, Mary rang up the newspapers, in alphabetical order, artlessly asked for the Features Editor, and, with the luck of the naïve, got through every time.

It was early April 1939 and, following the Munich crisis, the papers had a lot of pages to fill, but with a declaration of war anticipated, editors were looking for cheerful, upbeat stories to counterbalance the gloomy world news. Apart from the serious *Daily Telegraph* and *The Times,* most of them sent reporters around to New Bond Street, and Godfrey Winn, a very well-known and popular journalist, did his whole column in the *Sunday Express* about the strange but intriguing phenomenon and its charming proprietors.

Near the end of the week, with Mary and Heather's pictures in every paper except the more sedate ones, Heather thought she should telephone her mother and father. She had not told them or her autocratic grandmother what she was up to, nor that she was using the name Jenner, which came from her mother's family, rather than her real surname, Lyon—she thought Jenner went better with Heather. Brigadier and Mrs. Lyon read only the very staid *Morning Post,* but Heather knew that news of the Marriage Bureau would eventually percolate through to them.

Heather hoped her mother, the less reactionary of the two, would answer the telephone, but she got her profoundly conservative father and, taking a deep breath, she broke the news. To her amazement he merely snorted, "Thank goodness somebody in the family is trying to make some money at last!" The next morning he and some club cronies came around to the office, fizzing with charm and enthusiasm, laden with a huge box of chocolates and a magnificent bouquet of flowers, the lilies dripping orange pollen all over the furniture and exuding a hothouse scent.

Mrs. Lyon was annoyed, but the Brigadier, blessedly converted to the whole venture, won her around. Curiously enough, it turned out to be almost the only thing Heather ever did of which her ninety-six-year-old dragon grandmother approved. "My generation, my dear Heather," she breathed fierily down the telephone, "had a dreadful time marrying off our daughters. As you know, I did not succeed with all of mine, not for want of trying, I assure you. And the cost of the balls and parties and other shenanigans was astronomical, far higher than the fees of your organization—your 'Marriage Bureau,' don't you call it? I wish you good fortune."

Heather's grandmother sent around two dozen red roses. Perhaps luckily, she did not read a less than encouraging piece in an Australian newspaper, in which Brigadier General S. Price Weir, described as "Australia's only marital conciliator," censured the Marriage Bureau as "a very stupid and dangerous enterprise" which would cause people to marry in haste and repent at leisure. "Surely," blustered the Brigadier General, "there are no people so incapable of finding a partner in life that they have to use such a crude and ridiculous means of finding one?"

"What a pompous twerp!" cried Heather. "And I have no

idea what a 'marriage conciliator' is, but he doesn't sound remotely conciliatory!"

On the morning of Monday, April 17, 1939, Mary and Heather arrived at the office at 8:30. They paused momentarily in the street
to admire the wooden notice board, its silver lettering standing
out clearly against the black background: MARRIAGE BUREAU:
PRIVATE AND CONFIDENTIAL. Anticipating having nothing to do,
and having always thought she wanted to knit, Heather strolled
in carrying knitting needles, wool and a pattern book. Mary put
in the drawer of her wobbly desk her intended reading: *Contract
Bridge in Twenty Minutes*.

Heather never learned to knit, nor Mary to play bridge.
Thanks to all the previous week's publicity the postman had
put so many letters through the door that they had difficulty
in opening it. Having fought their way in, they each started on
half of the letters, assigning them to one of three piles: "Men,"
"Women," and "Uncertain," on account of dreadful handwriting
or a dubious photograph (the prospective client as a baby, flat on
his or her tummy on a tiger-skin rug, sucking his or her thumb,
labeled "Me aged 7 months").

A knock at the door interrupted the sorting.

"It must be a client!" whispered Mary. "Quick, let's toss to
interview whoever it is!"

Hastily she flipped a sixpence and Heather won. At the second impatient knock Mary took some letters out into the passage while Heather opened the door.

Major A. was a smart, upright, retired army officer in his middle forties. A kindly soul, and no doubt a good leader of men, with great courtesy he took Heather through the interview rather than the other way around. To her horror he paid to register—the fee was five guineas (to be followed by the After Marriage Fee of ten guineas each if a couple married through the Bureau). He filled in his form, very politely gave a little bow, and said goodbye to a stunned Heather.

"Mary, come and help! He's too old for any of our girlfriends—they'd all think him middle-aged. What shall we do?"

"Look at the letters!" ordered Mary, holding out a handful. "There's a woman in at least half of these envelopes! And if we can't find anyone suitable we'll keep his money for a few days and then return it to him."

Mary and Heather busied themselves with the letter opener and were relieved to discover several possible wives for Major A.

"Whoopee!" cried Mary as she read another letter from a promising woman. "We—"

She was cut off by another knock at the door.

It was a young man, very haughty and full of himself, who refused to sit down while telling Mary that several of his connections were titled, and that anyone to whom the Marriage Bureau introduced him must be in The Book.

"Titled, my eye!" declared Mary, raising her eyebrows and grinning, as she heard his footsteps descending the stairs. "He's all puffed-up pretense, the titles are 'Mr.,' 'Mrs.,' and 'Miss,' I'm sure! And does he mean the telephone book or *Debrett*, do you think? What a conceited ass! But he's paid, and he's coming back for an interview tomorrow as he has some very important appointments today—the dentist, I would lay odds on it! He just wants to dazzle us."

The British press remained on the Bureau's side. In July the *Daily Mail*'s Charles Graves wrote enthusiastically about the venture of "Miss Jenner, a magnificent blonde, and Miss Oliver, an entertaining brunette," and was so intrigued that he asked them how often they were proposed to themselves, to which Heather coolly replied, "As a matter of fact most of the men propose to us. But really it is a matter of politeness and they don't mean it. I can tell you, though, that we both often get quite attached to some of the clients."

The telephone rang incessantly, most calls coming from inquirers, others from well-wishers, journalists, and the model agency for which Heather had worked, begging her to do another show for them.

Clients poured in, and as there was no waiting room they had to queue up the narrow stairs. When the staircase was full, Mary would give the hopefuls her most appealing smile and guide them to a decrepit ladder leading up to a small trapdoor, saying apologetically, "So sorry, we shan't be long, would you be so kind as to wait a few minutes up on the roof? Thank you so much!"

Beguiled, nobody ever protested, and they climbed the

ladder, probably anticipating a scenic roof garden full of flowers and elegant benches, only to find nothing but a dirty bit of concrete surrounded by smutty chimney pots.

The clients came from all levels of society. One newspaper quoted Heather as saying that they ranged from plumbers to peers, and from charladies to countesses, which was true, as she wrote later:

> The first five hundred men did indeed include a plumber and an earl, as well as businessmen, farmers, landowners, members of the armed forces, labourers, stable boys, postmen, clergymen, lecturers, waiters, motor drivers, architects and doctors. We had a London, Midland & Scottish Railway Traffic Officer (a poppet), an owner of a factory making artificial limbs, a nib-maker who examined our fountain pens with a critical eye, a manufacturer of silk stockings whose eyes kept wandering toward my legs (which are rather splendid), a rat-catcher and a "cowman in charge," whatever that means—I am not a country girl.

Some letters brought not clients but strange requests and offers: some from charitable organizations, one from a man who wrote that he would not mind marrying either Mary or Heather if it was going to cost him only five guineas.

Some clients turned out to be practical jokers: during a difficult interview, Heather was interrupted by the door opening to admit a man with a blackened face beneath an exotic turban, demanding replacements for his harem. Heather recognized the voice of an old friend, and was not at all amused by his idea of humor, nor by other acquaintances who telephoned, disguising their voices to give impossible requirements.

One real client was an MP. "Goody goody!" exulted Mary. "If we get him married off he'll tell lots of people in Parliament and in his constituency!"

"I'm not so sure," said Heather. "He's noted for raising tricky questions in the House, and confounding those who oppose him with smart answers, and crowing over them in the bar afterwards. He's not a nice man. He might even raise a critical question about us and the Bureau, so be careful."

The MP was fifty-five, tall and, at first glance, quite good-looking in a traditional English way, though his chin flowed over-smoothly into his neck, the continuous curve giving him a faintly reptilian look, enhanced by smallish eyes that darted hither and thither like a snake's. He reminded Heather of cobras she'd seen performing at the command of fakirs in India. He was dressed in a Savile Row suit and a tie from one of those antique gentlemen's clubs that women—if admitted at all—have to enter through a small side door at the bottom of a flight of outside steps. He had a dry, sharp, put-down manner, and Mary particularly disliked the arrogant way in which he addressed them as if they were servants, demanding introductions to young women aged no more than thirty-five.

"My wife died before we had any children," he snapped. "Most inconsiderate of her, although I suppose she did not choose to contract scarlet fever. I want an heir; I have a position and the wherewithal."

Heather stifled her laughter as she wondered exactly what he meant by "wherewithal." The MP was not a man with whom it would be wise to attempt a joke. He was adamant that his prospective wife must be a lady, English, of good birth, educated by a governess or private school, Church of England, Conservative, of independent means (through inheritance, not anything so vulgar as working), cultured, refined, in good health, well dressed, slim, not too brainy, accustomed to moving in the higher echelons of Society (he talked as if the word had a capital *S*) and single or widowed, without children.

Unsurprisingly, the young women under thirty-five thought him far too old. Generally they disliked him. "He believes himself to be a wonderful catch," commented a young woman who met all his requirements but was too intelligent and far too nice. "But whoever marries him will pay a high price. He is looking for someone to add luster to himself—woe betide her if she falls ill, or produces a sickly child."

"I am not surprised that he has not found a second wife in the past twenty years," reported another. "I found him far too dictatorial and set in his ways, and not at all interested in me, just in what I might do for him. He is much too glorious for me!"

The MP was chillingly critical of everyone he met, until Heather introduced him to Lady M., a rather dim, reasonably pretty, aristocratic girl, whose main aim in life was to get away from her overbearing mother, whom she constantly disappointed by her inability to find a husband. Lady M. would put up with anybody rather than have to remain under Mama's roof, and the MP liked her looks, her social standing, her income, her lack of brainpower, her gratitude, and her willingness to comply with whatever he wanted. He wrote a curt note acknowledging that the Marriage Bureau had fulfilled its part of the contract, and paid the twenty guineas. Mary and Heather jointly breathed a gusty sigh of relief, devoutly hoping never to hear from him again. And they never did.

Many of the women who approached the Bureau did not have paid jobs but lived on an allowance from their father, or an inheritance. An earl's widow had money but no occupation, and was as bored and lonely, festering away stitching appliqué to linen hand towels in her drafty country house, as the penniless little seamstress client straining her eyes sewing black sequins onto black silk evening dresses in her dingy bed-sit.

The daughter of another aristocrat turned up dressed in the dowdiest old coat imaginable, a curious, ancient, hairy gray sack lashed to her shapeless form by a broad belt, which seemed to be made of knitted string. The Honourable Priscilla's tyrannical father gave her a most miserly dress allowance—"I spend in a week what he gives her for a year, the rotter!" protested Heather, for whom good clothes were as essential as food and drink.

This parsimonious and backward-looking patriarch did not

hold with girls being educated, nor even, felt Heather, clothed; but when he died, his downtrodden daughter would inherit a sizable amount. The Honourable Priscilla was too nice and too meek to hope that this happy event would come soon, but was concentrating on finding a husband who would take her away from the gloomy old pile her family had occupied for generations.

She was just one of many young and not-so-young women living drearily at home, housekeeping for parents or brothers, financially completely dependent apart from little jobs such as making and selling sheepskin toys and embroidered table linen. Their only hope of a life of their own was marriage. But where were they going to meet a man? "I feel so sorry for the Honourable P.," muttered Mary, a protective glint in her serious brown eyes. "She's just the kind of girl we want to help. I know exactly what it feels like. The thought of still living on the farm with my parents, being a dowdy daughter and a big disappointment for not marrying, gives me the shudders."

Although the matchmakers had thought only the relatively well-off would apply, many poorer people saved up to become clients and the Bureau charged some impoverished girls only three guineas, or even less. Some low-paid young men also had their fee reduced or were allowed to pay in installments. Many of the female clients were paid scarcely a living wage, as lady's maids, beauticians, shop assistants, nannies and nurses, stenographers and shorthand typists, comptometer operators, dressmakers, milliners, cooks, governesses and companions. Slightly better paid were a professional violinist and a dreamy cellist, a fearfully efficient LCC social worker, a model for paper patterns, a traveling auditor who quibbled about the fee arrangements, a matron at a school for blind boys and men, and a Hoffman Presser in a big laundry.

"Oh, I do remember Miss Hoff Press!" recalled Heather. "She was dressed in an impeccably clean, crisp suit over a starched white blouse, with little pleats all pressed as sharp as a carving knife. She made Mary and me feel grubby and crumpled and blowsy—which we were, of course. We were so busy that we lived like nuns, seldom left the office until late at night, never had time to go to a hairdresser or dressmaker, and lived on fishcakes from the restaurant below the office. They were less fattening, we thought, than sandwiches, and easy to eat cold in one hand as we answered the telephone or wrote out introductions with the other. But they were greasy so sometimes we got marks on our clothes."

A few of the female clients had their own business, usually inherited from their father, such as a large, square, red-faced woman who lumbered up the stairs puffing and coughing, dumped herself down on the chair, which protested but fortunately held, got out a packet of cigarettes, and proceeded to smoke throughout the interview.

Miss Doris Burton had a small tobacconist's shop that brought in £3 5s per week, had always worked, and never married. Mary interviewed her, categorized her as *Better Than Some*, and reported to Heather: "She says she's thirty-nine but that's a whopper, she's nearer forty-nine. It's the smoking that's done it. Her face reminds me of smoked salmon, leathery with an orangey tinge. When I half-closed my eyes I could feel the fire burning in the smokehouse and smell the fishy smoke as she gently cured. No makeup, and that broad figure, cropped mud-colored hair, and severe black suit, make her look distinctly mannish. But she wants a sound, reliable, steady, homely gent with a decent job and no children. No elderly parents, or a dog or cat either (I rather wondered if she'd accept goldfish or a parrot, but thought it undiplomatic to ask). She doesn't mind how ugly he is—that's just as well, as he'll certainly have to have the same view about her! Not a gambler. Preferably an abstainer, though she would be agreeable to an occasional pint. Of course, he must be a smoker. She is offering sufficient furniture and linen for a flat, plus expectations from an old aunt, and wants the man to have sufficient income to provide the home. She's a challenge!"

The story of the Marriage Bureau's first wedding, of a bride aged sixty-eight to a seventy-year-old groom, delighted the press. British Pathé made a two-minute documentary film showing the matchmakers—"Cupid's labourers"—in action. A deluge of inquiries came from both the United Kingdom and abroad: missionaries, rubber planters, colonial servants, managers of tea estates, mining engineers, soldiers in Malaya, Tanganyika, Ceylon, India, South Africa, Egypt, Rhodesia, Uganda, Sudan, Nigeria. They had leave infrequently, so they were put in touch with suitable women by post, and some marriages followed lengthy correspondence.

"Poor wandering ones," cried Mary. "Just the kind of men we set out to help!"

The original idea had been to answer all letters by hand, for, as Heather recalled, "in those days you didn't type letters—it was considered a little ill-bred—but Mary couldn't spell and my handwriting had always been difficult to read, and in any case there were far too many letters for two people to deal with. On opening day alone we received 250, and the pattern continued. So we needed not only another office but also a secretary."

The landlord offered a small empty office on the same landing for £1 a week, and the employment exchange could supply a secretary at £3—but she would need a typewriter. Even though there was a steady flow of registration fees, after the rent, yellow paint, solicitors, telephone bills, stationery, fishcakes, and other vital expenses, the cost of an extra office, secretary and a typewriter was daunting.

Heather went off to Harrods, where she had an account, and bought a typewriter on the never-never. Mary greeted her as she carried the precious machine through the office door.

"Goody goody! I have just sent out application forms to a hundred people, and I can't write another word!"

The interviewing never let up. As Mary took charge of the typewriter, in walked Rosemary, a charming twenty-two-year-old ex-deb of, Heather guessed, pretty conservative outlook and behavior. She was polite, correct and unimaginative, but with the naïve charm of an unspoiled girl. She was pretty, slightly plump, wearing expensive but matronly clothes better suited to her mother: a well-cut but dull coat and skirt over a classic silk blouse, a pearl necklace, handmade shoes, a hat and gloves.

Rosemary lived at home and had an allowance from Daddy, a distinguished professional man who had been knighted. She had very few ideas of her own, and had difficulty articulating her requirements to Heather. "Someone older than me, I think, perhaps about forty—what do you think?" she managed after some thought, giving Heather a childlike, trusting little smile. "I mean not too old, but older, a man who knows more than I do, because, you see, I don't know very much. I've only been a deb, which was fun, but I don't know much, except I'm good at riding. I love horses. And flowers. I'm good at arranging flowers for dinner parties. Perhaps a man in the army, a good regiment, of course, because I should love to live abroad, I think. I know people who live there and they say it's great fun. Not a native, of course, and not a man who has been married before, and he must be a gentleman. And Church of England of course, even if he lives abroad. What do you think?"

As Rosemary stumbled through her appeal, Heather half-drifted into a reverie, reliving her own life in India. She pictured Rosemary in an agreeable hill station, gracefully riding side-saddle on a white horse in the cool of the day, in the evening changing into a simple but perfectly cut silk dress adorned with a regimental brooch, and talking—or rather, mostly listening—to the dinner guests, to the proud satisfaction of her heroic husband.

Heather could not think of anybody suitable among her friends in England, but perhaps that polo player from Colombo she had put on the books might fit—he was coming home on leave soon. Or maybe Mary had some suitable friend. Or the perfect man might come in tomorrow. Or perhaps he was already lurking in an as-yet-unopened envelope.... Cogitating about Rosemary, coloring in a mental picture of her Mr. Right, and how he was to be discovered, Heather felt a growing and glorious conviction that she had found her true vocation.

4

The Capitulation of Cedric Thistleton

Pondering on her newfound feeling of vocation, Heather came to recognize that she had always had it in her. "I suppose I am what is called a born matchmaker," she reflected later. "Ever since my fifth birthday, when I announced my engagement to two small boys at once, I have been busy marrying people off. Matchmaking was my hobby, so it was logical that it became my business too. I match people up with all the ardour of a philatelist with his stamps, or an entomologist with his butterflies."

For Mary, though, the prospect of guiding a stranger toward a potential spouse felt novel and disquieting, and it was with trepidation as well as excitement that she anticipated her first interview with a man. It was April 18, the day after the Bureau had opened. The matchmakers had just finished touching up the paint on the ceiling, so Mary took off her overalls and headscarf to receive Cedric Thistleton. He had visited the day before, accompanied by a faint aroma of bay rum and dropping heavy hints about his importance, and now he had returned for an interview.

He was a businessman of thirty-three, tall, dark, and exceptionally, classically good-looking, radiating confidence and A-1 health from his lightly sun-kissed face to his expensively shod feet. His dark navy suit was faultlessly tailored; his dazzlingly white silk shirt sported tasteful gold cuff links. Without waiting for a polite invitation he sat himself down opposite Mary, while casting appraising glances at Heather as she climbed down from her painting ladder to sit at her own desk. Then he fixed a questioning but commanding look on Mary.

Silenced by Cedric's self-assurance, Mary returned his gaze. She had expected her first interview with her first man to be fraught with difficulty, for surely he would be nervous or shy, needing her to encourage him to speak. Or he might be longing to spill out his hopes and needs without letting her get a word in edgewise—Mary had envisioned various scenarios, and had worked out how she might proceed. But none of her imaginings had foretold Cedric's abrupt opening: "I have five weeks' leave before I return to Malaya with my wife. She must be socially acceptable to my employer and my social circle. It is your job to find her."

"Oh!" gasped Mary.

Cedric made it clear that he expected entire satisfaction from his contract with the Bureau: a girl of impeccable breeding (as if he were buying a racehorse, mused Mary), under twenty-one years old, willing and able to bear children, sophisticated, self-assured and worldly wise. She must be capable of entertaining the grandees they would invite to dinner, and of managing a large house with several servants. She must be upper class or at very least from the top ranks of the middle class (to compensate for his own lack of class, suspected Mary), with not even a hint of anything so scandalous as drink, divorce, debt, or any other form of dishonesty. This paragon was to have no encumbrances such as children or dependent parents, and no desire to do anything but glorify her husband and impress all in his circle. He was unconcerned about his bride's looks or tastes or character, and the possibility that she might not enjoy life in a far-flung continent had cast not even the slightest shadow over his mind.

To Mary's intensifying dislike was added anxiety, for most of the girls who had so far inquired were not of the class Cedric obviously thought he deserved. He would assuredly raise Cain if introduced to a shop assistant or a parlor maid. Among Mary's friends were some upper-class girls, but she was not prepared to sacrifice friendship to the cause of appeasing this obnoxious client. So she played for time, diverting him by requesting more details about himself and the bride he sought.

Cedric expanded so loudly and fulsomely on the subject dearest to his heart—himself—that he failed to notice Heather aiming kicks at the telephone bell underneath her desk, which made it ring. She then apparently took calls from gloriously aristocratic young ladies all agog to meet a Cedric Thistleton lookalike.

Cedric sidled crabwise away from Mary's questions about his background and education. Having herself adopted a new name and persona, which involved fending off inquiries about her fictitious debutante year, in a twinkling of an eye Mary spotted the evasiveness with which Cedric ducked and dived about his "public school." She grew convinced that he had left a council school at fourteen. But he waxed lyrical about his income of £800 a year and his progress up the ladder of a company that exported rubber. Hard work (and slimy toadying, Mary was certain) had elevated him to a position that would be further improved by the addition of a suitably superior wife, and he intended to gain promotion, adulation and envy by marrying into the aristocracy, or as near as possible to it.

Quite casually, Cedric informed Mary that he had been on the verge of becoming engaged to eighteen-year-old Miss G., the youngest of five daughters of titled but impecunious parents. Choosing an engagement ring had focused his mind, and in the jeweler's shop, fingering the little gold bands with their single large diamond, he had concluded that, despite her pedigree, Miss G. lacked the sophistication and social assurance to impress his circle. So he had summoned her to what she had doubtless imagined would be a romantic proposal of marriage, and told her he was of the considered opinion that she would not do.

Mary was outraged. "Oh, how my heart bleeds for that poor child," she burst out as soon as she had reluctantly accepted Cedric's registration fee, and closed the Bureau's door firmly behind him. "I met many 'Miss G.'s when I was with Uncle George in Assam. They were all young and ignorant, with no proper education, brought up purely and simply to get married. Just like me, in fact! And you too, Heather! I know to the last sleepless night and anxious day what they felt like, and if I'd married either of the pompous idiots I was engaged to in Assam I'd have ended up like so many of them, locked in a gruesome marriage, a prison with no escape until death us did part. Or else I'd have been a spinster forever, paid a pittance by some tyrannical old dowager, or by rich parents needing a governess for their wretched infants."

"Calm down, dear Mary—it wasn't always as bad as that," objected Heather. "Some of those girls ended up as happy as anyone ever is."

Mary fell silent, meditating on the fate of Miss G. Immediately after he'd cast her off, Cedric had told her, she had married a widowed colonel of forty-two. She was friends with his daughters, who were her age. They were distraught at the death of their darling mama, who had not been sufficiently robust to cope with the Malayan heat. Mary felt sure they had leaned on Miss G. to marry their papa, even though he was twenty-four years older than she. But what was Miss G. to do otherwise? She must have been terrified of being left on the shelf, and with the reputation of being a reject, for everyone in that closed, gossipy little world would have known she should have married Cedric. She would have been pitied, despised, patronized. Now she would at least have some status as the Colonel's wife, and with luck some nice children of her own, and friendly stepdaughters.

"She might not have done any better if she'd come to the Bureau!" said Heather. "Anyway, did you get sufficient information from Cedric?"

"Oh yes," sighed Mary, "he added pages of detail to his

registration form. But heaven knows whether we'll find someone for him. He's like a clockwork toy you wind up that just keeps moving and jerking and ticking until the little wheels slow down and come to rest. All he wants is for his social circle to kowtow to him, and a nonpareil wife will make that happen. Given half a chance he'd marry you, Heather!"

"He did rather remind me of my former husband, so no, thank you. I noticed him staring at me, though not admiringly. I'm sure he disapproved of my wearing slacks, and was wondering whether my family appears in *Debrett*!"

Mary was dispirited but resolved at all costs to find Cedric a bride, in order to get rid of him. The young women under twenty-one currently on the books were a milliner, a domestic servant, a cake maker, an art mistress and a lady's companion, none of them a potential Mrs. Thistleton. But two days later in walked a girl of twenty who worked in a very recherché art gallery owned by a baronet. Mary immediately telephoned Cedric and arranged for him to meet Miss Plunkett for luncheon the next day.

When Cedric swanned into the office the following afternoon he did not express gratitude. Drumming his well-manicured fingernails on the desk, he complained in clipped tones that for him to marry a person who was in trade was totally impossible. He failed to comprehend how Miss Jenner and Miss Oliver could have even considered such an introduction. Mary's chest swelled in indignation. "If being in rubber is not being in trade, what on earth is?" she muttered to herself.

Oblivious of the impression he was creating, Cedric added

more criticism: baronet he might be, but the gallery owner had been scandalously divorced, he sniffed, lifting his chin. He frowned, while contracting his nostrils and tweaking the pristine silk handkerchief from his breast pocket, as though to protect his delicate nose from an indelicate odor. So would Mary and Heather kindly try harder?

As Cedric left, Mary turned to Heather, speechless with indignation. The telephone rang, and Heather picked it up to hear Miss Plunkett's icy voice. "He was *frightful,* truly frightful. His brain cavity is filled with rubber, and his heart with copies of *Debrett*—shredded very fine as there is virtually no space in the teeny-weeny void that should contain his vital organ. He is the most snobbish and the most obtuse man I have met in my entire life. He could talk of nothing but his employer and his social circle in Malaya—but I do not believe that in Malaya or anywhere else in the whole wide world anyone at all is interested in him. His own self absorbs all the interest in people of which he is capable: there is not the smallest sliver of love or kindness or interest or concern or even common courtesy left over to bestow on anyone else. If he is a true sample of your male clients kindly return my registration fee forthwith."

As Miss Plunkett paused for breath Heather adopted her most soothing yet commanding tone, assuring her that Cedric regrettably failed to understand that mores in England are different from those in Malaya, and that, equally regrettably, there were some English girls not dissimilar to him who would find him congenial. Had Mary but known Miss Plunkett a little longer, Heather insisted, she would have realized it was not a good match. Heather then diverted her still-fulminating listener with a description of a clever, kind and open-minded young man whom she could meet immediately. Almost mollified, Miss Plunkett accepted and put the telephone down.

"Thank you, Heather," murmured a chastened Mary.

"No thanks are due, dear Mary. There will always be clients who complain, whether justifiably or not. And it is true that there are young women who share Cedric's unfortunate characteristics, and others who want at any cost to escape their fate by fleeing to another country. We shall have to hope that some equally unpleasant or thoroughly desperate damsel darkens our doors before long."

"There are certainly young women who loathe their drab life here, and sigh for some exotic far-flung continent, especially with a gallant husband adding to the rosy adventure."

"Mrs. Thistleton would be assured of an adventure, though rosiness with Cedric is difficult to imagine."

Mary thought long and hard before introducing Cedric to the next candidate. Miss Jenkins, a very smart former debutante, lived on an allowance of £500 a year from her father. With no need to work, she spent her days buying clothes, having beauty treatments, and lunching with girlfriends. She had been engaged three times but always (according to her) had broken off the engagement, and although most men insisted they did not want a hard-boiled wife, Mary felt that a soft-boiled one simply would not survive Cedric.

The meeting was not a success. Cedric stormed into the office to castigate Mary: no sooner had Miss Jenkins sipped her sherry than she had told him—horror!—of the three fiancés, and—unspeakable horror!—had confessed to having had an affair with a married man. Cedric was mortally offended. How dare Mary introduce him to such a fast, loose, dishonest female? He could no more marry such an improper person than fly. His friends would be incensed; his employer would give him the blackest of marks.

Heather was unmoved. "The silly girl should not have told him, of course," she drawled. "But his shock was pure playacting, for he has no idea what an affair is. He has no acquaintance with real human experience, and is devoid of any true feelings. He is, in truth, rather pathetic. You are doing your best for him, dear Mary, so keep smiling. However, I seem to remember that Miss Jenkins has made such confessions to other clients. She needs to be told to stop, for she is ruining her chances, and if she does not find a husband soon she certainly will be on the shelf."

Heather asked Miss Jenkins to come into the office, sat her down, and looked her straight in the eye. "It is most unwise for a woman to confess to some past misdemeanor of which she is ashamed, such as an affair with a married man. It is especially unwise to make such a confession to a potential husband, for he is bound to wonder if a woman who has been complicit in one married man's unfaithfulness might behave in the same way again."

Miss Jenkins gave a defiant little sniff. After all, her married man had felt no shame, so why should she? She drew hard on her cigarette, twitched her skirt, crossed and recrossed her legs, and half-rose to leave. But as Heather was poised to continue, she settled down and listened, albeit with the air of a child compelled to endure a ticking-off.

As both she and Heather well knew, at twenty-six and not married, Miss Jenkins was beginning to become something of a social pariah. Most of her friends had a husband, and children, and the majority now lived out of town and had exchanged gossipy girlfriend luncheons for couples' dinner parties. Miss Jenkins had never felt any inclination to train for any profession, and was alarmed to realize that, with little to occupy it, her life was emptying. The thrill of affairs had diminished since the wife of the married man, discovering the couple in bed in a hotel, had raved and stormed to such effect that the cowardly husband had meekly slunk back to the marital lair like a mauled fox, swishing his drooping tail in farewell.

Terrified of the nothingness of spinsterhood, Miss Jenkins earnestly hoped Heather would rescue her from the gaping hole of her future. Her only concept of somethingness was marriage, so she forced herself to smile and listen as Heather elaborated on the importance a man considering marriage places on moral behavior. Miss Jenkins was not at all sure she understood but, needing to ingratiate herself with Heather, she mouthed her agreement, and thanked her potential savior profusely.

But it was too late for Miss Jenkins and Cedric. Heather and Mary kept trying, consulting their registration cards, forms and books. "What about Miss Read-Melville?" wondered Heather. "She's a terrible snob—when I interviewed her she went on and on about the family estates and acres and ancestors. If she and Cedric got off, we would kill two difficult birds with one stone!"

"That would be truly wonderful. But I doubt she would think his background good enough, especially as I don't think he's got any background. Miss R.-M. requires a pedigree dating from William the Conqueror, and I feel in my bones that Cedric's started with a gentlemen's tailor circa 1910!"

"Well, what about Arabella Scott? She would adore to live abroad, and boss a lot of servants around and run a grand house. She would out-memsahib all the memsahibs in the entire social circle!"

"Yes, and she'd boss Cedric too, and serve him jolly well right. He'd soon rue the day and demand his money back. But Miss Scott lives in Aberdeen, remember, and she's not coming to London again before Cedric goes back to Malaya."

Mary managed to introduce Cedric to one or two young women who were so desperate that almost any husband would be better than none, but every girl squirmed at his arrogance, while he haughtily dismissed them as inadequate for his requirements.

With only two weeks of Cedric's leave to go the two matchmakers were in despair, until out of the blue, with no appointment, in walked the future Mrs. Thistleton, escorted by her father.

Lord W. was a chivalrous old peer with courtly manners who doted on his only child, the Honourable Grizelda. Late in life he had fallen hook, line and sinker for a much younger, fragile girl and married her, only to stand helplessly by as she died giving birth to their daughter. Lord W. was now in his seventies,

Grizelda twenty. What would become of her when he was no more? She was not an appealing girl, entirely lacking the alluring grace of her mother. She would never be short of money, for he was inordinately rich, but he had set his heart on finding her a husband and a home.

Before inheriting his title, Lord W. had managed a rubber plantation in Malaya. After his wife's death, a charming childless widow, Mrs. R., now in her fifties, had befriended him and helped him to bring up Grizelda, and now they wanted to marry—once Grizelda was established. Ten years ago they had moved back to the Old Country so that Grizelda could go to an English school; but they felt lost in a drastically changed England, and yearned to return to their beloved Malaya. So on hearing that the Marriage Bureau received many applications from that state, Lord W. speculated about the possibility of Heather finding a husband for Grizelda, and a new life for him and Mrs. R.

After they had ushered Lord W. and Grizelda out, the matchmakers faced each other across the desk. "Here's a dilemma!" lamented Mary. "Cedric is the answer in so many ways. But though she's far from pretty, the Honourable Grizelda is a nice child and it would be like throwing a Christian to the lions. I'd feel like a cold-blooded murderess! Anyway, he doesn't want a wife with dependent parents, so it's a nonstarter. But he's the only possibility."

"Grizelda is certainly not a star attraction. Her skin's too sallow, her eyes too close-set, her lips too narrow, her hair too lank, and her clothes are quite simply deplorable. But Cedric's not concerned about looks. It's social status he's entirely focused on, and Grizelda has that in spades. I agree she is a nice child, but I think there's more to her. I was watching her all the time her father was talking: she didn't utter a squeak, but I could see her mind working—she was chewing her lower lip and twisting her hands from time to time. I bet my bottom dollar she has views of her own. Let's get her in by herself. As for the dependent parents, Cedric assumes they would be financially and socially embarrassing; but imagine the stupendous kudos of pa-in-law being a Lord, and a rich Lord too! A full-blooded aristocrat! It's beyond Cedric's wildest dreams. He'd be over the moon!"

So Grizelda was invited back, and to Heather's gratification the silent girl waxed so loquacious that Mary had difficulty in absorbing the whirlpool of words that cascaded from her thin lips. Much though she loved and appreciated her father and Mrs. R., Grizelda felt crushed by their anxious concern. "I am perfectly capable!" she exploded, thumping the desk with her fist, "and I should love to run an establishment and have a husband, though not one who fusses over me as if I'm a fragile flower. My father is the darlingest of men, but he cannot see that I am a cactus. Nor that worrying over me achieves nothing except to worry me! And my 'mother,' Mrs. R., is devoted to him, which is simply heavenly, but she sees me only through his eyes. I should adore to go back to Malaya, and as long as he's not a lunatic or a savage, I don't care what my husband is. I am perfectly able to manage. Pa doesn't have an inkling, but last year I had a fling with a gorgeous man in the village, until he got too uppity and I had to see him off. This candidate of yours sounds possible: kindly arrange for me to meet him."

Flabbergasted, Mary organized the introduction and, a day later, was further stunned when Cedric telephoned to recount, in curiously stifled, subdued tones, oozing meekness and gratitude, what had transpired.

He had been first taken aback and then taken over by the Honourable Grizelda. The minute they had finished luncheon at the Dorchester, and were drinking their coffee, she had laid down her terms for their marriage: she would retain her title and the vast sums of money she would inherit on her twenty-first birthday and on the death of her father. She would if necessary make her husband an allowance. They would marry immediately and sail to Malaya on the first available ship. She would manage their house and entertain lavishly. Her father and his new wife would live in the vicinity. She would do all in her power to produce a son and heir. Was Cedric content with the proposal?

Cedric had capitulated.

Torn between laughter and tears by this chillingly unromantic outcome, Mary alternately chortled and wept as she repeated to Heather Grizelda's matter-of-fact summary: "Cedric is magnificently, superbly, ravishingly good-looking, simply the most sensational man I have ever set eyes on, and I am not at all attractive, I know. But I have what he wants. So you see, we are equal. And whenever I'm fed up with him I shall simply sit and stare at him!"

5

The Perfect Secretary and Other Learning Curves

In 1939 fear of war pervaded and polluted the atmosphere. You could feel it, almost touch and hear and smell it. The rumbling tension concentrated the minds of unmarried people, bringing into sharp focus their desire for a spouse, a steady ally in a threatening and uncertain world. The Marriage Bureau offered hope to the ever-growing numbers of people who climbed the Bond Street stairs in the summer heat, overwhelming Mary and Heather, who worked flat out to keep up with the demand. Something had to be done.

More clients meant more money, so there was now enough to pay a secretary. Mary engaged one. "She's perfect!" she reported to Heather. "Just wait till you see her. She has impeccable references—I spoke to her former employer over the telephone. She'll change our lives!"

The Perfect Secretary seemed to embody all the respectability and discretion her former employer had emphasized. Aged about fifty, she looked eminently reliable and competent, her gray hair parted down the middle and drawn back into a neat bun, and no visible makeup. She wore a plain, tidy gray coat and skirt over a high-necked, demurely frilled cotton blouse, sensible black lace-up shoes and thick brown lisle stockings. Her hat was a sort of gray felt pudding basin with a limp felt flower stuck incongruously on one side—"Left over from her youth in the 1920s," judged Heather—and her gloves were so heavily padded that had she been younger she might have been taken for a lady fencer. She peeled them off to reveal strong square hands with short stubby fingers, which were soon flying like gunshot across the keyboard of the Harrods typewriter.

The Perfect Secretary was a flawless typist, and she could spell and punctuate to perfection. Mary and Heather had only to say, "Please send Mr. X to Miss Y," for her to rattle off the introduction, meticulously observing special requirements requested on the registration form: "Do not post any letter on a Friday as I am out at work early on Saturdays and my mother will open my letters. I cannot stop her." Or, "Use only the envelopes I have supplied—the Bureau's are too thin, you can read through them."

The Perfect Secretary could write too: she composed tactful letters to applicants who had paid their registration fee, but for whom after a few weeks there was still no suitable introduction, so Mary and Heather returned their money wishing them luck, and trying not to hurt their feelings. Mary was exultant: "She's a real gem! What a difference! Now we can take on even more clients!"

And so they did, interviewing, arranging introductions, and talking to applicants and clients on the telephone, while the Perfect Secretary kept her head down and typed, hardly pausing in her pounding to talk to the matchmakers.

With more clients came more registration fees. Heather was thrilled but taken aback: "We had thought small rather than big about the business, and the results of our publicity had caught us by surprise, so much so that we had not even opened a bank account. Now we were taking lots of cash, and we didn't want to leave it in the office over the weekend. So I put it all into a big brown paper bag, walked out into Bond Street, went into the first bank I saw, a Bank of Scotland, emptied the notes and coins onto the counter, and said to the cashier that I would like to open a business account. He looked a bit startled and said I ought to see the manager.

"The cashier showed me into an office where a benign and cherubic-looking man sitting behind a huge desk was smiling kindly at me. He introduced himself as Mr. Gentle, shook my hand warmly, and asked me to sit down and tell him about the business. So I did, and I told him that we would probably be returning most of the money we had taken. He was interested and not at all shocked, and said that would be quite all right, but if the business really got going we should become a company, with an accountant. He was marvelously helpful and we took this piece of advice, and several others that he gave us over the years. He became a father figure to me until he retired."

Perhaps affected by the unusualness of the Marriage Bureau, the Perfect Secretary started to display odd changes in her appearance. Heather described the evolution: "At first we thought the changes were for the better, when she started using makeup—just a little powder on her rather shiny nose, and a delicate pale pink lipstick. But every week the lipstick became rosier and brighter, until she settled into a garish dark red, which made her mouth look as if it belonged to a vampire who had just bitten into a deliciously tasty virgin. The harsh color did not become her at all, especially as her face was so at odds with her clothes. We didn't say anything, in fact we hardly ever talked to her, for she was always bent over the typewriter and repelled any overtures from us.

"Then her hair started to change color. First it went from gray to mousy-brown, and from there to a fierce chestnut, the color of a spaniel, but dry and woolly, not sleek and shiny like a dog's, and the next week it was a strange orangey-red carrot color. Until the chestnut stage it had still been done in a tight little bun, but between then and the carrot stage she had it cut off and permed. She appeared one morning crowned with an alarming frizz of very stiff, tight, carrot curls, sticking out at all angles. It put me in mind of an unexpectedly colored lavatory brush. I gasped when she opened the door, but as usual she didn't say a word, just made for her chair and attacked the typing."

To begin with, Mary and Heather were pleased, because they thought their secretary was enjoying her job, and that it was doing her good and making her feel more attractive. But as the changes became more eye-catching, and clients started to look shocked when they saw her, Heather wanted to say something. She didn't like to criticize, though, because both she and Mary thought it would be impertinent.

"If she had been our own age," reflected Mary, "we would have been bolder, but as it was, we just tried to whisk clients past her very fast, talking to them nineteen to the dozen, so that they didn't have a chance to stare at her."

Early one morning a very rich client of the Bureau, an industrialist in Birmingham, rang and said curtly that he had a serious complaint to make, so would one or other of the partners kindly meet him for a drink after work that evening?

Mary and Heather fell into a flutter of anxiety. They had had nothing but very minor complaints—a letter not arriving in time, a client turning up late at a meeting—and Mr. Baldwin was not only a very nice but also a very important client. He was forty-nine, a widower who had hesitated for weeks before plucking up the courage to come to the Bureau. Despite his huge wealth he was a modest, quiet, polite man, a proper gentleman. Heather, who had interviewed him, was terribly keen to find him the right wife, and to make him feel at ease with the process. She had so far introduced him to two candidates, both of whom he had liked and remained on cordial terms with. His letters had been considerate, courteous and approving: "I deeply appreciate the confidential nature of your ingenious operation, which as you know is of great importance to me and for which I am most grateful."

"Mr. Baldwin is my client," pronounced Heather, "but I'd like you to come with me, please, dear Mary. Let's make ourselves as soignée as possible. You don't really need much makeup with that complexion of yours, but try a little more this evening. Here, have some of my lipstick: we need war paint for this skirmish!"

Heather dabbed her own and Mary's wrists with her favorite Gin Fizz scent and pinned an elegant flowered hat with a flirty little veil on top of her chignon. Emboldened, the two match-makers stepped into the bar of Brown's Hotel with a confident air. But they had had all day to wonder what on earth could have happened, and to worry themselves to distraction. Mr. Baldwin must have realized how upset they were, for he settled them in deep armchairs (Mary's feet did not reach the floor, she was so tiny) and gave them each the strongest G&T they had ever tasted—strong even by Heather's standards—before launching into his cautionary tale.

Mr. Baldwin disclosed to his matchmakers that a woman had written him a very good letter telling him that his name and particulars had been given to her by the Marriage Bureau. She was a widow of forty-two living in London, having moved there from the Midlands in 1928, when she married. She wrote that she had no children, a very good income as her husband had been wealthy, lived a pleasant life meeting friends, going to concerts and theaters, but that she was at times lonely, and although she enjoyed all the activity in London she yearned to return to her home territory. She sounded intelligent, pleasant, friendly, unassuming, and not a gold-digger (what had finally driven him to the Bureau was a spate of impoverished Birmingham widows who had descended on him from the very day his wife died). So he agreed to meet her. Her name was Mrs. Gladys Robertson.

"She's not one of our clients!" exclaimed Mary. "She can't be! I remember all the names!"

"Mary's right," agreed Heather. "What was she like?"

Mr. Baldwin grimaced. "She was awful. You cannot imagine how awful. You remember that I asked you to introduce me to ladies in their late thirties or early forties? Well, this, this . . . female . . . was fifty-five if she was a day. But her age was the least of the horrors. She was made up like a tart (forgive me, ladies), with blood-red lipstick smeared all over her mouth, heavy white powder on her face except for around red clown blobs on her cheeks, eyes she could hardly see out of, the lids were so weighed down with green muck and some kind of waxy-looking black stuff on her lashes. Her hair looked like a ginger tomcat who'd seen the vet bearing down on him with a castrating knife (forgive me again, ladies) and had leaped in terror onto the top of her head.

"She was squashed into a bright green shiny dress, much too tight, with a very low neckline filled with a cheap flashy necklace, and a nasty bit of moth-eaten musquash around her shoulders. Her legs were encased in those black stockings full of holes— what do you call them? Fishnets? And she tottered on her shoes, which had arrow-shaped toes and ludicrously high thin heels. She had a hideous old handbag from which she took a bottle of scent and poured some onto her wrists. The smell was so sweet and at the same time sour and musty that it made my stomach heave. And when she'd done that she ferreted around in the dreadful bag and got out the bloody lipstick (forgive me, ladies) and painted her mouth, as if it wasn't dripping with gore already. She did all this in front of me in the bar where we met. I had to buy her a drink, then I turned on my heel and left. I didn't care what happened to her. If she'd gone out into the street and been treated like a whore (forgive me, forgive me, ladies) I wouldn't have helped her—that's what she was asking for. How in heaven's name did she get to know about me?"

All through this dreadful saga Mary and Heather had been thinking the same thoughts and coming to the identical conclusion: the Perfect Secretary would have to go. They explained to Mr. Baldwin, apologizing with every other sentence they spoke. Very luckily he sympathized and took their side, and for the rest of the evening he regaled them with stories of tricky and recalcitrant employees of his factory. They parted the very best of friends and, to Heather's particular delight, a week later he met a perfect candidate, a charming widow of forty-three who, as it turned out, had known and liked Mr. Baldwin's wife, but had been too reticent to contact him after her death for fear of being thought grasping. She was his match in money, modesty and simple niceness, which they both recognized in each other the minute they met.

Fear of war looming made Mr. Baldwin and his beloved act quickly: they married a few weeks later. The Bureau sent them a congratulatory telegram, ambiguously worded so that nobody at the reception would guess how they had met. In return came the sweetest thank-you letter, with a check, a huge bouquet of red roses ("Bloody red!" grinned Mr. Baldwin on the telephone), and a little white and silver box containing two slices of wedding cake.

As for the Perfect Secretary, Heather and Mary both jibbed at the prospect of dismissing her. Mary wanted them to toss a coin to see who would have the unsavory task, but Heather refused and they agreed that it would be a joint effort.

The interview was painful but brief. The Perfect Secretary remained mute throughout, but she knew she had been caught red-handed, and when Heather and Mary stopped speaking she picked up her handbag, put on her coat, hat and gloves, and walked out without a word or a backward glance. Heather sent on what she was owed in wages, and thankfully she faded out for ever.

Mary was very cautious when choosing the next secretary; but she struck lucky with Miss Blunt. "I hesitated about Miss Blunt because she was so terribly young, but there was something so grown-up, so reassuring about her, she positively glowed with competence and calm, and she had the most captivating smile imaginable. So I took a chance, and am eternally grateful that I did for she turned out to be really perfect for us. She started as a junior at thirty shillings a week, for she was only just sixteen, but her typing was as good as her predecessor's, and she developed the most extraordinary filing system, which could produce anything you wanted in a matter of seconds. She always seemed to know by instinct the people to whom we wanted to talk on the telephone, and the ones we wanted to avoid."

Mary heard the superbly efficient Miss B. flummoxed only once, when a man telephoned: "I hope you have someone who might suit me. I'm keen on fellatio."

"Oh," replied Miss Blunt eagerly. "That's stamp collecting, isn't it? Yes, I am sure we can help you!"

The caller promptly put the telephone down, leaving Miss Blunt perplexed and wondering anxiously if she had somehow offended him.

Miss Blunt stayed on as a full-blown secretary at £3 a week until after war was declared, when she was called up to work in a Ministry. She grew achingly bored because there was very little to do, and she was so efficient that she could do a day's work in two hours, so she used to go back to Bond Street and type the Bureau's letters in her lunch hour. She would fly in, dash off scores of letters, and rush back to the Ministry, waving her sandwich and mouthing, "Goodbye! I'd better skedaddle! I'll see you tomorrow!"

Mary and Heather were growing practiced in the art of interviewing and dealing with their many and varied clients. The grander, aristocratic ones tended to get on well with Heather, whose cool style they understood, while Mary's warmth and sympathy particularly appealed to the poorer, humbler clients.

In 1939 nobody, rich or poor, was used to talking much about themselves, their feelings and hopes, especially to someone they didn't know. Nor were they used to filling in forms about personal matters, so the Marriage Bureau's registration form had to be short, asking only for dry facts such as name, age, occupation and marital status, which did not provide much insightful information to the interviewer. The two matchmakers grew adept at encouraging applicants and making them feel relaxed—sometimes so relaxed that they poured everything out without a pause. "Awful talker," wrote Mary as she interviewed a middle-aged woman who bent her ear for an hour. "Extremely nice gent," she noted of an elderly widower, "charm. Talked but also listened. No left hand but is not incapacitated in the least by his disability. Wants to meet a lady who is interested in humanity, like himself."

Such comments helped to fix a client in the interviewer's mind. So too did clients' own descriptions of themselves and their desired spouse. "I have always lived in the country," stipulated a herdswoman of forty-one, "so do not want to meet an urban type. Someone unafraid of cows and dogs would suit, though I am not a dog worshipper, and with a thoughtful frame of mind and of course a dash of humour (NOT a parson)." A South African gentleman farmer required "Good old family, good health, good rosy colour, auburn hair, not moon-faced, not bandy-legged, in fact good to look at. Not prudish. Not subject to mooch. Must be prepared to live in South Africa. Must have £800 unearned, free of tax. Ought to be mainly self-supporting after my decease."

Both matchmakers felt that their desk was a useful aid to conducting an interview. "One becomes vaguely disembodied," recalled Heather, "like a hairdresser or a dentist, who traditionally receive the most astounding confidences. And one must be prepared for the unexpected—one man, as I entered the interviewing room, turned pale and exclaimed, 'Good heavens, you're the image of my fourth wife!'"

Everyone who found their way to the Marriage Bureau got a sympathetic and constructive hearing from Heather or Mary, or from the new interviewer, who was needed by June. But the office was too small, even with the extra room, so when the matchmakers heard of a good space to let on the first floor of a building just up the street, they hurried to look at it. The tenants had left London, along with many other people who could see that war was certain to break out. There were a few weeks left on the lease, which the tenants offered to Heather and Mary, saying that the landlord would surely be reasonable if they renewed the lease at its end. Heather's solicitor friend Humphrey, who had been helpful from the outset, warned that they would be taking a bit of a chance, but thought the landlord was unlikely to be unreasonable, indeed that he would be thankful to have a tenant in such uncertain times. However, he advised spending the minimum on any equipment so that they could move quickly if necessary.

Heather and Mary moved in, and were so delighted with their new premises that they became overconfident. They painted the walls, festooned the windows with lilac satin curtains that framed lovebirds in a pretty cage, and laid pale carpet on the floor—only to find that all their friends swarmed in for coffee and a chat in such pleasant surroundings. Far worse, the landlord insisted on a new seven-year lease at a much higher rent.

"What shall we do?" wailed Heather to Humphrey. "We're doing well, but not enough to afford the rent they want—it's extortionate. And who knows what will happen when we're at war, as we surely shall be? And we've got only three weeks left on the lease!"

Humphrey advised sitting tight until they had found somewhere else. The lease was in Heather's name so, in Humphrey's opinion, if the landlord sent in the bailiffs, it should be easy to avoid them as it was only Heather they were out to catch: they were not interested in Mary or anyone else.

There were two doors to the new office and a fire escape, so twice, warned by the invaluably quick-witted Miss Blunt that a bailiff was approaching, Heather managed to disappear just in time. Heather cast her mind back to what happened next. "After three weeks of living in a state of siege we found another suitable office, and I was due to sign the lease a few days later (I always did the business side, Mary not being interested). Vastly relieved, one evening after the staff had left we settled down to finish off the day's mating—my favorite occupation! I adored plotting and planning who should be introduced to each other! We forgot to lock the door as we usually did, and suddenly it flew open and a respectable-looking man asked, 'Miss Jenner?' Automatically, without thinking, I said, 'Yes.' Without more ado he banged a writ down on my desk.

"I was appalled, but tried to remain calm, and asked him to sit down and tell me what I was meant to do next. He chose a swivel chair which we had just bought secondhand, and as he leaned back in it something snapped, and he did a backward somersault onto the floor (we never have had much luck with swivel chairs, somehow). We all rushed to help him up, and luckily he wasn't hurt, in fact he softened up and confided that in his line of work he usually had a far more unpleasant reception. He dealt with really gruesome types, he said with some relish, robbers an' crooks an' wide boys of all 'orrible sorts, not nice ladies like our good selves, who he could tell hadn't done nuffink properly wrong, bless our hearts: 'Crikey, you two young ladies wouldn't know how to do nuffink a person could rightly call wrong!' (Little does he know.) He said we should see our solicitor, so we did, and the blessed Humphrey saved us again."

A week later Heather signed the lease for a spacious office on the second floor of 124 New Bond Street. It had four rooms: a waiting room, a secretary's office, and two front rooms, one for interviewing and one for doing the mating. This office became the permanent home of the Marriage Bureau. In 1939 Heather paid the princely sum of thirty-five pounds, four shillings and elevenpence.

Mary and Heather felt that the Bureau was now securely established in as safe a home as possible. But in August 1939 nothing was secure: everything was uncertain and potentially dangerous. Closing the office every evening, Mary and Heather joined the people scurrying along Bond Street, their faces set and tense with anxiety.

In September, Heather, who was virtually bilingual in French, was due to spend a weekend with friends in Le Touquet; but the news was so threatening that, reluctantly, she canceled her ticket. Knowing that at any minute war would be declared, she and Mary went down to the River Hamble for a "last" weekend's sailing on a friend's yacht. Heather reclined languidly while Mary put all the knowledge she had gained as skipper of a forty-five-foot sloop to good use.

It was a golden weekend, until Sunday, when it was devastatingly shattered by the Prime Minister's grim announcement on the wireless:

> This morning the British Ambassador in Berlin handed the German Government a final Note stating that, unless we heard from them by 11 o'clock that they were prepared at once to withdraw their troops from Poland, a state of war would exist between us. I have to tell you now that no such undertaking has been received, and that consequently this country is at war with Germany.

Mary and Heather knew that everything had changed irrevocably. "We sat down, feeling weak at the knees. Darkness was descending. The world as we knew it was at an end."

6

New Clients Wanted—but No Spies, Please

Britain's declaration of war with Germany on September 3, 1939, had an immediate effect on the Marriage Bureau. People behaved as if frozen, so chilled by shock and hideous memories of the Great War that they were unable to act except robotically. Going to a Marriage Bureau was not a priority. The phenomenal rush of clients generated by the press publicity only five months earlier, when the Bureau opened, was not sustained. The papers were focused on the war, as too were people's minds. Mary and Heather were deeply concerned.

"I've just been to the bank," announced Heather, her voice darkening, "and our account contains precisely elevenpence. No pounds, not even any shillings. Just eleven pence. Mr. Gentle was sympathetic but when his secretary put our statement on his desk he could not help but look somber."

"Whatever shall we do?" An anxious frown marred Mary's pretty and usually smiling face.

"First, chase up the After Marriage Fee from existing clients who are about to tie the knot. War will sharpen the focus of everyone who is thinking of marrying—the uncertainty will make them want to get on with it quickly."

"Not a good reason for getting married, but you're right. We can't force them to marry, though, and in any case a few After Marriage Fees won't be enough to keep us going, will they? We must get more new clients or we'll have to close down, won't we?"

"Over my dead body!"

"Well, what *are* we going to do? More publicity? The press have been very good to us ever since we opened. I'm sure we could persuade them to give us a bit of extra help now. What do you think, Heather?"

Mary spoke tentatively, for she knew that Heather had reservations. When Mary had first suggested, in early April, that they contact the newspapers, Heather had been alarmed and argued against it. Mary had been amazed, but came to realize that there must be some reason for Heather, usually so poised and commanding, to be apprehensive. She had pressed her friend, who eventually confided that when she was eight, one of her cousins had been kidnapped. Her family had been horrified by the publicity about the case, for fear that the girl might have been raped (though nobody uttered that fearful word), and that the press would report the whole story. If they did, neither the girl nor the family would ever be able to escape the notoriety. The child had been rescued and restored, unharmed, but the family still recoiled from the memory, judging the press as terrible people, to be avoided at all costs. The prejudice had stuck in Heather's mind. She left the journalists to Mary, whose turn of phrase delighted them, as in August when her stout defiance of critics of the Bureau was reported: "Miss Oliver considers she is performing a national service, and adds that if she established a bureau in Germany Hitler would see it in the right light."

Soon Heather began to accept that the situation was critical, and that her reason for disliking the press was irrational. She could also see that Mary was very popular with the journalists, and that their articles brought results. So with Heather's blessing, in the dark days of September 1939 Mary assiduously wooed journalists as if they were potential husbands. She buttered them up, flattered them, sympathized with them (she was a devoted listener), got to know their personal histories, and genuinely liked them. They responded to her cajolery and to the story of the Marriage Bureau: a wonderful tale of imagination and initiative, a welcome contrast to the unremitting gloom of war stories. They delivered a fresh round of positive stories featuring the two charming matchmakers, their novel ideas and their marvelous success.

Mary also devised a small brochure to help people understand what the Bureau was doing. She wrote:

POSSIBLY YOU MAY be feeling a little uneasy at having this brochure in your possession. The English still regard marriage in rather a sentimental light, and forget that in most Continental countries it is rightly considered as a contract of such importance that it is carefully arranged—not left to chance.

THERE IS NO reason to feel ashamed because you want to marry the right person. Indeed, you should congratulate yourself on your good sense in trying to make sure that you have every opportunity of meeting and getting to know the type of person whom you would like to marry. You would consider yourself unwise and improvident if you did not make provision for other aspects of your life—how much more important is this question of making the right match!

THE MARRIAGE BUREAU will put you in touch only with people who fulfil the qualifications you demand. Afterwards it is entirely for you to decide whether you want to marry—for, needless to say, mutual attraction and affection cannot be guaranteed! We cannot play the part of Cupid, we can only introduce you to people who have already expressed a wish to marry somebody like yourself.

TWO SENSIBLE PEOPLE who know what they want are introduced to each other. If they are not attracted—if friendship does not "ripen into love," as the saying goes—no harm is done, and it is our business to try again on behalf of both our clients until they are satisfied.

Slowly, thanks to press articles and Mary's reasonable and reassuring words, the Bureau welcomed more new clients, including increasing numbers of foreigners. Heather and Mary were legally obliged to report to the police any non-Allied potential clients, who might be enemy aliens: fifth columnists trying to infiltrate themselves by marrying an English spouse. Most of the foreign applicants were men, though more and more women, often Austrian, turned up at the Bureau, anxious to marry an Englishman and thereby avoid internment and the restrictions on aliens. The police were concerned about illegal marriages, such as one, reported in the press, made by a father of eight whose hapless wife discovered that he had bigamously married a German Jewess. So Mary and Heather sent off to Scotland Yard details of foreign nationals who applied, but they seldom discovered whether those they had interviewed, but who subsequently did not register, had been interned, or had simply decided not to proceed with the Bureau.

One day, Mary interviewed a forceful man who exuded both a seductive magnetism and a sinister aura she found disturbing and threatening. When he had telephoned to make an appointment Mary had puzzled about his accent: he spoke English fluently, but with odd hints of an American twang— and surely a guttural, Germanic note crept in too. The minute she set eyes on him she felt instinctively that there was something false about him, something "actor-y," which put her on her guard.

Clicking his heels together and nodding a little bow, the well-dressed, stoutish visitor held out his hand and gave Mary's such a firm shake that she winced. He produced his registration form, already filled in in clear, bold handwriting and, without waiting for her to ask questions, proceeded to fire facts at her as if shooting bullets at a target. He was a German count. He had been born and brought up in America. He was an insurance agent. He was fifty-six. His many English friends had begged him to leave Germany in 1938. He was passionately attached to England. He was residing at the Hampden Club in Marylebone. He was buying a flat in Knightsbridge. He had divorced his wife. He had a son living in South America. He had a good income and wide interests. He wanted to marry a well-bred lady of good family, figure and income. She must have been previously married.

Mary mouthed "Yes" and "Certainly" and "Naturally" and "How interesting" as the Count fired on, ignoring her. When he came to a halt he thrust his head forward questioningly and switched on a dazzling smile.

"I felt as if I was about to be interrogated," Mary recalled. "He unnerved me. I felt certain that he was acting, especially when he smiled at me: his lips curved, but his eyes did not follow suit: they were cold and hard and dangerous, like little lumps of coal. I stalled, told him I would contact some ladies on his behalf and write to him when I had a positive reply."

Mary reported to Heather, who immediately dispatched the Count's details to Scotland Yard. Three days later, a high-up friend in the Yard informed Heather, confidentially, that the man had spied for Germany in the Great War, but had somehow offended his government and so was persona non grata in both Germany and England. The high-up thanked Heather for helping to put the Count where he should be: in prison.

One foreigner considered safe by the police was "the Sheikh." But once again, Mary's bones urged her to beware. In her view, the police must have been so baffled by the Sheikh that in the end they gave up. He claimed to have been born Lebanese, of a French Christian father and a Syrian Mohammedan mother who moved to England in 1890, when he was only ten, and got themselves British passports. He did not know why they left Lebanon. He was fluent in French, English and Arabic, so he worked as a translator, then fought in the British Army in the Great War. He survived the trenches, though he was vague about that period, and then moved to Wales.

"I asked him, why Wales?" said Mary. "But he was elusive, just like Cedric Thistleton was about his background—remember, Heather?"

Heather did indeed remember, but she was more perturbed by the Sheikh than by Cedric, who had been all bluff and self-important bluster but basically harmless. Though she trusted Mary's bones when they sensed a good introduction, she placed less reliance on her friend's intuitions of dark and possibly unsavory secrets, putting them down to oversensitivity. But there was something about the Sheikh that Heather could not put her finger on, something oddly disturbing. Perhaps it was just his unfathomably black eyes, hooded like a hawk's. Otherwise, his appearance was faultless: of medium height, clad in an expensively well-tailored suit, a large red rose in his buttonhole and a matching silk handkerchief in his top pocket, his surprisingly small feet shod in fine leather brogues. Though a shade saturnine, his face was attractive, his features sharply boned, his nose a curved hook—like an eagle's beak, thought Heather, who found herself constantly reminded of a bird of prey.

The Sheikh spoke perfect English with an engaging little lilt—no doubt acquired in Wales, presumed Heather. He bowed to the matchmakers as he made his entrance, kissed their hands, disposed himself in the chair, and lit a black and gold cigarette. The aromatic fumes rapidly filled the small office, mingling with the faint whiff of attar of roses he exuded. Heather and Mary observed his coal-black hair (suspiciously uniform in color, judged Mary), sleeked down with Brylcreem, and his gleaming white teeth (a fine set of false snappers, thought Heather), curiously at odds with his fingernails, which were unattractively overlong and edged with grime.

The Sheikh's wife had died some years ago, for reasons he declined to give (nothing about the Sheikh was ever glowingly clear). Now he wanted to marry a very smart lady who would entertain his guests in style. "She must be charming and sophisticated," he explained, waving his cigarette perilously near

Mary's face, causing her to cough. "Alas, such ladies do not exist in Wales. They are all Welsh there," he added cuttingly.

Mary, proud of her part-Welsh ancestry, bristled, but kept silent while the Sheikh enumerated his other requirements: "It is imperative that my bride is English, elegant, slim and beautifully dressed, by couturiers." He winced in aesthetic pain as he added, "Not clothes off the peg, *no*! *Never*! She must also be without children, not even grown-up ones, for I am unable to abide children of any age. She must be not a day over forty-five, and not an inch over five foot three. It is also vital that she is wellborn, an aristocrat or at least of your noble upper class. She must have knowledge of the world and its ways. Finally, she must have an excellent income to match my own."

Despite much skillful probing, the matchmakers failed to establish either the size or the source of the Sheikh's income. As with everything about him, the subject was mysteriously cloudy. He was enigmatic, even evasive, as he deflected Heather's questions onto yet more requirements of his dream wife: though a sophisticate, she must not be an entirely urban lady. She must like the country, birds and animals. "I do not mean that she should be adoring of dogs or dedicated to horses," he elaborated, "as so many of you English ladies are, but only that she should have an affection for our friends who are not human, but who are as deserving of our love as many people. Perhaps more deserving."

"That's easy, at least," declared Mary to Heather after he had left, "since so many of our female clients describe themselves on their registration forms as 'fond of animals and children.' Only the British put animals and children in the same category," she added, with uncharacteristic acidity.

Heather and Mary picked out a Mrs. Pratt-Evans, a widow, barely five feet tall, extremely smart, expensively preserved, beautifully coiffured and manicured, and something over forty (unclear how much, probably quite a lot; but luckily her daintiness suggested youthfulness). She loved music, the countryside, fashion, theater-going, and, especially, animals. She lived in London and in her husband's family home in Shropshire, a convenient thirty miles from the Sheikh.

Heather wrote to Mrs. Pratt-Evans, describing the Sheikh, listing his interests: languages, country life, fine porcelain, the animals and birds he owned. "Oh, I speak Spanish and French, and I am utterly convinced that I shall adore his pets," she gushed down the telephone, "for I adore all God's creatures! I seem to understand them, you see, and they will do anything I require of them. My little pooches would die for me if I asked them to. Isn't that too divine?"

Mary was quite sure that Mrs. Pratt-Evans had no more love of animals nor influence over them than Heather, who greatly disliked all four-legged friends except for Blanche, her own beloved Peke. She was equally sure that Mrs. Pratt-Evans was desperate to marry again, knew her chances were diminishing daily, and would claim anything at all that might help her to capture a suitable man.

Mrs. Pratt-Evans had been married to a Welshman with whom she had emigrated to Uruguay, where he ran a ranch until a bull went berserk and gored him so badly that he slowly expired in a great pool of blood, witnessed by his mesmerized wife. She had recounted this shocking story to the two matchmakers in such a dispassionate way, as though his frightful death had been no more than a tiresome interruption to her ordered life, that they felt sure she could hold her own with such a forceful character as the Sheikh.

Mrs. Pratt-Evans and the Sheikh exchanged several letters before he invited her to luncheon, sending her directions. After days of indecision she settled on a simple floral frock, perhaps a trifle girlish, but it suited her lightsome mood of excited optimism. She applied her makeup with exceptional care, coaxed her slightly thinning hair into a becoming bob, topped by a delicious little veiled hat, and drove off humming happily in near-ecstatic anticipation.

Expecting a sheikh to reside in a grand mansion with sensational views, Mrs. Pratt-Evans was disturbed to find herself following ever-narrower, overgrown roads before arriving in a bleak valley. She stumbled up a rutted path between neglected flower beds, avoiding two chained dogs that growled menacingly as she knocked on the door of a small, down-at-heel cottage. She perked up at the appearance of an elderly retainer, though he was dressed in flowing white robes and looked her up and down with an inscrutable yet somehow critical eye. He addressed her in fierce tones, in a language that might have been Welsh or Arabic. Flummoxed, Mrs. Pratt-Evans nodded and smiled nervously, clutching her handbag in both hands and extending one foot over the threshold.

"No!" shouted the retainer in recognizable English, gesticulating wildly toward the side of the building, from where the Sheikh suddenly materialized, as if Aladdin had rubbed his lamp.

Encouraged by Mary and Heather's glowing description of the Sheikh's style and suavity, Mrs. Pratt-Evans had pictured an elegant, mature man, perhaps wearing sharply creased cream flannels with a silk shirt and cravat, who at first sight of her would fall into a stunned silence of worshipful disbelief. He would be enraptured by such a vision of delight, so miraculous a blessing, a dream of surpassing elegance: his ideal bride.

But advancing toward her was a scruffy man dressed in a grubby nightgown, carrying a tin bucket in each hand, his shoulders hunched to support a large bird whose glittering eyes regarded her with such malevolence that she recoiled as from the devil incarnate. Parts of the infernal creature's body showed pink where its feathers were molting, and from its beak there dangled the remains of a baby chick, its dear golden fluffy little body streaked with gore and falcon dribble—for the hideous carnivore was indeed a falcon, such as had recently terrified Mrs. Pratt-Evans during a visit to the zoo. She paled and stepped backward, and when the bird uttered a great screech, letting fly the pathetic remains of its feast, unfolded its disintegrating wings and launched itself from its human perch toward her, she fell to the ground in a faint.

As she revived, Mrs. Pratt-Evans felt hands around her waist and chest, pulling her up. Glancing down at her torn frock, spattered with unspeakable remnants of baby chick, she wrenched herself free and fled to her car, abandoning her hat, which had flown off. Gripping the steering wheel in hands trembling with shock, horror and disgust, she ground the gears and roared away, watched impassively by the Sheikh, his retainer, and the glassy-eyed bird.

Two days later, Mrs. Pratt-Evans stalked into the Bureau.

"Why, Mrs. Pratt-Evans!" Mary sang out. "Did you have a delicious luncheon with the Sheikh?"

"I had no luncheon." Mrs. Pratt-Evans spat the words out. "But luncheon was indeed had."

Mary looked puzzled.

"Luncheon was partaken of not by me, nor even by the Sheikh, as you call him, though I call him a complete charlatan. Luncheon was partaken of by a foul, no doubt pestiferous, disgusting, diabolical, repellent, moldering, cruel-eyed, savage, utterly ghastly bird. A bird of prey, to be precise. Or rather, the devil in avian form. The property of his hellish, filthy, accursed, be-nightgowned, utterly monstrous master, the Sheikh of Araby or Llandudno or wherever he is from." Mrs. Pratt-Evans paused in her tirade, searching for more excoriating adjectives to hurl at the bird and its owner.

Stunned by her client's vehemence, and still at a loss as to its cause, Mary persisted. "But did the Sheikh not give you luncheon?"

Now near hysterical, Mrs. Pratt-Evans poured out the entire saga. Mary was shocked and at first disbelieving, but the lady was so emphatic, so precise in her descriptions, from the Sheikh's dirty nightie to the bloodstains on her frock, that eventually Mary came to believe her.

At last Mrs. Pratt-Evans departed, leaving a depressed and deflated Mary to recount the hair-raising drama to her fellow matchmaker. Heather was normally much more cavalier and contained than her feelingful friend, but the more she heard of the Sheikh the more concerned she became for the reputation of the Bureau. She wrote an appeasing letter to Mrs. Pratt-Evans, explaining that the police had cleared the Sheikh, that she was very obliged to her valued client for bringing the matter to her attention, and would waive any After Marriage Fee that became due—as Heather hoped it would—from Mrs. Pratt-Evans. She received a grudging but mollified reply.

Mary and Heather decided to erase the Sheikh from the books. So they were appalled when he appeared, without warning, in the Bureau. He looked as immaculate as on his previous appearance, sat down without a by-your-leave, frowned ferociously, and lit a cigarette. Then, the veins in his neck bulging, the lilt in his voice submerged in an aggressive growl, he let off a furious volley: "She is a fearful, ghastly female. She is unfashionably dressed—by D. H. Evans of your so frightful Oxford Street, a common department store, I am sure, or perhaps Marshall & Snelgrove, which is a little superior but not good enough. Before I even met her she bored me to death with letters recounting innumerable dull anecdotes of life on a ranch in Uruguay and servant problems and bulls and her dogs and her dead husband. And she insisted that she loves all God's creatures, as she kept calling them. So I decided to invite her to my raptor's luncheon, and if she truly adored him, I would then take her to luncheon at my house, which is very beautiful, and not where I keep my birds. But I took an instant, vehement dislike to her, and she to my bird. And what is worse"—his voice rose to a higher note, his upper lip curling insolently as he blew a scornful cloud of smoke—"she has *only one breast*!"

The Sheikh leaned back and, oblivious of Mary's coughing and choking, exhaled clouds of cigarette smoke as if blowing Mrs. Pratt-Evans to the four winds. He raised his eyebrows, a look of contempt in his black-currant eyes. Imperiously, Heather returned his gaze. Without uttering a word she contrived to imply that she knew all about Mrs. Pratt-Evans's breasts, both of them, but deemed them none of the Sheikh's business, and considered it odiously ill-bred of him to raise the subject. Mary was so incensed by his daring to come near the Bureau again that she remained mute with fury.

For a few seconds a silence of almost audible antagonism reigned. Then Heather stood up, towering over the Sheikh, and hissed with all the considerable venom she could muster, "We are unable to assist you in your search for a wife. Kindly desist from any further contact with the Bureau. We shall refund your registration fee. That is all. Goodbye."

The Sheikh knew he had gone too far. With an insubordinate sniff he stubbed his cigarette out on the desk, leered wolfishly at Mary, who was clutching a large sheaf of papers in front of her chest, sneered at Heather, and vanished down the stairs.

"I thought I'd better protect my breasts!" said Mary, putting her papers down on her desk. "I didn't want him expanding his knowledge on me!"

7

Mary Transforms Myrtle

When Mary caught sight of Myrtle Glossop edging her way into the office, her hand flew to her heart and, as she screwed her eyes tight shut in fleeting horror, the words flashed through her mind, "There but for the grace of God went I!"

After the long-dreaded announcement of war, with children and pregnant women hastily evacuated from cities, millions of gas masks issued, sandbags piled up outside buildings, and couples rushing to marry before the men were conscripted, nothing seriously warlike happened, and the panic soon lapsed into bemusement. Life became punctuated by inconveniences and restrictions, but not by violence, terror or death. Indeed, on October 6, 1939, Hitler offered peace. In this preternatural Phoney War calm, business in the Marriage Bureau continued apace. Myrtle Glossop was one of hundreds of anxious yet hopeful new clients.

It was to divine grace that Mary attributed the rebellious spirit that had enabled her to escape her destined role in life: childhood as a farmer's daughter on a windswept East Anglian farm, to be followed by womanhood as a farmer's wife on a similar farm. But poor Myrtle, scuttling through the Marriage Bureau's doorway like a little brown crab, had resignation written all over her. Though she was only twenty-six, her shoulders sagged, she drooped like an old lady, and was dressed like one, in an all-enveloping grayish-brownish-greenish tweed coat. Her hat, pulled down over straggly brown hair, was in a thick matted beige felt, an amalgam of flowerpot, pudding basin and policeman's helmet. Her small face was devoid of makeup, the mouth turned down at the corners as if she was struggling to withhold tears. Her gloves and shabby handbag were of a matching muddy brown, her thick woolen stockings visibly darned, her feet encased in clumpy, old-fashioned lace-up shoes that gave the impression of being too big.

"*Quelle horreur!*" whispered fashion-loving Heather to Mary. But Mary's kind heart melted at the sight of the prematurely elderly girl, whom she took by the woolly arm and guided into the interview room.

Prompted by Mary, in a light, timorous voice Myrtle embarked on her tale of woe. She was the only child of elderly parents, long dead, whom she had hardly known. Her father, Horace Glossop, had been a civil engineer constructing dams and irrigation systems in India, so passionately consumed by his work that, though craving an heir, he was forty-five before he met and married the only female available, a thirty-eight-year-old Scottish missionary, who renounced the unequal task of converting the natives for her last chance of marriage and children.

After a protracted and agonizing labor, at forty-two Mrs. Glossop gave birth to a daughter, only to hear the doctor's stern warning that another pregnancy would kill her. She blanched at the news, and at Horace's grim-faced reaction. He largely ignored his poor substitute for a son, but Mrs. Glossop was overwhelmed with adoration of little Myrtle.

However, the wretched mother scarcely ever saw her beloved daughter. Mr. Glossop insisted that Myrtle be cared for by native ayahs while her mother behaved like a lady of leisure, calling on local European bigwigs and holding polite tea parties and picnics. When Myrtle was nine, despite her mother's tearful entreaties, the child was dispatched to a prep school in Sussex, to be as properly educated as would have been Mr. Glossop's son and heir.

In the unheated school Myrtle turned so blue with unaccustomed cold that she could scarcely speak, and when she did open her mouth, she was mercilessly mocked for her singsong tones, copied from her ayahs. She learned little either at school or in the holidays, spent with three devout, impoverished maiden aunts in their comfortless house on the Isle of Wight. They were kindly disposed to their little niece, and welcomed the pitiful sums of money sent from India for her keep; but Myrtle's life revolved around formal tea parties, wind-buffeted seaside walks, dutiful letter-writing to her unknown parents, stitching samplers, and lengthy church services, with no companions of her own age. Thousands of miles away her mother wept as she penned letter after tear-stained letter to her daughter.

After leaving India for Sussex, Myrtle had not seen her parents again until they came to Europe on leave, when she was fourteen. The family admired museums, opera houses, quaint ceremonies and ancient buildings, which they discussed in exhaustive detail over meals. Strangers, none of them knew how to talk personally to the others.

Seven years later Mr. Glossop retired. He and his faithful weary wife, yearning to see the daughter she scarcely knew, were days away from sailing back to the Old Country when they succumbed to cholera and were swiftly cremated. The government pension, for which they had sacrificed all hopes of seeing their daughter, immediately expired.

The aunts had imperceptibly languished and died, one by one, so, aged twenty-one, with only a legacy of £300 a year, no job, and no qualifications, Myrtle had had no choice but to accept the charitable offer of a home with Godmother Augusta. When she ventured up to London and the Marriage Bureau, Myrtle had been ensconced in Cornwall with this benign but parsimonious ninety-year-old for five tedious years.

"How do you spend your time?" inquired Mary, who could herself have given Myrtle's answer.

"Most days I walk my godmother's dog in the village, taking some soup to anyone who's sick. If it's raining I stay in and help the maid with the laundry—it's much easier folding the sheets with two people. Or I do some sewing—there are always clothes to be mended or altered. Or I read to my godmother—her eyesight's not very good. On Saturdays I pick flowers and take them to the church, and put them on the altar and on the grave of my godmother's husband. If the Rector's there he talks to me, which is lovely—he's very nice and not as old as everyone else. On Sundays I go to church with Godmother Augusta, and I help with the children at the Sunday School—they can be quite naughty, so I tell them to be quiet. The Rector helps too, which is very nice."

Mary's assessment was that, lacking money, education, family and friends, poor Myrtle was imprisoned by poverty on all fronts. Immediately after the outbreak of war, excitement had briefly enlivened her humdrum life when a pregnant mother and her three-year-old identical boy twins were evacuated from the dangerous East End to the safety of Cornwall. An administrative cock-up had billeted this forlorn trio on Godmother Augusta, whose rambling house had enough empty rooms for a small army.

The cock-up led to disaster. Neither Godmother Augusta nor Myrtle had ever encountered any but clean, well-dressed, well-spoken, polite, lice-free, house-trained people. Godmother Augusta's cook, Mrs. Castle, took one look at the dirty, unkempt, incomprehensibly cockney, blue-languaged, lice-ridden evacuees, and wasn't having any of that sort in her domain thank you very much, madam. The final revolting insult was that, in the absence of an outdoor privy, which they understood, the twins used their bedroom wall as their own private lavatory, competing over who could spray the wall the highest.

Mrs. Castle waged a relentless war of attrition to rid the household of the despised and detested cockneys. She deferred not even to her employer, who was troubled by the tension. Mrs. Castle forbade the family to enter her kitchen, fed them on the congealing leftovers from Godmother Augusta's meals, made sure that the boiler ran out of hot water just when the family were due to wash, and daily concocted new obstacles and humiliations.

After only a month Mrs. Castle emerged triumphant. The mother came to view the East End, even with the prospect of Hitler's bombs, as a haven of delights compared to Godmother Augusta's hostile house and Mrs. Castle's persecution. The cook flailed the air with her great rolling pin and hissed "Good riddance!" as the heavily pregnant mother fled, cursing, dragging her distraught toddlers in her wake. Myrtle looked on in despair, for she had delighted in the rampageous little boys, running races with them in the orchard, binding up their wounds when they fell out of trees, teaching them to stand up straight and sing "God Save the King," laughing at their incomprehensible jokes, feigning despair at not being able to tell them apart. She had never played with anyone before.

Mary listened with rapt attention. Myrtle had stumbled across the first person who had ever taken a real interest in her, asked her personal questions, and examined the answers. Her soft voice grew more robust, her little heart-shaped face brightened.

Myrtle reminded Mary of a baby mouse awakening from sleep, its whiskers twitching and its tail uncurling and frantically waving, as she grew ever more garrulous and animated.

"I came here six months ago," confided Myrtle. "Godmother Augusta comes to London once a year to make sure her solicitor and her stockbroker are doing the right thing. She's not very rich, you see, so she's careful about money. I came to help her, and she told me to collect a fur muff from the furrier downstairs here. I saw your Marriage Bureau sign, and when I came out of the furrier's the nice girl who had wrapped up the muff for me came out too, and she said, 'That's for people looking for a husband or a wife. Are you looking for one?' Well, I didn't know what to say, so I just walked down the stairs and back to the hotel, and the next day we went back to Cornwall. When we got home I thought and thought about the Marriage Bureau, and about the smart people wearing nice clothes in London. And I thought I'd like to get married, but I wouldn't find a husband in the village in a thousand years, especially not looking like this in these clothes."

Myrtle glanced disconsolately down at the faded navy dress under her hideous coat. Mary judged it to be an ancient gymslip—the crease where it had been let down from schoolgirl length still showed. She was right: all Myrtle's adult life almost all her clothes had been either lengthened school uniforms or an aunt or godmother's castoffs, taken in at the seams, shortened, and clumsily restitched.

In London, Myrtle had felt a tidal wave of repulsion for her looks, and had resolved that when Godmother Augusta had accumulated some more city errands, she would offer to go to London for her. She would take £25 of her carefully hoarded savings and buy herself some delicious new garments. Godmother Augusta's eyesight was now so dim that with luck she would never notice any difference. "Only there are so many shops here I don't know where to start," admitted Myrtle.

Mary beamed at the mournful young woman, leaned across the desk, patted her hand, and, on the spur of the moment, inquired, "Would you like me to come with you? I am not busy for the next hour or two, so we could have a little excursion!"

Cinders Myrtle's fairy godmother had tapped her on the shoulder with her magic wand and wafted her to heaven. Nobody had ever made such a suggestion. "Oh yes!" she whispered. "Yes, please! Now?"

So Mary steered Myrtle into Swan & Edgar, the large department store at Piccadilly Circus. In the changing room, she helped Myrtle to shed her matronly disguise, starting with the gymslip and a drab gray blouse, then a voluminous petticoat of coarse cotton, secured around Myrtle's dainty waist with heavy tape. An oversize camisole—a Godmother Augusta castoff, decided Mary—swamped the girl's chest, flattening her bosom, for she had never even heard of a bust bodice. Myrtle's slender body was laced into stout, peach-colored stays reinforced with whalebone, beneath navy knickers made of thick wool, matted and scratchy from years of being washed in carbolic soap.

Soon, flushed and giggling with excitement, Myrtle pirouetted in front of the long mirror. It reflected a sweetly pretty girl wearing a becoming dress in a delicate blue, under a soft, light cardigan fastened with pink pearl buttons. Not visible, but known and felt and gloated over by Myrtle, was a set of silk underwear, including a lacy bust bodice adorned with a pink rose and blue satin bow, which she could hardly bear to conceal.

An hour later, complete with a blue coat, lighthearted hat, smart shoes and silk stockings, Myrtle emerged from her caterpillar carapace into Regent Street: an entrancing butterfly poised to spread her decorative wings and fly into a man's heart.

Back in the office Mary asked Myrtle for details: what kind of man would suit? What age, height, religion? Living in the country or in town? Or abroad? What about children? Divorce? Money?

Myrtle listened, but suddenly dropped her head to her chest, her hand clutching her neck as a rosy flush crept over her face. She was filled with a mixture of intoxicating anticipation and pure panic. Was she embarking on something terrible, even immoral? What would Godmother Augusta say? And the dear Rector—would he cast her out of his flock as a shameless hussy?

Mary perceived that transforming Myrtle's attitude would be much more difficult than changing her appearance. Luckily the girl was by now happy to place her trust in her fairy godmother, who through gentle coaxing managed to persuade her that she was doing something wholly natural and normal.

Myrtle had to return to Cornwall immediately. She traveled in a daze, abruptly curtailed as she was greeted at the front door by Mrs. Castle announcing that Godmother Augusta had tripped over her ancient dog and was in hospital, in a parlous state. Pausing only to hang her new clothes in her wardrobe, Myrtle seized her bicycle and pedaled to the rectory, from where the dear Rector drove her to the hospital.

For a month Myrtle shuttled to and from the hospital and London, from where she returned with Godmother Augusta's solicitor, summoned to the bedside. She read to the quailing, shrunken old lady, sang melodies in her small but tuneful voice, brought her little pots of Mrs. Castle's blancmange, stroked her cold, wrinkled hands, entertained her with stories of village people and the evacuees.

But nothing could prevent Godmother Augusta from dying. Myrtle found herself in charge of organizing the funeral and, to her amazement, enjoyed the responsibility. She was even more flabbergasted when the solicitor announced that Godmother Augusta had bequeathed her house to the church, but a small fortune in stocks and shares to Myrtle.

Thunderstruck, Myrtle protested, "But that is not possible! Godmother Augusta was poor!"

The solicitor gave a knowing little cough. "Indeed, Miss Glossop, your godmother believed herself to be in financial straits, and ordered her life accordingly. She labored under a misapprehension of her situation, of which I frequently attempted to disabuse her, but in vain. I assure you that a substantial amount is yours, and that I await your instructions."

Completely bewildered, Myrtle's first thought was of her

fairy godmother. She rushed up to 124 New Bond Street and poured out her miraculous tale to her astonished but delighted ally.

Myrtle and Mary worked out a plan. Myrtle would spend a few weeks in London, making necessary visits to the solicitor while staying in a quiet, eminently respectable hotel. From there she could meet some agreeable men, none of whom would have any idea she was an heiress. Mary would ensure that all of them had a more than adequate income of their own, and were not angling to marry for money.

Myrtle took to town life like a duck to water, reveling in her transformed looks, her freedom to spend money on clothes, makeup, and scent, visits to the hairdresser and beauty parlor, singing and dancing lessons, and anything that took her newly released fancy. Cornwall faded into the misty past, along with Sussex and the Isle of Wight. She was joyfully preoccupied, oblivious to what was going on in the world—she was even amused by having to take her gas mask to the cinema in order to be allowed to buy a ticket. Despite the blackout she blundered excitedly around the West End, and steeled herself to go down the moving staircase to the underground train. Thrilled by her own courage, she promptly took the up staircase and descended again. She haunted the department stores, buying herself the first pretty blouse she had ever owned, dotted with rosebuds and daisies. She wore it with a delectable pink skirt when she met the first of "Mary's Men," a kind, reliable civil servant who would, Mary felt, give her confidence in the male sex.

At 8:45 on the morning after this meeting Myrtle was waiting outside the Bureau's door when Mary arrived. Tearfully, she blurted out that the civil servant had kissed her! On her lips!! What should she do? Was he not a wicked man?

Mary realized that Myrtle's sheltered background had given her no inkling whatsoever of how men (other than the Rector) might behave to a woman. She was aching with anxiety to please a man but had no idea what to expect from him. Mary sought advice from Heather.

"Myrtle is dying to do the right thing, but she is too eager—it's small wonder our nice civil servant kissed her first time. It's pitiful, like the way she used to arrange the church flowers, and then go to early morning communion *and* matins *and* evensong, *and* help with the Sunday School, hoping her adored Rector would notice. What shall I do, Heather?"

"Sit her down and go through a few simple facts about men," advised Heather with her usual practicality. "Myrtle's intelligent, though woefully ignorant. Persuade her to look at men more calmly—and keep calm yourself. I've been observing your Myrtle, and I am certain she will manage."

Myrtle rented a flat in Kensington and met more of Mary's Men, not revealing to Mary whether they kissed her or not. But she gave her fairy godmother happy descriptions, such as of an evening in a dance hall, where the civil servant had introduced her to the Palais Glide. "I've never danced before! I adored it!"

Myrtle and the civil servant liked one another, but neither envisaged a future together. Mary's Men included also an MP, a

clergyman, a country solicitor, a naval officer and a businessman.
Myrtle wrote Mary lengthy letters giving her views.

She heartily disliked the MP:

He kept questioning me about politics and I did not
know the answers. I am certain that he knew that I could
not answer, and that he kept asking merely to make me
feel embarrassed. His only concern is politics, which do
not interest me a jot. He has a very good opinion of himself, but I found him badly wanting in good manners.

The clergyman irritated her:

He is the most frightful fuddy-duddy, nothing like my
old Rector, who was a dear. He sermonized and I was
bored.

She was offended by the solicitor:

I am sure he was at least fifty-five, though he said forty-
five (which was too old anyway). He took me to an afternoon tea dance, where tea in the ballroom cost 2s 9d, but
at the entrance, only 1s 6d. He said that the ballroom
was full, so we would have tea at the entrance. But there
were hardly any couples dancing in the ballroom, it was
just that he was too mean to pay. And he wore a toupee
which kept slipping down his forehead.

She was attracted by the naval officer:

He is a very handsome man, and very pleasant too. We spent an enjoyable evening at the theatre and I should have liked to hear from him again.

The businessman's appearance did not have the same effect on her as hers on him:

He is not a cultured man but certainly successful—he informed me with great pride that his income is about £2,000 a year. But his suit was of purple checks and his waistcoat scarlet, he carried a black silk top hat which was unsuitable for the occasion, and his short socks revealed an expanse of pasty white lower leg which repelled me.

Myrtle assured Mary that she followed her advice by not behaving too eagerly, yet all the men referred directly or indirectly to her advances.

The MP dismissed her out of hand:

She is uneducated, ignorant and overbearingly flirtatious. Flightiness is most undesirable in a politician's wife.

The clergyman wrote:

Her conversation was limited to clothes, which are of no concern to me, and dancing, which to me is an athletic activity verging on the pagan. She appears to regard her religion merely as a social activity.

The solicitor was disconcerted:

She planted a large kiss on my unsuspecting lips as we were dancing, at our first (and only) meeting. In endeavouring strenuously to please, she fails to understand that she denies any man his role of seducer.

The naval officer was nervous:

She is engaging and warm-hearted, but I fear that when her husband is at sea, such a gregarious soul would hanker after the company of other men. Her need of affection is touching in its transparency.

The businessman was not altogether negative:

She dresses in a style of which any husband would be proud, and her conversation has a girlish appeal. She combines an engaging youthfulness with a most tasteful and inviting appearance. She will make an ideal wife for

a man who loves both the innocent girl and the uninhibited woman in her.

Mary sighed gustily as she read between the lines: Myrtle
was frightening off any man she liked by setting the pace. Her
little virgin was mutating into a man-eater. So when Roderick
O'Rawe wrote from Ireland Mary held her breath, for every line
spoke the single word: *Myrtle.*

Roderick was thirty-six, the inheritor of a ramshackle Irish
estate that he farmed single-handedly, despite bouts of asthma.
He wanted a wife to contribute vivacity and gaiety to his solitary
life. The local Catholic girls were too bashful, shy and provincial
for his taste, unblessed with the zest and exuberance for which he
hungered. He was coming on a quick visit to London next week:
could the Bureau help?

Mary never forgot her joyous amazement at the turn of
events. Rory and Myrtle met in London on Monday, Tuesday,
Wednesday and Thursday. On Friday they married, Mary standing witness. On Saturday they set off for Ireland, from where
Rory shortly wrote:

She is enchanting, ravishing, so pretty in her dainty
clothes, always smiling. Her joie de vivre lights up my
life. She makes me happy as a pig in muck! Myrtle too
is tickled pink, she is helping me to plan improvements
to the estate, which I can now afford. She is learning the
lovely Irish songs and jigs, and she entertains me in the

long evenings. Her singing and dancing transport me to realms of wonder and glory. She is also learning to play the darling Irish harp. I am in heaven, bewitched by my golden-haired angel. We shall remain grateful to you for ever and a day.

Rory's extravagant signature, all curls and flourishes, was followed in Myrtle's childish handwriting: "PS I adore him! THANK YOU!!"

"Well done, dear Mary," Heather applauded. "I only hope that the magical enchantment will endure longer than the golden hair—which must benefit from an exceptional Irish hairdresser, for it was surely a nondescript brown!"

8

The Mansion and the Mating

By the autumn of 1939 new applicants were visiting or writing to the Marriage Bureau hourly. The *Daily Mail* reported that "among the businesses that are booming since the outbreak of war is the Marriage Bureau conducted by Miss Heather Jenner and Miss Mary Oliver in Bond Street. Last week eighty of their clients married—making, therefore, forty marriages." Heather was quoted: "There are so many young men wanting to marry before they go to the Front, or at any rate to have someone waiting for them when they return and to write to while they are away." And women, remembering the dire shortage of men after the slaughter of the Great War, were anxious to secure a husband, even though he might be killed later.

Heather and Mary were becoming increasingly skilled at matching clients, and both were deeply committed to their work. But like everyone running a business, they were profoundly apprehensive about the likely effects of war. The certain prospect of bombing, which might destroy the office and all its records, brought them out in a cold sweat.

Stubbing out her cigarette, Mary shuddered. "A single bomb could wipe us out. And I wouldn't put it past that Hitler fiend to drop a multitude of bombs on London."

"You're right, he is the devil incarnate. And he could obliterate the Bureau as if it had never existed."

"And us too."

"Never mind us—we must do something about the Bureau. We should make copies of all our records and store them in a second office, in another street."

"But that could easily be bombed too. Nowhere in London will be safe. Or in any other big city, come to that. But what about the country? We could have an office somewhere rural and quiet, somewhere unlikely to be a Hitler target."

This somber conversation took place as the two matchmakers were driving from London to visit friends near Aldershot. Steering her precious Morris 8, Heather's eyes were fixed firmly on the road ahead while Mary looked out of the window, relishing the vistas of trees and green fields—until she turned to Heather, her eyes sparkling. "What about near here? The Hun wouldn't waste his precious bombs on farmland, with hardly any buildings. Look, there, above that high wall, there's a house agent's board. Let's investigate!"

Heather drove through two huge, rusty, wrought-iron gates, propped open and leaning at a perilous angle across a graveled drive that led to a Victorian redbrick mansion smothered in Virginia creeper. Tentacles of blood-red leaves crept across the windows, giving the impression of half-closed eyes in a building fallen asleep, with no doubt a somnolent princess reclining inside, waiting to be kissed awake by her resourceful prince.

Heather stretched out her fingers to grip the immense black knocker and rapped firmly on the front door. After a few minutes it creaked open, to reveal a buxom, middle-aged Mrs. Tiggy-Winkle wearing a sober gray dress and starched white apron, who introduced herself rather frostily as Mrs. Plum, the housekeeper.

Heather explained that she and Mary were looking for an office out of London. Unaware that Heather was using her increasingly well-honed interview techniques to extract information, Mrs. Plum thawed and grew garrulous, telling Heather all she wanted to know.

While Heather and Mrs. Plum chatted, Mary gazed at the imposing hall, crammed with velvet-upholstered chairs, dusty tables with tops and legs so thick it must have taken a small army to move them, and cabinets filled with military medals, tarnished silver snuffboxes, ancient coins, and miniatures of women in powdered wigs and men lounging in poetic poses. The gentle wind outside stirred the Virginia creeper, causing the thin streaks of light that filtered in through the filthy windows to flicker as they played on the marble walls and fluted pillars.

Leaving Heather and Mrs. Plum absorbed in conversation, Mary peered around a half-open door into a shadowy room in whose cobwebby recesses she glimpsed three once-glossy grand pianos. She stole across the parquet floor, scattered with fabulous Persian rugs, while from the paneled walls swarthy grandees, framed flamboyantly in gold, sneered down their cliff-edge noses at her. In the half-darkness, their haughty eyes, bejeweled silver swords, and arrow-shaped beards resting on stiff ruffs inspired in Mary a frisson of rapture and fear. She turned tail and escaped back into the hall.

"Ah, there you are, Mary. Mrs. Plum tells me the house belongs to a foreign diplomat who has fled back to his country, where he imagines Hitler will not find him. It is to be let with all furniture, four servants, twenty-five bedrooms, about twenty bathrooms (nobody has counted them accurately), and twenty-three acres. I have agreed to take it for an initial three months. We must hurry now, or we shall be late for our friends. Come along!"

"But, but—" Mary stammered as Heather strode to the door. "Are you serious?"

"Yes, aren't you? I thought you'd love it, dear Mary, it's such a romantic place, exactly your style!"

Mary took a deep breath, and turned an ecstatic face to Heather. "Yes, it's the most romantic house imaginable, magnificent and scary too. And there's pots of room for our records, and bedrooms for our newly married couples who loathe living with their parents but can't find anything else in wartime. And in Aldershot there are soldier husbands who don't like living in army quarters but have to be near. And—"

"And it's only twenty guineas a quarter! An entire mansion and acres of grounds for far less than our minuscule office!

Mrs. Plum wanted twenty-two guineas, but I pointed out that it is far from spick and span, and persuaded her that she would never find such good and honest tenants as we."

A week later, the two matchmakers and two reluctant secretaries transported themselves, their clothes, and boxes of writing paper, air letters, envelopes, record cards, ledgers and registration forms to their new home.

Mrs. Plum welcomed them in some amazement. "Where are the servants?" she inquired. "The house needs fifteen."

"We have brought two secretaries," replied Heather in her most authoritative manner, indicating the two girls, who were looking distinctly unenthusiastic.

But even just keeping the rooms clean was far too much for the Bond Street contingent plus the four servants included in the rent: Mrs. Plum, a "tweeny" housemaid who flicked her feather duster right, left and center, gaily redistributing the dust, and two ancient sisters whose rheumatic joints (or was it gin?) confined them to the servants' wing. Heather and Mary spent their days cleaning, or typing out circulars extolling the glories of the mansion and the success of the Marriage Bureau, which they put in their bicycle baskets and distributed around Aldershot.

For days nothing happened. The matchmakers were beginning to despair when an elderly admiral telephoned, gave his name, and abruptly demanded the price of a room. But he immediately put the phone down, cutting Heather off before she could reply.

So it was a surprise when the next evening the Admiral

marched up the drive, carrying a battered suitcase and tugging a drooping bloodhound with a hangdog look in its bloodshot eyes. Uttering not a word, he barged past Mrs. Plum and set off up the stairs. He aimed straight as an arrow for the largest of the immense ex-diplomatic bedrooms, where he sniffed and harrumphed at the expanse of four-poster bed draped in faded, moth-eaten velvet. Silently, he inspected the pink marble bathroom and the shelves of leather-bound books. Then he dumped his suitcase unceremoniously down on a fragile, exquisitely inlaid writing table, Heather squirming at the thought of the replacement cost, and gave voice. "Used to live here myself. Wife's family built it in 1870. Wife died. Too expensive to run. Damn foreigner bought it off me for a song. Dog can sleep in the kitchen. What time's dinner?"

The meal was not a success. Neither Heather nor Mary had any culinary skills, and the secretaries, exhausted by the daily cleaning and typing, refused point-blank even to enter the cavernous kitchen. The ancient mystery sisters both claimed via Mrs. Plum that their joints and hearts were so dicky that they could not even walk, let alone cook, and Mrs. Plum, usually cooperative, tartly advised Mary and Heather that cooking was no part of her duties. So they had advertised locally for a cook, and had had no choice but to employ the sole respondent, a slatternly woman with a cigarette hanging out of her mouth who claimed to be a good basic cook.

"She's gloriously basic," groaned Mary, as the Admiral stomped furiously up the stairs after a dismal repast of cabbage so overboiled it looked and tasted bleached, a scrawny boiling fowl and rock-hard gray potatoes, followed by a lumpy pink blancmange sprinkled with what looked suspiciously like cigarette ash.

"She'll have to go," said Heather, who was beginning to regret her impetuousness in taking on the mansion.

At breakfast the next day Mrs. Plum planted herself in front of Heather, arms akimbo.

"That vile dog has diarrhea. All over my kitchen floor. It's more than flesh and blood can stand. I am not clearing it up." Uttering a snort of disgust and scorn she turned sharply and stormed off.

At that very moment the Admiral banged his way downstairs, purple-faced, cursing and swearing as if castigating sailors, hitting the furniture with his suitcase, bellowing, "Appalling! Ruddy bed collapsed! Didn't sleep a wink! Saw mice! Bathwater muddy! Filthy food! Disgraceful! Not paying a penny! Out of my way! *Out of my way!*" Hearing the familiar voice, the sickly dog slumped out from the kitchen, shooed violently by Mrs. Plum, and slunk off with its master.

Although brought up on a farm, Mary had a horror of sick animals, and even the thought of canine diarrhea made her retch. So it fell to Heather to clean up the kitchen, after which she downed three large gins. She listened as Mary sighed that they were losing clients in London, for whom Aldershot was too far, especially with petrol rationing.

"Nonsense," retorted Heather. "Chin up! It'll just take time. Anyway, it gives us a chance to get on with some mating. Come on."

Mary had persuaded a local newspaper to take an advertisement under the heading MATRIMONY. Giving the Bureau's address and telephone number, it stated that introductions were AVAILABLE FOR ALL CLASSES. English society was very class-conscious, and clients almost invariably wanted to meet someone from their own background—"Except for people like Cedric Thistleton," observed Heather, "who want to rise far above their own background by hitching themselves to a superior spouse!"

So Mary and Heather had developed a "mating" system, based on the all-important distinctions of class. It assigned each client to one of these categories:

Lady and *Gent*
Upper class, not necessarily titled but definitely
of superior breeding.

Gent For Here and *Lady For Here* (*GFH* and *LFH*)
Upper middle class, public school educated.
(*Here* being the office, i.e., *for our purposes*).

Near Gent and *Near Lady*
(or *Half Gent* and *Half Lady*)
Middle class, with a professional background.

Gentish and *Ladyish*
Lower middle or working class.

WC (Working Class)

Used in the very early days of the Bureau;
soon replaced by *MBTM (Much Better Than Most)* and,
a smidgeon lower, *MBTS (Much Better Than Some)*.
Both could have an added *V: VMBTM (Very Much
Better Than Most)*; or even a further addition,
GOOD, creating *GOOD VMBTM*.

+, ++, or −

All categories could be modified with plus or minus
signs which enabled the client to be introduced to the
next category (up or down). For example, *Ladyish ++*
could meet *Near Gent −*. Similarly *Gent For Here* could
be matched with *Near Lady +*.

Just

Another modification: a *Near Gent, just* could
be introduced to a *Near Lady*, though
probably not to a *Near Lady ++*.

A client in the *Gent For Here* category would almost invariably specify "She must be a lady." The interviewer knew exactly
what he meant, and immediately searched for a woman who had
been to private or public school, spoke without any local accent,
and moved in social circles similar to his. Similarly, a *Much Better*

Than Some woman would ask for "a plain ordinary working-class man," and be matched with a man categorized as *Much Better Than Some* or *Working Class*.

The interviewers recorded each client's name, religion, age, profession, income and place of residence in a volume called the Black Book. Each client's town was also entered alphabetically, since geography was a critical factor, especially with the difficulty of traveling in wartime. Index boxes contained a card for each client, recording his or her registration number, details about the client and about the type of person he or she wanted to marry. On the back of each card, the interviewer wrote the registration number of all that client's introductions, thereby avoiding the risk of sending the same introduction twice. There were so many clients that most letters of the alphabet needed two separate index boxes, one for men and one for women. Some smaller groups, of country or religion, such as clients living in India, or Jews, needed only one box for both men and women.

It was a very complicated set of records, "but," recalled Mary, "finding the right husband or wife, in the right place, at the right time, was a complicated business. And the system worked!"

Doing some mating in the increasingly chilly mansion one autumnal day, the two matchmakers assessed the situation. Heather was huddled in her fur coat, Mary shivering despite wearing layers of underwear, vainly attempting to warm herself with cigarette after cigarette. Mrs. Plum had just disclosed that in winter the fires burned a ton of coal a week, and the central heating about the same of coke. The diplomat had installed the newfangled system years ago when it was a daring innovation. According to the housekeeper, the diplomat's entourage and hangers-on had been greatly impressed, but even though the boiler was perpetually ravenous, the radiators remained tepid. As for the price of such a quantity of fuel, even in peacetime it was punitive, but wartime prices were rising daily to ever more astronomical heights.

As the matchmakers glumly examined the newly delivered coal bill, a mangy cat stole into the room. Before she had even seen it, Heather, who had a violent allergy to cats, sneezed uncontrollably, her eyes swelling up pink and puffily, tears ruining her makeup. As she struggled to stem the flow while aiming a kick at the offending creature, Mary answered the telephone.

"I must speak to Miss Jenner," wailed the secretary left behind in Bond Street, so loudly that Heather heard too. "I cannot cope any longer. There are far too many letters to answer, and I cannot manage them and answer the telephone too, and there are some nasty clients to deal with. I shall have to hand in my notice."

"That's the very last straw!" exclaimed Heather. "Come on, Mary, let's get packed. I'll tell Mrs. Plum. We shall pay the rent as we are obliged to, but we are leaving today."

Two heavily laden car trips later, back in Bond Street, Heather, Mary and the two secretaries swiftly and joyfully restored all the papers, listened to the incumbent secretary's tales of woe, and set about sorting the mountain of post. Mary stopped short at a long air letter, sent from Australia by a young man, Fred Adams.

Fred's story wrenched Mary's tender heart. He had been born in Suffolk, on a farm which he dimly remembered. By the age of three he was an orphan: his mother died in the ravaging Spanish flu pandemic of 1918, just after she'd heard that her husband had not survived the combination of gangrene contracted in the trenches and the consequent amputation of both his legs.

Fred was bundled off to a spinster aunt living on the next-door farm, who brought him up because it was her duty. Auntie Ellen did not love him: he was nothing but a nuisance to her, and she resented having to feed and clothe him. She was an old maid because her soldier fiancé had been shot as a deserter, and she was bitter to her bones about everything and everybody (not surprisingly, thought Mary). Fred wrote that Auntie Ellen had never had much love in her, but what little there was had been knocked right out of her. The fiancé was not in fact a deserter: he'd simply gone so mad after being gassed that he'd run away. The search party found him crouching in a ditch sobbing his heart out; though he didn't cry when they stood him up and shot him.

Mary paused to dry her eyes so that she could read on.

Fred decided life could only be better somewhere else. At fourteen he left school—which he had scarcely attended, since Auntie Ellen had always found jobs for him on the farm—and went out, steerage, to Australia. Auntie Ellen was glad to be rid of him, so she gave him a bit of money and a ticket on the ship. In Australia he did odd jobs and lived hand to mouth until he was fifteen, when he joined the Royal Australian Navy (lying about his age). He was now twenty-four. In September, when Australia joined the war, he had heard rumors that his ship would shortly be sent to England. He didn't know exactly when, but he did know that he wanted to marry an English girl because, though he liked Australia, he rated Australian girls flighty, hard-boiled and harsh-voiced. He had had a childhood sweetheart in Suffolk, Elsie, when he was a little boy of ten, whom he remembered as the dearest little thing.

"Oh, Heather, it's a most touching story, we must help!"

"It certainly is," agreed Heather. "But how did he know about the Bureau?"

"The article in that Queensland newspaper *The Morning Bulletin* in July, remember? The one that said the Bureau gets three hundred letters a day, many from Australia, New Zealand and South Africa. It had the story of me chaperoning that glamorous Arabella Pickering to Paris to meet that wealthy businessman. And it said that half our female clients are mannequins, and we introduce them to eligible bachelors from the Dominions who want decorative wives. It quoted us as saying, 'We call ourselves Empire Builders!'"

"As indeed we are! Yes, I remember now. You are very good with journalists, dear Mary. I doubt that half or even a quarter of our girls are mannequins, but no matter."

Fred's letter told Mary so much about himself that she quickly formed a mental picture of the future Mrs. Adams, and was overjoyed that it echoed Fred's description of his childhood sweetheart, who remained vivid in his mind: "I want you to interduce me to a nice quiet affekshunate girl with dark flashy eyes," wrote Fred.

I remember elsies eyes they were big and dark brown they were allmost black and her hair the same colour and shiny and long all down her back. I want a girl who nos her way about and will help me to settle after ten years in australia I will feel out of things in England. elsie was a very kind harted little girl she used to slip biskits from her tea into her apron pokitt and give them to me the next day at school because she new my arnt didnt give me much to eat. elsies parents were kind to but they were poor with not enuff money to feed themselves and 4 children. I am 5'6" tall and please find me a girl shorter than that a dainty girl and a chased girl. I dont mind what rcligun she is or if shes forrin but not german or australian. Please send me some girls but please do not put marriage bureau on the letter or your name please put arnt mary I dont want navy officers to see.

Mary was completely won over. "Poor lamb, his spelling's even worse than mine, but his heart's in the right place. I can think of three or four girls who might suit."

On a plain air letter, including some misleading information about imaginary friends, and signed *Aunt Mary*, Mary sent Fred details about Nancy Patch, a shy, stuttering young woman who had rushed along to register with the Marriage Bureau in her half-hour break from working as a nippy at Lyons Corner House next to Charing Cross.

"It's ever so busy," Nancy had panted, "us waitresses have to be really n-n-nippy! There's lots of young m-m-men come in for a cup of tea and a bun, and they're lonely and want to chat, but we can't talk to them, only t-t-take their order and their money. I live in digs with my sister, she's shy like me so we don't nev-nev-never go out and we don't meet no young m-m-men. I'm twenty-three and my mum says I'm on the shelf, cos she was m-m-married at seventeen."

Mary had assessed Nancy as *WC+*, and from his letter thought Fred was probably the same. She was a pretty, dark-eyed girl, her long hair coiled on top of her head "so it don't fall in the customers' soup." Mary imagined Fred feeling protective of this sweet young soul, who stood only five feet one inches tall. So she was dismayed when a few weeks later Nancy flew into the office, flushed from running, blushing apologetically as she broke her news.

"Oh, Miss O-O-Oliver, I'm ever so sorry, I'm in a pickle, you see I got a nice letter from Mr. Adams but I've said I'll marry Trevor Potts that you sent me in J-J-June. He's ever so keen and he wants us to marry n-n-next month before he gets called up. But Mr. Adams sounds ever such a nice gen-gen-gentleman and he sounds just right for my little sister Elsie. She's a ni-ni-nippy like me, she's like me in mostly everything, but she's only just started work, and she hasn't got enough m-m-money to join the Ma-Ma-Marriage Bureau. What ever shall I do?"

Mary's mind was in a whirl. Elsie. Could it—might it—no, it wasn't possible—but it might—yes—no—yes . . .

"Are you and Elsie from London?" she asked a startled Nancy.

"No, we come here to work because there weren't no jo-jo-jobs at home, we wasn't big and strong enough for farmwork."

"So where is home?" inquired Mary, her thoughts racing.

"We was born on a f-f-farm. It's not near anywhere, there's only f-f-farms."

"Do you know which country?"

"Oh, yes, c-c-course I do, it's Suffolk."

Mary was gripped by a wild hope. "Well, I think we could change the rules a little. Your sister could pay us two shillings and sixpence and I'll tell Mr. Adams about her. If she marries him she'll have to pay the After Marriage Fee, though. Would that suit?"

"Oh, oh, oh, thank you ever so much, Miss O-O-Oliver. I've got a f-f-feeling about Elsie and Mr. Adams. One of them feelings, you know."

"Yes, I do know," agreed Mary with fervor, adding to herself, "and I hope and pray this one is right!"

9

Mary's Bones and Babies

"They're just children, babies," sighed Mary after interviewing a succession of bashful but eager young men. "They're still wet behind the ears, little puppy dogs fresh from being licked clean by their mother. I can almost sniff that soggy-doggy scent. They shouldn't be going off to fight, and nor should they be getting married."

It was 1940 and, since the Nazis did not invade, many evacuees had returned to the cities, where they learned to pick their way with caution through pea-souper fogs along the blacked-out streets. People grew more casual about taking their gas masks everywhere, but everyone knew that savagery and anarchy were inevitable. The first to be called up for military service were fit and able men of twenty and twenty-one, the single before the married. Many rushed to the recruiting office, while more timorous young men hurried to the Marriage Bureau in hopes of putting off the evil hour.

"So what are you going to do about your puppy dogs?" demanded Heather.

"You know as well as I do: I'll look for some equally young and scared girls. The Black Book is full of them. I had such a nice child this morning—Ada Burn, a shy little elf with a voice so gentle I could hardly hear her. She's only eighteen, but she's been working as a milliner's assistant since she was fourteen, and she's living with her mother and a new stepfather who frightens her. He goes down the boozer, she says, and comes home drunk and bashes her mother. She's tried to help, but the woman insists that he hits her because he loves her, and she loves him. Daft. So poor Ada's longing to get away and marry some quiet, home-loving young man who's kind to people, that's her main consideration. 'Someone not too gay or too energetic,' she put on her registration form. 'Any decent type will do.'"

Heather considered, and suggested Fred Adams, who would be over from Australia very soon. Mary agreed that he sounded the right sort, but that he would probably return to Australia after the war, while Ada wanted to stay in England—she'd never been farther than Clacton in her life. In any case, Mary was anxious to see what happened with Fred and Elsie before trying anyone else for him. Elsie's protective sister Nancy had told Mary that Elsie and Fred were corresponding.

"I have a feeling about that pair," mused Mary. "My bones go a bit soft, as if I've had too many gin and limes."

"Soft in the head, more like! You have the most speaking

bones I've ever known! Ask them to tell you the name of some nice man for your Ada."

Mary scoured the Black Book and the record cards, soon lighting on a young man who spoke to her bones: John Parker.

John was a cabinetmaker of twenty-one, working with his father in Bethnal Green. His mother had died giving birth to him, and his stepmother regarded him as an unwelcome intruder in her life. She had once whacked the inquiring toddler across the mouth for reaching up to her favorite vase and bringing it crashing to the floor. Little John had bled so profusely that for once his father had rounded on his wife and hit her. Since then she had hardly ever touched John, and spoke to him only when she couldn't avoid it.

But his grandmother and he had doted on one another. He had always loved old Mrs. Zambrovsky's graphic stories of his lost mother—her favorite, forever-mourned daughter. Instead of playing outside with the children of the street, John had stayed in his nan's stuffy parlor listening enraptured as she told him rambling tales of his mother's talents and charm, and described her own childhood in Russia, and her arrival in bewildering London. She had stood in the street for hours to catch a glimpse of Queen Victoria—who had graciously waved directly at Mrs. Zambrovsky! Picked her out in the seething mass and waved at her and her alone! The old woman's wrinkle-scored face always glowed at the memory, whose glory illuminated John too as he hugged his beloved nan.

In his grandmother's final harrowing illness, John had spent days and nights at her bedside holding her hand, listening, laughing, stroking, soothing, looking after her with an instinctive loving-kindness that baffled his father. "It ain't natural, the way that boy carries on. It's woman's work wot 'e's doing."

But John's stepmother wanted nothing to do with either her stepson or the drooling old Jewish woman. "Shut yer mouth and let 'im get on wiv it, wontcher?" she screeched at her husband. "Thank yer lucky stars you and me don't have to look after the old witch. I can't never understand wot she's saying, in that forrin voice of 'ers. She'll be gorn soon and good riddance I say!"

So John had quietly taken charge. To the chagrin of the family, his nan bequeathed him her tiny terraced house, so with deep relief he had moved around the corner and gradually mended the furniture and cleaned the rooms and washed the curtains until he had a very pleasant, comfortable, cozy bachelor home. He was horrified at the prospect of being called up to fight, for he was a gentle, domesticated soul who, since the death of the one person with whom he had known what it was to love and be loved, was happy only when absorbed in making a piece of furniture, or restoring a beautiful antique. He had heard of Conscientious Objectors, who were exempted from killing by doing war work such as driving ambulances. But he knew with what scorn and even violence his father and friends would treat him if he became a despised "Conchie," so the only tactic he could think of that would at least delay his call-up was to marry.

"I think you and your bones may be right, dear Mary," said Heather. "Ada and John are well worth trying. I remember him: I interviewed him. Didn't he say he wanted to meet a quiet, homely girl, perhaps one who has helped old or sick people?"

"Yes, he did. And you liked him: you wrote on his card, 'Nice boy, working class, split lip, lovely hands, v. blue eyes, own house and furniture.' It's very unusual for such a young man to have his own home; it'll be an attraction."

"It should be, though last month I wanted to introduce him to a girl who said she wouldn't even go near the East End, not for all the furniture in the world, not if you paid her, it's full of cockneys and Jews."

"What a nasty little madam. John's well shot of her."

Mary wrote about John to Ada, who replied that she would like to meet him, and sent him a letter giving the address of the milliner's shop where she worked rather than her home address, for fear that her stepfather might get wind of what she was doing and mete out the same viciousness to her as to her mother. Mary waited; but no news came.

"What in heaven's name is the matter?" cried Heather two weeks later, as she observed Mary clutching a flimsy air letter while laughing and crying simultaneously.

Miraculously, Mary's bones had been right: Nancy Patch's

little sister Elsie was the very girl Fred Adams in Australia had known all those years ago. They were going to meet as soon as he came to England; they were both overjoyed. So too was Mary, though the emotions overcoming her were mixed: "Fred and Elsie are jumping up and down like jack-in-a-boxes and almost planning the great day and shall he bring some sultanas for the wedding cake and it's wonderful but I can't bear it because it's too fairy tale and I'm sure they'll take one look at each other and think 'Oh, NO!' and their golden dreams will go up in gray smoke and it'll be all my fault and—"

"Such nonsense!" Heather broke in. "Really, Mary, you are taking off at as great a speed as if Hitler has dropped a bomb at your feet. Fate has played one of its tricks, aided and abetted by you—and by Elsie's sister too, let me remind you. If it ends happily ever after we shall all bless fate, and if it ends in tears we shall all curse fate. It's as simple as that. Now do brace up and let's get on with answering all these letters."

Mary meekly picked up her letter opener, slit an innocuous-looking pale violet envelope, studied the violet-scented sheet of paper, and burst into peals of laughter. "Oh, Heather, you won't believe this one! We are invited to judge a baby show!"

"What? Why? I don't know anything at all about babies, and neither do you. Who's the invitation from?"

"The Lady Chairman of the Women's Institute of some place I've never heard of, in Surrey. She read about that scheme we had for rewarding clients who had a baby."

Heather grimaced, remembering the plan she and Mary had dreamed up to publicize the Bureau at the same time as being patriotic. They had offered £50 for each baby born to a client, on three conditions:

1. Both parents must have married through the Bureau (no payment to a client who had married "out," to someone who was not a client);
2. The father must be a member of the fighting forces;
3. The baby must be born within a year of the marriage.

The *Sunday Chronicle* had quoted Heather: "It is essential that the population should be maintained at such a time, and we hope we will have to make many £50 payments." Almost immediately, a recently married colonel client had written to announce that, ten months after his wedding to his much-loved Bureau wife, with whom he was deliriously happy, he had become the proud father of twins. Biting her lip, Heather had sent the now even more crazily happy couple a congratulatory letter enclosing £100. Her very next letter was to the insurance company, adding to the Bureau's policy a codicil insuring against future twins, triplets, quadruplets and quintuplets.

The violet invitation to the matchmakers was for a charity fete in aid of refugee children, mostly Jewish, whose parents had managed to get them out of Germany. When they arrived at a mainline railway station in London, with a label attached to their clothes and carrying only a small dented suitcase, the forlorn little mites were greeted in a strange language, in an alien country. They were then assigned to an unknown family who might welcome them, but equally might resent them and treat them shabbily. Mary and Heather were eager to help these pitiful lost souls.

So, on a boiling hot day a few weeks later, the two matchmakers motored in the Morris to a Home Counties meadow, dressed in their very smartest white outfits complete with kid gloves, jaunty hats, dainty handbags and snow-white shoes, Mary nursing a deliciously delicate white lace parasol, a relic of her Assam trousseau. Drawing near, they were astonished to hear raucous music and shouting: "Roll up! Roll up! Madam Arcati tells your fortune!" "All the fun of the fair!" "Roll up! Pin the mustache on Hitler! Roll up!"

As they rounded the last corner a great crowd of people hove into sight, garishly colored paper hats balanced on their heads as they stuck greedy tongues into swirls of frothy pink cotton candy, spluttering, laughing and giggling, pushing and shoving. Roundabouts were whirling, swingboats plunging and swaying, bumper cars bouncing off one another with alarming bangs, the drivers squealing with delight. Men, women and children were flinging balls at coconuts, aiming rifles at moving plastic ducks, trying their hand at hoopla, or thwacking a small sandbag resembling a rat as it hurtled down a chute. All were in high holiday mood, united in their determination to ignore the war and enjoy the sweltering afternoon to the full.

Following a sign pointing to BABY SHOW, 2 P.M., Heather and Mary fought their way around the stalls, tottering through the crowds on their high heels in the rough grass, to a roped-off part of the field. All around was confusion and noise, since hundreds of mothers had in tow not only their babies, wailing in the uncomfortable heat, but also their other children, who were too young to be let loose in the fete field, but too old to be remotely interested in a baby show. So they grizzled and grumped, to the frustration and rising anger of their mothers (their fathers having long since escaped to a beer tent tucked away in a corner of the field).

The Lady Chairman bore down like a ship in full sail to greet them, a formidable figure encased in a gown of intricately pleated and folded scarlet satin, strained to the splitting point by her redoubtable torso. She was immense, positively pneumatic, and as the matchmakers shook her plump hand, they observed the sweat stains on her gloves and under her arms, visible despite a wreath of silver fox furs around her neck, the black reynard eyes glinting glassily in the sunlight. Her width was to some extent balanced by her height, which was increased by a froth of a hat, a confection composed of feathers and bows and artificial flowers perched on top of a cascade of auburn waves.

Mary and Heather were marched off to a series of competitions: the Baby with the Bluest Eyes, the Tallest Baby (impossible to judge with any accuracy as none of the cherubs could stand), the Best-Dressed Baby ("but a nappy is a nappy, surely!" murmured Mary), the Happiest Baby ("meaning the one who cries the least," whispered Heather), the Fattest Baby, the Thinnest, the Prettiest, the Ugliest, the Baby with Most Hair, and many more.

The first competition was for the Most Healthy Baby. Perspiring in the heat of a large tent, Heather and Mary surveyed the hot, sticky, sniveling entrants, conferred, and decided that they all looked much the same.

"Pick them up and hold them in your arms," encouraged the Lady Chairman, demonstrating by scooping up a podgy specimen who howled himself purple in the face. "Like this. Then you'll get a good feel of their darling little bodies."

The prospect of proximity to the dribbling infants horrified the two judges, so they hastily settled on the cleanest, declaring him most wonderfully healthy, a tribute to his mother and certain to become a highly desirable husband whom they would one day welcome to the Marriage Bureau with open arms.

"What do you mean, a desirable husband?" squawked the indignant mother. "She's a *girl*!"

"In that case she'll be a beautiful bride to some very, very lucky man," declared Heather decisively, flashing a crushing smile as she swept on to the next competition, leaving the prizewinner's mother muttering, "Those two la-di-das don't know anything about babies, they're just posh friends of our Lady Chairman."

For every new contest, Mary and Heather walked up and down the aisles, inspecting with their untrained eyes the squirming infants laid out like so many freshly caught fish on the slab. They cooed at the contestants, smiled consolingly at the anxious mothers whose precious babes failed to win, commented as intelligently as their ignorance permitted, until at last every competition had been judged. But the weary adjudicators still had to face the prize-giving, which was to take place on a temporary stage cunningly concealed by large white sheets dotted with potted plants of patriotic red, white and blue flowers.

The Chairman introduced Mary and Heather to the dignitaries on the stage, representing the Women's Institute, Child Welfare Committee, church, and parish council, all seated on flimsy bentwood chairs. A reluctant little girl dressed like the Sugar Plum Fairy, with elaborate sausage curls tumbling to her waist, was shoved by her mother up to the stage. Her lips parted to reveal a hefty wire brace on her teeth as she scowled at Mary and Heather and thrust a bunch of wilting rambler roses at each of them.

"Oh, she was an evil child!" complained Heather later, as they motored home in the fading light. "I am convinced she had stripped the thorns off the stalks where she held them, but left the rest on purposely so that we should get pricked. My gloves are pierced beyond repair. I could have slapped her then and there."

"It's just as well you didn't. We were supposed to be representing the Marriage Bureau, advertising the civilized way we work. Walloping a child would have been truly frightful publicity."

"Yes, yes, I know. But I really cannot imagine what good publicity we achieved. It was after all a fairly disastrous occasion."

The disaster had been caused by the Lady Chairman's husband, a man as portly and as heat-struck as his wife, whose ample backside bulged over his modest-size chair. As Madam Chairman rose, like a whale ascending out of the sea, to introduce her husband (whom everyone present except Heather and Mary already knew and heartily disliked), he had lurched in her backwash and lunged toward Mary, imprinting a sweaty palm on her pristine white skirt. He then steadied himself, stood, and staggered toward the front of the stage.

With a protesting groan, the overburdened boards had yielded, tipping Lady Chairman, husband, dignitaries and guests into an undignified heap, spattered with small clods of earth and displaced flowers, horribly resembling disturbed graves. The chairs fell higgledy-piggledy, some of them disintegrating into broken flying sticks. The prizes and certificates, which had been proudly displayed on a rickety table, were torn and crushed in the melee.

The shrieks rending the summer air from the stage were as dozy murmurs compared to the hooting and yelling of the mothers, all ghoulishly rejoicing in the discomfiture of the Chairman's unloved husband. The babies bawled even louder than before, bursting their little lungs they knew not why, and the children, given license to shout and boo, hollered their juvenile heads off while rushing hither and thither, dive-bombing one another in an ecstasy of unrestrainable pandemonium.

Nobody was injured except in their pride, but the show could not go on. The Chairman's husband heaved himself up and, wisely skipping his not-longed-for introductory speech, made a blessedly brief announcement that the prize-giving would be deferred to a more auspicious occasion. Exhausted, and politely declining rather lukewarm invitations to stay for tea, Heather and Mary had pleaded anxiety about driving in the blackout and stumbled back over the meadow to their car.

"I wasn't overly fond of babies before today," groaned Heather, "but now I never want to clap eyes on another one. My gorgeous white suit is ruined by infantile dribble, my shoes are covered in grass stains, which are impossible to get out, my gloves are spoiled, and my precious chapeau fell off and got squashed when that pathetic stage collapsed."

"Well, at least your handbag's all right, unlike mine. And my pretty parasol, which Uncle George gave me for my trousseau when I was supposed to marry that dreary man in Assam, was trampled on and torn. But you must admit that the day had its moments. When we all fell like nine-pins I was stunned at first, then a great slippery gleaming mass rose and fell inches away, like a beached whale. And four wicked little jet eyes winked in a knowing kind of way at me, as if to say, 'How are the mighty fallen!' It was the Lady Chairman, of course, rolling around in all her satin and foxes!"

"She was truly as blubbery as any whale. She put me in mind of lots of little barrage balloons stacked on top of one another. And wasn't the face of the Ugliest Baby's mother a sight to behold? It was the most hideous fizzog, all huge hooter and mean piggy eyes. The wretched baby had just the same features—like mother, like daughter. I was longing to announce that the winner obviously took after her mother!"

"Oh, Heather!" hooted Mary, "I thought you knew a lot about sex but you've got some really glaring gaps. The Ugliest Baby was a boy, not a girl!"

"You never can tell precisely at that age unless you unpin the nappy," said Heather defensively. "And I certainly wasn't going to do that!"

Two days later, Mary opened another violet-scented letter from the Lady Chairman, thanking them effusively for their gracious presence and their marvelous skill in judging the delicious little angels. "And I wonder," she concluded,

> if you would help a friend of mine, Etheldreda de Pomfret? She has been married three times, but, alas, her husbands did not survive, and so she was compelled to consign them to her past. She would so love to find a worthy husband, and I should so love to help her. I have given her your name and address and told her to write to you, or telephone. She will do as I say for she is a most dear friend, a friend of my bosom, we are like two peas in a pod.

"Never mind peas in a pod, more like whales on a beach! Etheldreda sounds ghastly. Even her name is fearsome. I pity all three consigned husbands from my heart. What shall we do, Heather?"

Heather did not yet know. She was becoming increasingly aware of how odd and difficult some clients could be. Recently a Mrs. Barnabas had telephoned demanding to speak to Miss Jenner and only Miss Jenner. She had read that Heather's birthday was, like hers, in February, and that Heather's eyes were green, like hers. This meant that they were in sympathy, and that

Heather would indubitably find her a man born under Taurus, whose lucky color was aquamarine and whose guiding number was eight. Mrs. Barnabas accepted that Heather would not automatically know all the relevant facts about her clients, but if Miss Jenner would but present Mrs. Barnabas with a selection of men, she herself would contact them all to ask if they satisfied her criteria. Heather had had great difficulty in shaking her off.

However, Heather did know, adamantly, that never again would they judge a baby show. Never. Not even if it were the most wonderful publicity in the world.

Mary nodded her agreement, only half-listening. She was already bending her mind to possible husbands for Mrs. de Pomfret. Which of the clients might be persuaded to marry a woman the same age as the Lady Chairman and probably equally mountainous, who had somehow seen off three husbands. What on earth had happened to them? Had she poisoned them?

As Mary reached for the Black Book she noticed an unopened letter, the envelope addressed to her in uneven block capitals. She extracted a thin sheet of lined paper carrying a penciled message: DEAR MISS OLIVER JOHN PARKER AND I ARE SUITED THANK YOU YOURS FAITHFULLY ADA BURNS MISS BUT SOON MRS.

"Hooray!" Mary waved the letter in Heather's face. "It worked!"

"And a special hooray for your sagacious speaking bones! Whatever will they tell you next?"

IO

While Bombs Fall the Bureau Booms

The Phoney War came to a devastating end in the late afternoon of September 7, 1940, when more than 250 German aircraft dropped 625 tons of high-explosive bombs and thousands of incendiaries on London's docks and East End.

For the next eight months Londoners trod fearfully along blacked-out streets shrouded in dense fog, strewn with scorched bricks and wood, broken glass, twisted metal, shrapnel, and forlorn remnants of people's lives. They breathed in the mortar-laden dust, smelled the acrid stink of high explosives, seeping gas and sewage, their ears attuned to the ghastly drone of approaching aircraft, the wailing of warning sirens, and the heart-stopping whine of diving bombs. The living comforted the sick, wounded and homeless, and buried the dead, knowing that at any minute they too might die. Some despaired and chose death, committing suicide by cyanide, but many sought life and love. The Marriage

Bureau was inundated with people in many states of mind, from the pitifully lonely and fearful to the determinedly optimistic and defiant.

"Three hundred applications today," counted Heather. "If this keeps up we shall have to employ another secretary, and that will be expensive."

"But if a bomb razes us to the ground, as it very likely will," countered Mary, "we shan't have that or any other problem!"

"That's why we must think again of storing a second set of records somewhere safe."

"But what about a second set of us?"

"*Courage, mon vieux*—or rather, *ma vieille et chère* Mary! We can but start with the records. I have arranged to see Humphrey and ask his advice."

Humphrey listened attentively, as he always did to one of his favorite (and increasingly lucrative) clients. He told Heather that she would certainly be well advised to keep duplicates out of London, since the situation was looking far from good—indeed, in his candid opinion the prospects were diabolical. Heather and her Bureau had been fortunate so far, and their luck might hold; but as her legal adviser, and indeed her friend, he urged her as a matter of priority to seek a repository as safe as anyone could hope for.

"I foolishly thought that diplomat's mansion was safe," admitted Heather, "but I shall not repeat such a sorry mistake! I realize we had a lucky escape, for the mansion was not far from

Aldershot. At the time we were optimistic and ignorant to the point of lunacy, but now we know a military centre is bound to be a target."

Humphrey nodded sympathetically as a possibility struck him: the clerk of a solicitor friend in Maidenhead, a town he imagined to be as safe as anywhere, had been called up. There were therefore two office rooms to spare. Would Heather like Humphrey to inquire?

Heather agreed with enthusiasm; the friend proved willing; the rent was modest. So night after night the matchmakers laboriously copied their record cards, ledgers, registration forms, letters and press clippings, writing in the smallest hand possible, since paper was beginning to be in short supply. Then, one bleak November day, they motored down to Maidenhead in the heavily laden Morris.

Several months later, Heather and Mary opened the Maidenhead office for two days every week. On the first afternoon, in glided a flawlessly chic designer, wearing a cape of American opossum over a perfectly cut two-piece of navy wool. She sat straight-backed, crossing her silk-stockinged legs, and explained that she had worked in Brook Street until a bomb had devastated her premises.

"Luckily it was December the twenty-seventh," explained Miss Easter to Heather, waving her ivory cigarette holder in a beautifully manicured hand, "and when the bomb fell I was having a little Christmas break, safely at home in Knightsbridge, but all my work went up in flames. I decided to evacuate myself. And luck has struck again: I had been meaning to come and see you, since Brook Street is only just around the corner from Bond Street, and now here you are, two minutes from my digs! It must be fate!"

Miss Easter had lost her income and was living on savings and on rent from her flat, which she had let to a Free French officer "who'll convert it into a Gallic love nest, I daresay, but he does pay the rent." She was thirty-eight, and wanted to meet an older, settled, reliable gentleman of her own class: "Public school of course. I don't mind if he's divorced, though I should prefer him to have been the plaintiff. Children are all right, but not babies. Probably over fifty; too old to be called up. Tall and well dressed. Not a country squire with grimy fingernails and addicted to dogs and shooting, but not a dedicated townie nightclubber either. Church of England preferably, or Roman Catholic if he doesn't expect me to go to church with him. And . . ." Miss Easter hesitated, looking down momentarily and flicking her cigarette ash into the ashtray before continuing, softly but intensely, "And he must have honorable intentions. I am sick to death of dishonorable men."

Heather noted the sudden trembling of Miss Easter's scarlet lips and quickly assessed her abrupt lack of assurance. She had no doubt that a woman as well presented, charming and socially adept as Miss Easter had encountered numerous men with dubious intentions. But she reassured her that those who came to the Marriage Bureau were seeking a wife, not an *affaire* or a mistress (though some were certainly fleeing from such entanglements).

The Bureau would introduce Miss Easter to no man who was not, as far as could possibly be ascertained, a gentleman in all senses of the word.

Only that very morning Heather had listened to the description of a woman uncannily resembling Miss Easter, by Colonel Champion, a fifty-four-year-old widower, educated at Eton and Sandhurst. He had fought with distinction in the Great War, but a limp from a bayonet wound had put paid to his army career. He had recently retired as a stockbroker to concentrate on charitable work for servicemen, and now wanted to marry a lady capable of providing social background for his "rather exceptional" fifteen-year-old daughter.

"He is a very doting father!" smiled Heather. "He's trying to make up for the girl losing her mother (in a car accident, sadly. She was driving.) He's interesting and humorous, old school but sympathetic. He does not, however, want a wife who is too much of a cocktail drinker, nor a chain-smoker. How much do you smoke?"

"Oh, only five or so a day!" said Miss Easter, a little too airily, thought Heather, whose sensitive nose twitched at the aroma of cigarettes lurking below her client's lily of the valley scent. "Perhaps a few more since the bombing started. A cigarette steadies my nerves. But now I'm out of London I'm sure I can cut down." Miss Easter filled in her registration form and paid her five guineas.

To Heather's delight Miss Easter's first meeting with the Colonel was such a success that she joined him and his daughter when he collected her from her boarding school. But there was one fly in the Colonel's ointment. "They cut me out!" he grumbled to Heather. "Those two girls spent the whole time talking about clothes and fashion and makeup—they took not a blind bit of notice of me!"

"How perfectly dreadful!" murmured Heather with a total lack of sympathy, as they both burst out laughing, and Heather accepted the bouquet of lilies held out to her with a heartfelt, "Thank you so much, m'dear, she's exactly the girl for me!"

Back in London, more and more people, particularly servicemen and women, undeterred by the difficulties and anxieties of venturing into the West End, arrived at 124 New Bond Street. One who poured out his heart to Mary was a thin, gangly twenty-three-year-old who gazed at her with eyes of such an intense sea-greeny-blue that she felt as if she might drown: Tadeusz Nedza. "The Scottish peoples call me Teddy. I am coming to you but not because I am sex-starved. I am luff-starved. I vant a vife to luff, and to luff me."

Teddy had been born in the sad, beautiful Polish city of Krakow, to hotelier parents who wanted him to take over the family hotel. He dealt very pleasantly with the guests, including the foreign ones, who were pleased that he spoke a smattering of their language. But in January 1939, with war threatening, he joined the Polish Army, to be trained in Morse Code so that he could take down intercepted German messages. When the Germans invaded Poland eight months later, he was captured.

Teddy and a fellow soldier escaped, throwing the Germans off the scent by dodging and weaving through the city's maze of little alleys, which they knew intimately. He was recaptured days later, and an exploding hand grenade, which killed his captors, badly damaged his legs. A Red Cross doctor—ironically, a German—saved them from amputation.

"So you can see," he insisted to Mary, banging his fist on the desk, "I hate the German peoples, but one German I luff."

Mary sat in silence, aghast, as Teddy continued his saga. Pronounced healthy and due to be sent to fight in Germany, he bluffed his way out of the hospital wearing a doctor's stolen coat and blessing his knowledge of German. He tricked a Gestapo officer who demanded his papers into falling to his death in an icy river. He outwitted slavering guard dogs, evaded wolves, and survived subzero temperatures as he made his painful and lonely way to Hungary. There he claimed to be a civilian, but his army haircut gave him away. Happily, friends came to the rescue with a ticket to a border river that he could cross into Serbia. From his breast pocket Teddy pulled a much-fingered ticket, that he first kissed and then held out to Mary. "Look, see, here is the ticket, my ticket to freedom. It is most precious to me, it is—how you say—my line of life. This ticket I luff."

At last, emaciated from malnutrition and seasickness, Teddy had reached France on an overcrowded and leaking ship. In a decrepit car he and other soldiers set out for Brittany, but a bomb dropped by a German airplane killed the driver. None of the other soldiers could drive.

"They said, 'You haf been on driving courses—you must drive us,'" Teddy remembered, pointing his finger at Mary and fixing on her his brightest blue stare. "I told to them, 'But I do not haf a permit to drive.' And they all laughed and shouted at me: 'Who is asking for your permit to drive? Is Hitler demanding to see it?!' So I drove. It was a terrible journey, the roads very bad and everywhere refugees pushing their carts with their old dying peoples, and animals starving and furnitures."

At last, in June 1940, Teddy arrived in Liverpool, where he spent his first night in Britain fast asleep on a bench in the Anfield football ground, looked after by the Salvation Army. The next day he went by train to Scotland, where he joined the Polish Section of the British Army, had a glorious bath—"Luffly hot water! And soap! And a *towel*!"—and set about taking down German messages and cracking the codes.

Teddy became more and more expert at his work, and was promoted to instructor. He spent some time in London, discovering in Piccadilly's American Hotel many other Poles eager to talk and drink and sing with him. Their convivial carousing left him feeling desolatingly lonely, homesick and lovesick. So when walking from the hotel to Oxford Street he saw the sign MARRIAGE BUREAU, on impulse he marched up the stairs.

"I was knocked sideways by his story," recalled Mary. "He was so young, and he looked so fragile, all bone and muscle, not an ounce of fat, and those luminous turquoise eyes which seemed to see into my soul. But he had killed and escaped and starved and dared more in his short life than almost everybody in their entire lives. How I wanted to help! I could think of lots of young women on the books who were loving and practical, which was what he asked for. But I wanted to find him a true match. I didn't quite envisage a young woman who had murdered an enemy, as Teddy had murdered his Gestapo man; but an equally strong girl who in the face of unspeakable odds would be courageous enough to do something equally nightmarish."

Mary put Teddy in touch with several young women. He was delighted, particularly with a Hungarian nurse whose prescient parents had fled to England in 1936. Ilma worked in a military isolation hospital where, to Teddy's dismay, not long after meeting him she fell in love with a Hungarian patient, and sent a heartbreaking farewell letter to Teddy.

"I luffed Ilma and she luffed me, but not enough," concluded Teddy, part angrily, part sadly, on a visit to London.

When Gertrude Hart appeared, Mary uttered silent cheers. "I knew immediately, my bones told me, and you can't deny, Heather, that I was right. She had 'Mrs. Nedza' written all over her. I was in a panic that after the interview she might not register, but thank heavens she did."

On her registration form, Gertrude described herself as "British, in the WRNS, age twenty-four, father a rancher in the Argentine (deceased), religiously tolerant." "British now," Mary noted, "but by birth a German Jewess, shy, quiet, strong, v. nice, v. difficult."

In 1935, when she was nineteen, Gertrude's South American father had died suddenly from some ferocious local sickness.

Her German mother had left the Argentine to return, with her daughter, to live with her frail parents, well-respected doctors, in Berlin, not realizing that it was the worst country in the world for Jews. On November 9, 1938, Kristallnacht (Night of Broken Glass), the Nazis attacked Jewish homes, businesses and synagogues in a sadistic orgy of destruction and plunder. Thugs smashed thousands of windows, including one that crashed onto Gertrude's grandmother. She died instantly, her head split wide open, spurting blood. When her grandfather bent to touch his wife, his heart failed and he dropped dead by her side.

Hearing her mother howling like a banshee over her grandparents' bodies, Gertrude seized a steel paper knife and rushed out of the house, brandishing it at the young Nazi standing outside the front door. He seized her wrist and, prodding her with his gun, pushed her back inside. There he released her, and whispered fiercely that he had been a medical student, a pupil of her grandfather's, forced against his will to join the Nazis, and had been on his way to warn the old couple. Gertrude and her mother must escape: they must not waste a moment, they must go to England *now*!

The two women took nothing, not even a suitcase, which would have advertised that they were leaving. All they had was the money for a train ticket to England. They arrived in London with no possessions, no home, no job, no friends, but were rescued by a Jewish charity and, after a spell in an internment camp, were cleared as "friendly aliens." It was all too much for

Gertrude's mother, though, and her spirit flickered out, soon followed by her body.

Gertrude joined the Women's Royal Naval Service to serve the country to which she was endlessly grateful for taking her in. An orphan, she took pleasure in the familial comradeship of the navy and made friends with several other Wrens, but although no longer classed as an "enemy alien" she felt herself to be a stranger. She was agonizingly lonely, longing to find a strong and loyal young man. She wrote on her registration form: "He would have a love of life and a big wish to live it fully with a wife he respects and loves. A man with morals and courage and sense."

Mary immediately put Teddy in touch with Gertrude, but as she was based in Portsmouth it was weeks before she could coincide with him in London. Mary was on tenterhooks, full of hope, but at the same time fearful that a meeting between a Pole and a German might prove disastrous. "They should be enemies, but oh, Heather, they are two of a kind, they will recognize each other, they will understand each other. I know, I simply *know*!"

"We shall see," was all Heather would say. Privately, she placed great faith in Mary's "bones," but she was also learning that the most promising plans can go awry.

Bombs continued to rain down on London. Though both Heather and Mary developed some immunity to the remorseless terror, sharing the "Blitz spirit" with other Londoners, the daily strain and the nightly lack of sleep were beginning to tell. Mary, living in a flat in Piccadilly, daily walked past scenes of hideous desolation, arriving at the Bureau in a jumpy and nervous state that no amount of cigarettes could calm. Heather, usually more resilient, had been shaken to the core in October 1940, when Curzon Street House, very near her flat, had been bombed. The 1930s block of flats was used by the War Office, so soldiers were among the thirteen killed and thirty wounded. Heather knew some of them by sight and had waved at them on her way to and from the office.

Heather also had friends among the regulars of the Café de Paris, a favorite haunt for nightlife, and she was a fan of its charismatic black American bandleader, Ken "Snakehips" Johnson. Being twenty feet belowground the famous Café was supposedly safe, but on March 8, 1941, a bomb whistled down a ventilation shaft and exploded in front of the band, blowing Snakehips' head off his shoulders, shearing off the legs of dancers, bursting the lungs of diners. Compounding the horror, looters were seen cutting off the fingers of the dead to steal their rings.

Bombs near home and bombs near the office: in April 1941 high-explosive bombs fell in Brook Street and Woodstock Street, just around the corner. Immediately around New Bond Street, the Blitz hit Bruton Street, the Burlington Arcade, Conduit Street, Dover Street, Oxford Street (John Lewis almost entirely destroyed, Selfridge's severely damaged), and Old Bond Street. On the night of April 16, a parachute bomb fell on Jermyn Street. The next day Mary and Heather held a small party in the office to celebrate the Marriage Bureau's second birthday.

The evening after the party, sitting in the office wondering gloomily how they could carry on, the matchmakers perked up at the sound of a familiar voice.

"Blimey, you two girls didn't oughter be still here. It's late, you should've gone 'ome. You look done in, you could do wiv a nice cuppa an' some grub an' a gasper. Lucky I come around. I said to meself, I said, Alf, Jerry's bin payin' partickerly 'orrible visits this week, so just you drop in an' see your girls is all right!"

Always chirpy and concerned, Alf was a middle-aged Special Constable who had registered with the Bureau and then taken a proprietorial interest in the welfare of "my marriage girls." As he patrolled Bond Street and around, he dropped in frequently to check on them and regale them with stories.

"I bin 'avin' a terrible time," Alf grinned. "Down Shepherd Market there's an 'ole lot of prostitutes, poor girls. I'm sorry for 'em, they're that desperate, they ain't got no money an' they're daft with fright an' the spivs an' the pimps an' the black market boys an' the pickpockets don't never stop cheatin' 'em. They 'ates 'itler for ruinin' their trade. The minute the siren starts it's my job ter get 'em off the streets to their 'ome or into a shelter, but they don't want ter go, they want ter keep tryin' for anuvver punter even when the bombs've started, you wouldn't credit it. So I have to chase 'em off. If they gets back ter their 'ome before I catch 'em they can't be persecuted, see. They're scrubby little things, but some of 'em can't half run. It's good exercise fer me, but—"

"Well, Alf," interrupted Heather, "you need exercise if we're going to find you the nice wife you want, because she'll be after some fit and healthy fellow who's handy in the house and the garden!"

"I know, I know. But you better 'urry up an' all an' find 'er cos I don't want ter keep running fer ever. There was a girl yesterday, can't 'ave bin more 'n fifteen, I'd say, skinny little madam, face made up to 'ell and falling out of 'er frock, if you know wot I mean, she had them high heels but she ran quick as a rabbit, till she caught 'er 'eel on a lump of rubble an' fell flat. I 'elped 'er up an' she'd twisted 'er ankle, so I 'eld 'er arm while she 'obbled to 'er 'ome. Effin' an' blindin' she was all the way—I was shocked, an' I've 'eard a fing or two, I can tell you. She nearly fell down the area steps, but I 'ung on to her an' left 'er in 'er 'orrible dirty room, stinkin' of cats an' cheap old perfume an' other nastier fings not for you girls' ears. She tried to get me ter come in, but I knew wot 'er game was and I was gone before you could say Jack Robinson!"

Alf poured cups of tea, handed around his cigarettes, and was about to launch into another story when the office door opened and in slunk little Nancy Patch. The last time she had been in touch had been to announce her impending marriage to Trevor Potts, and to tell Mary that her sister Elsie was happily corresponding with Fred Adams in Australia; so Mary was startled as Nancy, cowering and trembling, opened her mouth to speak, but burst into violent tears that racked her slight frame.

"Oh, Nancy, what on earth is the matter? Has something gone wrong between you and Mr. Potts?"

Gasping and straining to control her voice, Nancy closed her eyes, then opened them in a wild stare. "He-he-he's dead. Trev's copped it. And Elsie too. We was all in the h-h-house and the siren went off and Trev and Elsie rushed out to the sh-sh-shelter up the road but they was too late and the b-b-bomb got them. Killed Trev straight off. I'd been and left my p-p-purse in the house so I was a bit behind and the b-b-bomb just missed me. They took Elsie to hospital and she die-die-died this afternoon."

Heather sat frozen and mute, overwhelmed by a sudden memory of Sundays in the school chapel singing the words "the sharpness of death."

Mary rose shakily from her chair and wrapped her arms around Nancy. They stood, swaying, clinging tightly together, tears streaming down their faces.

Alf pulled the blackout screens down over the windows.

In the darkening room, the sound of infinite sobbing was drowned out by the ghoulish wail of falling bombs.

II

Sex, Tragedy, Success and Bust Bodices

In their first two years at the Marriage Bureau, Heather and Mary had learned when to ask a question and when to keep silent, when to give sympathy or advice or a warning, when to prompt a tongue-tied applicant and when to let her or him (usually a man) search for the words. Now, shocked and shaken themselves, they were at greater pains than ever to set their clients at ease, and found the difficulty was often not to persuade the hopefuls to relax, but rather to check the gush of words. The horrors of the bombing seemed to have toppled a great barricade of inhibitions. Clients now bent their interviewer's ears with intimate details, in startling contrast to the restrained, understated behavior of a year or so earlier.

"Several wanted to talk about sex," remembered Mary.

I found that very difficult. I was twenty-seven but I'd never been married, and my mother had never mentioned the subject. My family didn't talk about anything interesting! So I didn't know what to say when a client brought up the subject. I used to sit there nodding sagely when it appeared that I was being asked a question. It wasn't always a very direct question, more a slightly defensive half-statement, made with a meaningful look, asking for my approval, such as, "I don't think it's wrong to have two boyfriends at the same time." I used to look interested and thoughtful when they went rambling on, as though I was deeply knowledgeable and, with my vast store of experience, was weighing it all up in the most judicious manner. Heather was much better than I was about sex, so I tried to pass on to her any people I thought might want to wax on about it.

Heather's approach was matter-of-fact and practical, as she wrote later:

Luckily, from the age of eight I went to a boarding school in Devonshire which was near the kennels of the local hunt, and the woman who taught me riding was the girl-friend of the huntsman. I learned to take a keen interest in the breeding of hounds and talked freely about coming on heat and periods of gestation. Many of my fellow pupils came from farming families, and under their influence my interest turned to horses and cows.

Soon I could hold forth about slipping foals, mastitis and contagious abortion, but strangely enough I did not relate this to humans until I went to my public school, where I heard surprising stories about men and women which did not seem to relate to what I knew were facts in animals. However, after much thought, and reading *Lady Chatterley's Lover* (a private edition which was passed around the dormitory so we all took turns reading it, under the bedclothes by torchlight) I got a fairly clear picture of what probably happened.

That was just as well, since my mother never talked about sex to me, and the only advice I recall her giving me was, "Never trust a man with a small nose!" The term I left school I was a bit flummoxed when the headmistress asked me if I knew what was "worse than death." I didn't, but as my mind had flown to rape, which I did not feel I could possibly discuss with her, I mumbled "Yes."

Mary, of course, was a farmer's daughter, not the parson's daughter we said she was. I rather presumed that she would have acquired knowledge of sex in much the same way as I did, but she hated farm life, she had always escaped to London or Assam as much as she could, and she was squeamish, unlike me. She was wonderful with sick people, but animals, especially sick ones, made her feel quite ill herself. It was strange, but not important as long as I could deal with the clients who wanted to raise the subject. We didn't always manage to spot them in advance, and once poor Mary got stuck with a person who claimed to be both male and female, so could marry either sex! "It" wanted to have children too!

Heather was being wooed by several hopeful men. Many male clients were startled to find a glamorous, rather aloof and astonishingly young woman facing them across the desk, and, thinking fast, wrote "tall and blonde" and "I would not mind my wife working" on their registration form. The bolder ones followed up with an invitation to lunch at the Berkeley or dinner and an evening of gaiety in a nightclub. Heather accepted most of the invitations, but kept her client suitors at a distance, assessing them dispassionately while she laid other plans for them.

Clients were far from the only admirers. Heather was never short of offers of one kind and another from the many men brought to London by the war: debonair Free French supporters of General de Gaulle; Poles who had fled their devastated country, joined the RAF, and now flew on bombing missions with cavalier courage and panache; Australians and Canadians who had never traveled to another country, let alone another continent; Dutchmen, Czechs, Austrians, Belgians—men from all over the world who fetched up in a daily more ruined city, and were superficially ebullient, but in private petrifyingly lonely and hungering for love.

Even at home Heather had suitors. She lived in a small flat above the Mirabelle restaurant, in Curzon Street, Mayfair, a short walk from the New Bond Street office. In the flat above lived a dashing forty-five-year-old officer, Hugo, who was working on something ultra-secret for the War Office. His wife and child had taken refuge from the bombing with her parents in Scotland, so he hardly ever saw them, but was determined nevertheless to enjoy female company.

In pursuit of Heather, Hugo used to open his window and, paying out a length of rope, let down a basket containing a bottle of champagne. Often, when Heather saw the basket swaying gently outside her window, she leaned out and took the bottle, whereupon Hugo, feeling the loss of weight, would haul up the basket and hurtle down the stairs. If she was about to go out, or was already entertaining, Heather would ignore the basket, which a disappointed Hugo would then haul back up again, to drink the champagne in grumpy solitude.

If, one sunny day, Heather had not been lunching at the Ritz with a flattering rubber planter for whom she was finding a wife, but who would gladly have whisked Heather herself off to Malaya, Mary would have asked her to interview a sad-faced young woman who drifted into the office. She radiated desolation, thought Mary. Her eyes were cast down, long eyelashes shading the livid bruises that discolored the hollows below, her skin waxen and taut, her thin form disguised by a shapeless gray coat several sizes too large. She spoke softly in a slow, monotonous voice, as if reciting a roll call of the dead. "I must find a man to marry me," she implored, transfixing Mary with a penetrating stare from huge eyes as purple as the bruises. "I must, I must! Please help."

"But why must you?" asked Mary gently, sensing tragedy.

"Because I'm going to have a baby," whispered the girl, hunching her shoulders and gripping her handbag in her small white hands, the nails bitten to the quick.

"You poor thing!" Mary burst out, before collecting herself and offering Martha a cigarette, which she accepted gratefully. Mary lit one for herself, then, bit by hesitant bit, drew out the sorry story.

Martha Webb lived with her parents in a quiet street in Westminster where, before the war, she had spent many happy evenings with her fiancé, Eustace, a civil servant of her own age (she was now twenty-five). She had been an editorial assistant and occasional translator in a publishing company, a job that suited her very well, as she was an avid and sharp-eyed reader and liked helping people to enjoy books as much as she did. But as paper became scarcer, she feared she would lose her job.

Then, on December 29, 1940, the Luftwaffe had destroyed everything surrounding St. Paul's. Paternoster Row, home of booksellers and publishers, including the office of Martha's employer, was reduced to rubble. The numbness with which she gazed at the ghastly scene of burned-out buildings, charred scraps of paper floating forlornly in the air, soon yielded to a furious desire to do what she could to retaliate. She was quickly recruited to become a postal censor, monitoring letters written by prisoners of war in French, German and Italian, eliminating any scrap of information that might help the enemy if it fell into the wrong hands. She also signed on as a volunteer Air Raid Precautions warden, spending her evenings checking that no windows or doors let any light out into the street, and rushing to the scene of an air raid to pull people out from the rubble, administer first aid, and comfort the dying, the wounded and the dispossessed.

Equally patriotic, Eustace had joined up at the first opportunity, and their comfortable meetings had been reduced to occasional snatched weekends when he was on leave from the army. The last time Martha had seen Eustace was at the beginning of May, in a café near Victoria Station, when all he could tell her was that he was due to be sent abroad—where, he either did not know or could not say. Stricken with all-consuming fear for her beloved, and with his declarations of undying love glowing in her heart, Martha had experienced a passion to match Eustace's own. It obliterated the scruples of her Catholic beliefs, which forbade sexual relations outside marriage. Martha and Eustace had seized each other's hand, rushed into a small, dingy hotel, and consummated their love only just in time for Eustace to catch his appointed train.

A month later, Eustace's mother had accepted from the telegraph boy the dreaded telegram telling her that Eustace was dead. He had been shot through the heart: a swift and painless death.

Martha's grief paralyzed her. But it also intensified her anger, so she refused to abandon her duties, and on the evening of

May 10 she went out on ARP patrol as usual. She did not know that it was to be the worst night of the Blitz, and the final one. By the bright light of a full moon, 505 Luftwaffe bombers unloaded 711 tons of high explosive and 86,000 incendiaries on the already-stricken city, killing 1,436 Londoners, seriously injuring 2,000, and totally or partially destroying 10,000 buildings.

In the hellish inferno Martha heard screams coming from a half-destroyed terraced house, which through the murk she could just see was swaying precariously. She ran, but in the darkness tripped on a sandbag that had burst, spilling its contents onto the pavement. Flinging her arms wide to grab hold of a nearby railing, she lost her grip on her torch. Too anxious to stop and search for it, she followed the eerie howling down the imperiled house's outside steps, and then into the coal cellar under the pavement. There, in the dust-laden smoky darkness, she stumbled over a woman crouching against a wall, jabbering and whimpering incomprehensibly.

To Mary's unspoken question Martha replied, "I grabbed her coat and pulled her up, and she could stand, so she hadn't broken a leg, so I pushed her up the steps. I was desperate to get her out before the house collapsed on top of her. She didn't make any sense, she was bleeding and crying, and choking on the plaster and coal dust, and vomiting, and when we got out onto the street I could only just make out that she was saying something about a baby. She hit me in the face, screaming at me to let her go back into the cellar, and I realized there might be a baby left down there; it had been too dark to see. Luckily another ARP warden came along and I shouted at him to look after the woman and I rushed back down the steps.

"Down in the cellar all I could do was to shuffle and flounder around, and feel with my hands. I couldn't see anything. But I thought I heard a noise, and I made out a big hole in the wall where the Council had knocked the cellar into next door, so that if one house was bombed people could escape from their cellar into the next one, and then the next—all the way along the terrace. And—" Martha stopped abruptly. Her body curled in a profound shudder as a spine-chilling yowl of pain broke from her. Quivering, Mary took the cigarette from Martha's shaking fingers. Suddenly the girl jerked bolt upright and continued her story.

The noise Martha heard was made not by a baby but by a man, who shoved her violently through the opening into the next cellar and back against the wall, seizing her forehead in one hand and clamping the other across her mouth. In a rough voice with a strange guttural accent he ordered her to be silent or he would kill her. Then quickly and very calmly, without uttering a word, he ripped open the buttons of her trousers, yanked her panties down, raped her, and pushed her into the first cellar. He strode back to the steps, bounded up them, and melted into the all-obliterating blackness, just as the remains of the house gave a great elegiac groan and disintegrated, hurling dust and bricks and glass and furniture in all directions. Martha staggered up to the street just in time and ran for her life, clutching her trousers, narrowly escaping a flying sideboard and a glittering shower of jagged glass. Retracing her steps with immense caution when she could see that there was nothing still standing, she almost tripped over the ARP warden, cradling the stricken woman in his arms.

Mary felt as if a bomb had landed on her heart. She sat in silence as Martha faced her, her eyes dry but huge with anguish. "So you see, I am going to have a baby, but I do not know if the father is my dearest love or a crook—perhaps a deserter or a pimp or a looter, a black-marketeer or even a murderer. If there was a baby in the house whom I might have rescued, the man is certainly a murderer, for nobody could have survived when it collapsed. It is terrible for me and will be more terrible for my child, so I must find for him (or perhaps it will be a girl) some good man to be a father. My parents are fine people: they will help, even though they will be sick with shock. But they cannot find me a husband, so I appeal to you. One good man, a Roman Catholic, like me. I do not care about anything else at all."

Mary had never faced such an impossible request, and was 99 percent certain she would never, ever be able to produce anyone for Martha. In a profound quandary, all she could do was stall: she told Martha that there was nobody suitable, but that new clients registered every day, so she would telephone the minute a possible man appeared.

Martha duly wrote her telephone number on the registration form, and gratefully accepted Mary's proposal that she should pay the registration fee only if an introduction were made.

As the door closed behind Martha, Mary burst into tears of commingled despair, pity and fear.

• • •

"Chin up, dear Mary! Here's a letter to rejoice your heart!" said Heather, glowing from a flirtatious lunch and placing a small close-written sheet in front of her friend. "It's from Gertrude," she added as she swept out to greet a good-looking new client.

As she read, Mary's spirits revived and rose and overflowed. Gertrude and Teddy had met and fallen headlong in love. As a token of his devotion he had given her his precious ticket to freedom—"a gift which goes to my heart," wrote Gertrude,

> but I am so afraid that I can lose it. Really, I want to give it to him again, but he insists. Also he insists that if he is Polish and I German (and South American and above all British too, of course) it is of no matter, for now we are not citizens of one country or another country but all are citizens of the world, only whether good or bad is of matter. Also, he insists that he loves me—he says "luffs," which is so funny but I must not laugh for he is so serious! And my English is not perfect too! My heart says to me that I love him also. We are to marry and to have many children. So with my heart I thank you, Miss Oliver. I shall send you more news.

As Mary hastily wiped her eyes and beamed a searchlight smile, the raised voice of the receptionist reached her, apparently remonstrating with some visitor, insisting that Miss Oliver was occupied and not to be disturbed. She did not succeed, for Mary's door was flung open to reveal a slender young woman dressed in a black skirt and close-fitting dark red jacket. She paused just inside the door, striking a pose, her head tilted theatrically to one side, her back slightly arched, throwing her bosom forward.

"Greetings, greetings! Miss Oliver, I presume?" she inquired; rather coquettishly, decided Mary as she nodded at the unexpected visitor. She imagined her to be a potential client—but why would the receptionist have discouraged her?

"Miss Oliver," the visitor gushed on, "my name is Miss Bud. I have read about you and your magnificent Marriage Bureau with considerable interest, and am vastly admiring of your inestimably valuable skill in working matrimonial miracles. I have something to assist you in your labors, something which all your felicitous brides will long passionately to possess. I have the ideal bust bodice! Observe!"

To Mary's outraged astonishment Miss Bud swiftly unbuttoned her jacket to reveal two firm, young, naked breasts, the nipples hidden by two small circular pieces of what appeared to be adhesive plaster, the point of each nipple peeping shyly through a hole in the center.

Mary was not so taken aback by this eye-opening revelation that she did not judge the visitor's breasts to be in no more need of support than a healthy stalk of Brussels sprouts. Her immediate inclination was to tell the visitor to do up her buttons and leave forthwith, but Miss Bud's recital of the virtues of her patent product—pronounced as if making a declaration of peace with honor—had a hypnotic effect on the matchmaker.

On swept Miss Bud. "This avant-garde bust bodice sustains all but the most matronly of bosoms, yet in no fashion does it confine those entrancing feminine curves in which men take such innocent, boyish delight. It is blessedly free of the clumsy shoulder straps of conventional bodices, which resemble the cumbersome harness used to control a horse. Such bindings frequently reveal themselves, to the detriment of the romantic picture which each one of your enchanting brides strives unceasingly to present to that perfect husband, to whom you have with such refulgent genius united her. It elevates any sad and weary breast which pines to sag. Do you ever experience a saggy bosom, Miss Oliver?"

This most impertinent of questions jerked Mary out of her trance to glare at Miss Bud. "No! Never!" she snapped indignantly.

Aware that her sales patter might have missed its mark, Miss Bud hastily buttoned up her jacket and threw onto Mary's desk a card and a small packet. "Try them yourself," she said, retreating through the door. "Then you will certainly recommend them to your clients. Farewell, farewell, Miss Oliver!"

The receptionist knocked and entered, apologizing for allowing Miss Bud in, for she had overheard the entire bizarre conversation. She was as nonplussed as Mary, who opened the packet and studied the bits of plaster, wondering if in some mystic way they might really have contributed to the undoubted robustness of Miss Bud's bosom.

· · ·

At home that evening in her Piccadilly flat, curiosity overcame Mary's skepticism. She pressed the intriguing little circles to her far from saggy breasts. Surveying herself in the mirror, she discerned no visible difference, and tried to peel them off. They would not budge. Worse, in bed, woken from fitful sleep by the cacophony of anti-aircraft guns, bombs and droning Luftwaffe planes, Mary felt a tickle, which burgeoned into an itch, which made her scratch away at the plasters—but to no effect. They were as firmly attached to the most sensitive part of her anatomy as limpets to a rock.

In a panic, Mary telephoned the ever-practical Heather, who was sympathetic but crisp: "I am staggered that you should have fallen for Miss Bud and her dubious bust bodices. She must be a first-class con woman! Try lying in the bath to soak the little blighters off. Let me know what happens—but not this evening, I'm off to dinner with Hugo—he's so pressing. Must dash. Toodle pip!"

Mortified and dispirited, Mary put down the receiver. She always conscientiously bathed in only a few inches of water, and refused even to try lying facedown in the tub. She slathered her breasts with Pond's cold cream, confident it would do the trick. When that proved useless, she mixed a handful of Lux soap flakes into a large bowl of warm water, placed it on a table, leaned forward, and lowered her breasts into the bowl while gripping the top of a chair for balance. Ten minutes of this tricky pose made her twitch with such a disabling cramp that the bowl overturned.

In desperation, over the next few days Mary tried every

remedy she could think of, anointing herself with vinegar (horribly smelly), gin (awful waste), sewing machine oil (begged from the furrier below the Bureau), Brylcreem and even mustache wax, provided by a mystified boyfriend to whom Mary flatly refused to explain her request. As a last resort she spent an hour swimming up and down a nearby public pool. The plasters clung on.

Only weeks later did the valiant bust bodice give up the fight and, one evening, quietly fall to the floor. Wrapped in her dressing gown, weak with relief, Mary picked up the plasters and consigned them to the wastepaper basket, muttering, "So much for 'innocent delight' and 'perfect husbands' and 'enchanting brides'! As for 'refulgent genius,' 'simple idiocy' is more like it!"

12

A Sideline and Two Triumphs

When, in May 1941, Hitler stopped blitzing London to concentrate on invading Russia, nobody imagined that the end of the war was in sight. But the relief felt at not being under constant attack was profound. Mary and Heather, together with the population of London and other cities, started to recoup their strength. By the summer, the matchmakers were getting more sleep, feeling more buoyant, and widening their horizons. But they were still working extremely hard to keep up with the steady flow of clients: the nervous and the brash, the self-effacing and the arrogant, the domineering and the domineered, the delightful and the frankly ghastly. Heather often took clients' registration forms and the Black Book home with her, as her godmother discovered when she apologized for telephoning at nearly midnight and was reassured by a cheerful, "Oh, don't worry, I'm in bed doing my mating!"

Wherever she lived, Heather always transformed her rooms. She was as concerned to live in a stylish environment as she was to look elegant, in clothes that perfectly suited her coloring, height and carriage. She had an instinct for shapes and colors and proportions, an unerring ability to create a harmonious room that was as aesthetically pleasing as it was comfortable. She was also an exceptionally efficient administrator, so it was a natural progression from finding the right spouse to helping to choose the bride's trousseau, organizing the couple's wedding, even arranging the honeymoon and, finally, furnishing the house of those lucky enough to have their own establishment in which to embark on married life.

"I do wish you'd been there, dear Mary!" yawned Heather as she dropped her handbag on her office desk one Monday morning. "That wedding was exhausting. I certainly earned my fee."

Heather had organized the wedding of Winifred, a wealthy girl of twenty-four whose grim-faced mother had frog-marched her only child to the Bureau, insistent that she should find a husband. Mrs. Pinkerton-Hobbs had done her utmost to launch her unwilling and unprepossessing daughter into society, disbursing large sums to present her at Court and to ensure that she went to all the right deb dances, where she would surely meet and soon marry a suitable young man.

Far from grateful, Winifred had grown increasingly intransigent about being so overtly up for sale in the marriage market, and had been downright rude to several effete and penniless young "debs' delights" who would have forgiven her plainness and lack of femininity for the sake of the fortune that she would inherit. Mrs. Pinkerton-Hobbs drew even nearer to her wits' end when Winifred greeted the outbreak of war as a glorious opportunity to be something more than a tradeable commodity, joined the Women's Land Army, and was sent off to a run-down farm in distant Yorkshire.

For the first time in her life Winifred had a purpose. She hummed happily as, dressed in regulation fawn-colored, cotton-drill milking coat and dungarees, thick woolen socks and canvas gaiters, she obeyed the farmer's curt instructions: "There's the bucket, there's the stool, there's the cow. Sit down and pull!"

Ignoring the dull ache in her arms and the blisters on her hands, Winifred learned fast. She went on duty at 6 A.M., did the morning milking, then cleaned out the milking shed, pushed clumsy wooden wheelbarrows of dung to the pile, milked again, and was usually sunk in a heap in bed by 7:30 in the evening. She also learned to drive, not through lessons, but by trial and error. There was nobody to transport the milk to the local town, so Winifred was detailed to take the wheel of the small lorry.

"That's the brake and that's the accelerator," grunted the farmer, a man of very few words, most of them orders. "Now, drive!"

Weaving downhill, with the milk sloshing around in the churns, altering the balance at every bump in the rough road, fearless Winifred was exhilarated as never before. She had always loathed sipping cocktails with urban sophisticates in taste-fully decorated drawing rooms, but was at glorious ease in the company of her fellow Land Girls—a very mixed bag, from a former parlor maid to a millionaire's daughter as bolshie as herself. In the evenings they either darned their socks in the chilly farm kitchen, until there was so much darn and so little sock that they qualified for a new pair, or changed into the WLA walking-out uniform of greatcoat, green jersey and gabardine breeches and cycled off to the nearby Sergeants' Mess.

Mrs. Pinkerton-Hobbs trembled at the hideous possibility of Winifred contracting marriage with some unsuitable working-class soldier, and wept internally as she surveyed her daughter's wind-reddened face, cracked lips, broken fingernails and dirt-ingrained hands. How was the wretched girl ever going to catch a suitable husband? Her father would not have stood such nonsense, and would have more or less discreetly bribed and bought a husband, with a lucrative job or even hard cash. But what could she, a widow, do with so uncooperative a daughter? Her friends eyed Mrs. Pinkerton-Hobbs pityingly.

Fortunately, only the day after Winifred had unwillingly signed the Bureau's registration form under the eagle eye of her mother, there bounded up the stairs her destined man—for yes, it was destiny, Heather and Mary unanimously decided, destiny needing only a skillful little nudge.

Gyles Hopwood was a Lincolnshire landowner, producing quantities of grain and vegetables on the ancient family estate. "*Gent*," Heather wrote on his record card: "Merry twinkle. Fine big country type. Not the sharpest of tacks but nice. Knows his own mind." Gyles's application to join the navy at the outbreak of war had been rejected on grounds that supplying vitally needed food for a nation certain to be increasingly deprived of imports was a reserved occupation. Disgruntled, for he was a man of spirit and of action, Gyles had returned to his farm to work flat out, helped only by three aged laborers, greatly missing the four young, fit ones who had all been called up to fight.

Living alone in an imposing farmhouse, Gyles was receptive to the suggestion of an old girlfriend that he try his luck with the Marriage Bureau. Within five minutes of meeting Winifred he decided that she would make him a fine wife. She was practical, fond of the simple life, unperturbed by hard work, unaffected, blunt in her opinions, a lady and—a quality so desirable that he had underlined it on his registration form—she wore no makeup and confessed to a horror of painting her fingernails.

Decision was translated into action at top speed: after two hours, Gyles asked Winifred if she would do him the honor of marrying him.

"Why not?" she retorted. "I wouldn't have thought it possible, but now that you ask, it sounds a jolly good idea!"

Mrs. Pinkerton-Hobbs was shell-shocked but overjoyed. Heaven had answered her prayers (no doubt Mr. Pinkerton-Hobbs had cunningly bribed an influential angel). She sent an ecstatic letter and great sheaves of hothouse flowers to the Marriage Bureau, and set about organizing an elaborate church wedding complete with six matching bridesmaids and a choir of ten. Despite the limitations of rationing—food, clothes and petrol were all heavily restricted—her plans were lavish. In such a sublime cause she was prepared to turn a blind eye to the black market source of champagne and wedding cake. She made an appointment with her dressmaker to choose the wedding dress. Not for nothing had Mr. Pinkerton-Hobbs made a fortune out of steel before he expired. Money was to be no object in making this remarkable, long-longed-for occasion one to make her the envy of her friends.

But Mrs. Pinkerton-Hobbs had reckoned without Winifred's newfound confidence, with which she obstinately confounded her mother's plans.

"No, Mama, I don't want all that fuss and flummery, and neither does Gyles. We don't want to be some kind of sideshow, and I flatly refuse to look like a big white duck with a meringue on its head. We are going to be married in a register office with a good party afterward. I can't wear slacks so I shall be in my green frock, you know the one. I haven't got time to organize anything—I'm full-time and more on the farm—so I've talked to Miss Jenner and she will sort it all out."

Given a generous budget, Heather had done Gyles and Winifred proud, and had deflected a potential calamity when a doddering relative, clutching a bottle of champagne in each hand, had tried to reawaken his youth by demonstrating the whirling of dervishes he had so admired in Cairo. Swiftly assessing the damage that whirling bottles would inflict, and the risk of the ruddy-faced relative having a heart attack, Heather had smoothly de-bottled him, enticed him to a quiet corner, sat him down with a dish of cooling ice cream, and questioned him with intensely flattering interest about his Egyptian soldiering days. Mrs. Pinkerton-Hobbs had noticed this small pantomime, thanked her lucky stars and, brimming over with champagne and emotion, added a hefty "thank-you" tip to Heather's account.

Mary listened and laughed as Heather described the wedding, then held out an opened letter: "Now, here's another job right up your street! In fact, there are two jobs, this written one and one from a telephone call I've just answered. You'll never guess who it was."

"In that case I'll start with the letter."

A forty-five-year-old surgeon, Percival Gordon, living in Coventry, a widower who had just become engaged to Florence, a hospital almoner in London, had written to ask Heather if she would make his home more welcoming to his bride-to-be. The house, he wrote, was an ordinary one, but he was thankful to have anywhere at all to live since the Luftwaffe had flattened the city. Even before the war Coventry had been attacked: an IRA bomb had knocked Percival's pregnant wife, Amelia, to the ground with such force that five weeks later she died. "As you know," wrote Percival,

> I was aware when I came to see you six months ago that it might seem premature, indeed callous, to seek another wife scarcely a year after the death of Amelia and our unborn child. However, you listened sympathetically to me and I felt reassured that you understood how the

circumstances of war alter everything. They bring all aspects of life into sharper focus, so that in a curious way they simplify matters. When you are acutely aware that you may well not exist tomorrow, you do today what before the war you might have contemplated for months before taking any action. Moreover, as a surgeon I frequently confronted death before the war, so that, although not immune to it, I have a greater familiarity with it, and can better accept it as an integral and inevitable part of life than can most people.

In Florence you have found for me a perfect wife, not only because she is so loveable but also because through her work she too has much experience of death, and consequently an understanding of my situation (as well, I am happy to say, as a love for me which fills me with joy). We are jointly anticipating a new departure. After our wedding she will come and live with me here; but my house was made into a home by Amelia, and I want Florence to know that it is *her* home. I have very little time for matters other than my work, since there are so many sick and injured in Coventry that the hospital is always at full throttle. In addition, it is difficult for me to know what may most strike a woman's eye. So I should be most appreciative if you could see your way to visiting me with the aim of making some changes, and advising me generally. I should of course pay your fees.

"Certainly I'll go," said Heather, "though, heaven knows, it will not be an easy journey to Coventry. It could take me all day after the appalling bomb damage to the railway lines. I'll write to him. Now, what about the telephone call, dear Mary? Who was the caller I'll never guess?"

"Mrs. de Pomfret!" Mary burst out. "Mrs. Etheldreda de Pomfret! Dearest friend of the WI Lady Chairman at the baby show, remember? She's disposed of three husbands and wants victim number four! She spoke as if her mouth was full of sour grapes which she was trying to spit out at the same time as talking, and what she said was truly frightful. I told her the first step was to come in for an interview, and she made indignant exploding, swallowing, gurgling, spitting noises and let fly that she would do no such thing, who on earth did I think she was, only servants go for interviews! I bit my lip—you would have been proud of me, Heather—and with extreme calmness I explained to her that if, due to exceptional circumstances, someone was unable to come to the Bureau, you or I would, if convenient, visit the person at home, for an extra fee. She jibbed at the idea of paying, but I think she's desperate, since she agreed to an appointment with you next Monday."

So when Heather rang Mrs. de Pomfret's bell outside a solid Victorian block of mansion flats in Kensington, she was prepared for a haughty reception. However, staring up at Heather, Mrs. de Pomfret knew that she had met her match. Heather was a good foot taller than Etheldreda, who could have been mistaken for a vividly painted talking doll. She greeted Heather warily, but in exactly the strangulated tones Mary had described, ushering her through a narrow hall into a spacious and gracious drawing room.

Heather caught her breath, raising her shoulders and drawing her elbows in close to her sides. The room was a veritable museum. On every horizontal surface lay arrayed a multitude of precious objects: bejeweled presentation cups jostled with ostrich-feather fans, ivory chess sets sat on boards of ebony and mother of pearl, dishes edged with turquoise and gold were piled with silver fob watches. Candelabra of pink Venetian glass shone down on the enameled lids of tiny snuffboxes; a carved wooden monkey leered at a silver-framed photograph of an Edwardian patriarch.

The tops and shelves of the tables and cabinets bearing this dizzying collection were as invisible as the walls, which were concealed by a profusion of paintings, mirrors, light sconces, elephants' tusks, daggers and shields, the mantelpiece dominated by a manky but still intimidating tiger's head, mouth yawning open in a long-silenced yellow-fanged growl.

"It's my husbands', you understand," drawled Mrs. de Pomfret, clearly accustomed to the stupefaction of any newcomer and ready with the explanation. "They were all connoisseurs, men of great taste and of course wealth too. All three were collectors, and they were all besotted with me, so in their memory I like to display all their treasures."

With extreme caution, Heather threaded her way through the Aladdin's cave, only to stop dead in her tracks at the sight of a large black cat that uncurled itself from a deep chair. Immediately, Heather's cat allergy kicked in. She snorted and sneezed so energetically, bent almost double, and wept so copiously, that Mrs. de Pomfret, understandably misunderstanding, exclaimed: "Oh, please do not feel sorry for me, I am quite happy without my past husbands. It is most kind of you to sympathize so."

Between sneezes Heather explained the cause of her suffering, whereupon Mrs. de Pomfret led her into a small room. Recovering, Heather drew up sharply when faced with a stuffed brown bear, standing upright on its back legs. She put out a hand to steady herself, but jerked it back as she noticed a slight movement among the grizzly hairs.

Mrs. de Pomfret launched into a potted history of her matrimonial life. She had married at eighteen, straight from her Swiss finishing school, a pleasant man but weak—she dismissed Clarence as if he were a cup of underbrewed Earl Grey. She had been so devastatingly pretty that weeks after Clarence was killed in the Great War, she had accepted the proposal of Leopold, on leave from his regiment.

Alas, Leopold proved no more bulletproof than Clarence, and hours after his return to the fighting in France he was fatally shot. Once again Etheldreda donned her widow's weeds. Black suited her, especially black lace, and it was when wearing a particularly fetching Parisian *chapeau noir* with a spotted veil that her carriage had broken down in Hyde Park and Everard, taking his usual restorative morning promenade after a convivial evening, had rushed to the rescue. They had lived a life of content, with

Etheldreda organizing all their activities, which admirably suited Everard's indolent and pleasure-seeking nature.

True to himself, Everard was knocking back whisky on a grouse moor when, conforming to the pattern of Etheldreda's husbands, he was felled by a fellow sportsman's stray bullet. Etheldreda shed tears of irritation and set about finding a husband who might break the pattern. But the few men who had crossed her path since 1938 had not been attracted by the fading looks and sharp tongue of a middle-aged shrew. Etheldreda had confided her troubles to her ever-helpful dearest friend the Lady Chairman.

As Heather walked back to the office, deep in thought, she felt a tickle on her wrist. As she scratched, the skin reddened, and more tickles expanded into itches, which started to throb. Looking closely she was horrified to recall her early knowledge of animals and to recognize the unmistakable signs. "Fleas!" she yelped as she opened the office door. "That appalling, snobbish, conceited, heartless female has a cat with fleas! And they hop about on the bear too! A dead bear," she added hurriedly as Mary put a protective hand to her throat. "Not as horrific as the Sheikh's live falcon, granted, but certainly enough to deter any suitor. It is imperative that we find her a husband or we'll never get shot of her."

"What does she want?"

"Oh, the impossible: a public school man, well-off, a widower or bachelor, not a divorce unless he was the plaintiff, no children cluttering up the place (even a docile child would wreck that mausoleum of hers), a man of title preferably, though a bishop would do—her grandfather was a bishop somewhere in Africa. He must be a social asset, a connoisseur of objets d'art, and speak perfect French. Her most recent husband's ancestors were French nobility—though I'd be willing to bet that the *de* was not added to *Pomfret* before 1920. And if *Pomfret* is French, it must come from *pommes frites,* so she's really Mrs. Chips! She says she's forty-two and wants the next Mr. de Pomfret (because that's what he'll be, mark my words) to be from fifty to sixty, a mature man. But she's fifty if she's a day, though not badly preserved and wonderfully made-up. Her neck is shot, though, it's wrinkled like crêpe paper, and certainly half a century old! Oh, and just in case we were thinking of proposing any, no cads or bounders!"

Mary's mind flew to an amiable but rather feeble man who did something administrative for the Egyptian government. He was highly presentable but clueless; she had puzzled over how Egypt benefited from him. But she suddenly remembered that a colleague of his had written to tell them that he had been killed by some hotheads who had thrown a bomb into the English Club in Cairo, and fired guns through the windows.

"He might just as well have married Etheldreda!" remarked Heather. "He sounds just her type!"

In the Black Book and their card indexes Mary and Heather found three living candidates: a fifty-five-year-old bachelor colonial officer just returned from Nigeria, a divorced London art dealer of fifty-nine, and a widowed retired brigadier. All were pleasant, comfortably off, public school, Francophile, appreciative of the arts (except perhaps the Brigadier), and free from young children. And lonely.

Heather had noted that the colonial officer might be "a bit queer," but judged that sex was not a high priority for Mrs. de P. Like the art dealer, he was an agreeable rather than a forceful personality, likely to be happy to be bossed around. Not so the Brigadier, accustomed to controlling small armies of soldiers and dealing with the top brass of the War Office. But Mary wondered if he might not quite like a change, and enjoy being commanded rather than commanding.

First Heather sent the art dealer to Mrs. de Pomfret. He reported briefly:

> She has a firm view of the beauty and worth of her objects and of her own person. The former are, in my professional opinion, largely worthless. On the latter I shall not be so ungallant as to relate my conclusions. Suffice it to tell you that while Mrs. de Pomfret is an impressive lady, I can no more imagine marrying her than I can finding a Rembrandt in the attic (though I should live to regret the former but should rejoice and again rejoice in the latter).

After his encounter with Mrs. de Pomfret, the colonial officer walked directly to 124 New Bond Street to pour his tale into Heather's eager yet dispassionate ear: "She reminded me of a Nigerian chieftain. I used to have to deal with large black male Mrs.

Heather Jenner aged about twenty with her father, Brigadier Cyril ("Tiger") Lyon, in Ceylon, c.1934.

Heather and Mary Oliver relished "doing the mating." They searched the letters from potential and actual clients, the registration forms, index cards, Black Book and other records for suitable matches. Each took a proprietorial interest in the clients she had interviewed: "No, you can't have my Mr. Y for your Miss Z, I want him for my Mrs. A!"

The Marriage Bureau expanded so quickly that it moved
twice in its first few months, both times to offices very
close to the original office, in New Bond Street.

From its outset in 1939, hundreds of letters poured into the Marriage Bureau every week, some addressed to the Bureau, others to Miss Heather Jenner or Miss Mary Oliver, whose names were fast becoming well known.

Most letters were legible, but Heather and Mary despaired of some scrawled and rambling epistles, which they handed over to the secretary, who soon became indispensable.

GIRLS' "OLD MAID" PANIC STARTS MARRIAGE RUSH

MOST of the girls want to marry someone in the Royal Air Force. The Navy is still very popular, but the Air Force has outstripped them by a long way.

"In fact, ever since war began this has been our permanent headache because every other letter nowadays seems to have the phrase, 'I want to meet someone in the R.A.F.!'"

This statement appears in a most entertaining book published to-day, "Marriage Bureau," by Mary Oliver and Mary Benedetta, the two young women who established a successful marriage bureau in London three years ago.

They have between 9000 and 10,000 men and women on their books, including M.P.s, millionaires, and daughters of Peers, down to the very humble people who are also lonely.

The war brought them a deluge of clients. It was found the men wanted to get married so that when they went away to fight they had someone to come back to, and the women wanted to marry quickly because they were afraid of being left without a man at the end of the war.

"They did not say this in so many words, as, naturally, they did not want to look like chicken running after grain."

More men apparently want children in wartime, but fewer women want them which, Miss Oliver comments, is not surprising when they have to look after them alone in as much, if not more, danger than the husband, who is in the Army. Very few of the couples want to set up a home of their own in wartime.

Several men in the R.A.F. specifically asked to meet a girl who could go on living with her parents. "I suppose they feel happier about her if she is with somebody in case they get killed flying," says Miss Oliver

The bureau had applications from hundreds of Australian and Canadian soldiers who want to marry English girls, and the Australians, in particular, went like hot cakes. The girls were keen on the Australians because they found them sincere and because they want to go and live in Australia after the war.

In the case of the women who want R.A.F. men, it is generally sheer hero-worship. "These young men make wonderful husbands," says Miss Oliver, "not because of their deeds of bravery, of which the average pilot's wife says she hears little or nothing, but because of their outlook.

"**Their emotions are fewer and finer, and they have the best sense of proportion in the world. You cannot fight 1941 air battles and have a mind for petty quarrels and disturbances.**"

Miss Oliver says she is afraid of two things in these hero-worshipping wives of men in the R.A.F. One is that the

The Marriage Bureau had been set up to find wives for expatriate men on leave in London from far-flung continents; but the outbreak of war in September 1939 brought very different clients, including servicemen and, increasingly, servicewomen.

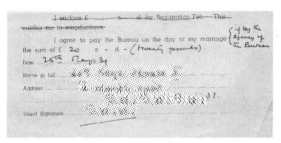

24.7.44

Strictly Private and Confidential

THE

"MARRIAGE BUREAU"

(Proprietresses: Heather Jenner and Mary Oliver)

125 NEW BOND STREET, LONDON, W.1

Telephone: MAYfair 9524. Office Hours: 10 a.m.–5 p.m. Sats. 10 a.m.–12.30 p.m.

CLIENTS CAN BE INTERVIEWED AT THEIR OWN APARTMENT IF PREFERRED.

REQUIREMENTS:

Age 22–26 Religion R.C. Height 5'1" to 5'4"

Figure medium (not thin) Income £250 a year (use) Nationality English, Scotch or French

Further particulars Colouring: brown. Social standing: unimportant.

Good looking rather than pretty. Education: good (particularly French language) Must know how to cook (if income below £350). Character: well balanced, etc.

DESCRIPTION OF APPLICANT:

Age 41 Religion R.C. Height 5'6'

Figure SLIM Income £700. P.A. Nationality English

State whether independent or in business ARMY.

If the latter, nature of business ARMY.

Interests and hobbies general interests country life

If married before NO Encumbrances if any NO

Home address

Business address

Name in full

Until Counsel had drawn up terms and conditions, the Marriage Bureau's registration form recorded only basic details. Registered in 1939, the fifty-fifth male client remained until July 1944. His requirements were discussed with the interviewer, who wrote them down. He had no "encumbrances" (children or other dependants).

I enclose £   s.   d. for Registration Fee. This entitles me to introductions.

I agree to pay the Bureau on the day of my marriage { if by the agency of the Bureau } the sum of £20 s. – d. – (twenty pounds)

Date 25th May 19 39

Name in full

Address

Usual Signature

While most clients were honest, some did their utmost to avoid paying the After Marriage Fee. Although happily married to a girl introduced to him by the Bureau, one client claimed that she did not comply with his stated requirements so he would not pay. Another did not immediately take to the woman he later married. He left the Bureau, met her again through friends a year later and refused to pay the AMF on the grounds that his friends had introduced them.

In her Curzon Street flat, Heather sorts through some index cards. The match-makers prided themselves on the efficiency of their elaborate systems for recording information, which were wonderfully backed up by their personal knowledge of clients.

The Bureau began without a secretary but almost immediately needed one, to transcribe information from each client's registration form onto an easily accessible index card.

Heather with her fiancé,
Michael Cox, and beloved
little dog, in 1942.

Heather posing for a 1943 *Tatler & Bystander* article about helping the
war effort by growing food. She was living in Scotland with her landowner
husband, Michael Cox, trying unsuccessfully to enjoy the country. If in color,
the photograph would reveal her uncountrified bright-red fingernails.

Heather's height, strong features, rich voice, authoritative
bearing and sense of style made her a charismatic interviewer.
Small wonder that many male clients wooed her.

In 1939, the press revelled in reporting on the extraordinary
Marriage Bureau and its alluring founders, Heather Jenner and
Mary Oliver. The Bureau remained a wonderful source of stories, as
this page from the Bureau's 1948 press-cuttings book shows.

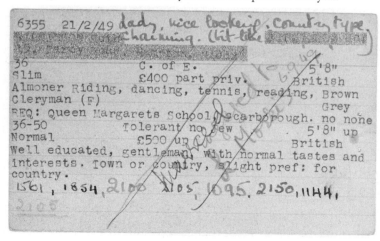

1095 NICE MAN. GENT. NICE LOOKING.
Duplicate. 17.11.47
no School teacher
AG 66   C.of.E.   6'
Very Slim   £1000 p.a.   British
Headmaster. Literature, Arts & Crafts, Dk Golden
Agent to Late Ld. Hillingdon(F) Music. Blue
       Plays, Dancing, Xxxxxx Country life.
REQ: Oxford   No   None
30-40   C.of.E. (Anglican) Not short
Not stout   Adequate.   British
Like partner to Have enough income to make her
completely independent for her own needs because
of my entry into the church. Resources to be
pooled. 4659. 4723.
         4403. 2731. 4611. 4504. 4269. 4617. 4657.
1583. 3095. 3045. 2088. 4006. 2397. 4235. 268.

Leslie M, a tall, very slim, country-loving headmaster of forty-six who was about to be ordained, was registered in November 1947. He was classified as a "nice-looking Gent," and met several young women before marrying Ruth W, a tall, slim, "nice-looking Lady" of thirty-six, an almoner with private and earned income, daughter of a clergyman. He sought a wife aged between thirty and forty, who was not stout, had some income and was happy to pool resources.

Ruth W registered in February 1949, seeking a normal-sized, well-educated gentleman aged thirty-six to fifty. Leslie's registration number, 1095, was written on her index card as a good introduction, and they married in September that year.

6355 21/2/49 lady, nice looking. country type.
                charming. (bit like ...)
36   C. of E.   5'8"
Slim   £400 part priv.   British
Almoner Riding, dancing, tennis, reading, Brown
Cleryman (F)   Grey
REQ: Queen Margarets School, Scarborough. no none
36-50   Tolerant no Jew   5'8" up
Normal   £500 up   British
Well educated, gentleman, with normal tastes and
interests. Town or country, slight pref: for
country.
1561, 1854, 2100 2105 1095. 2150, 1144,
2105

```
1289  working Class would like wives at once
                   as he is leaving for Australia

32                    Protestant              5'7½"
Medium        £15.p.m.       British(Australian)
Merchant Navy Greaser. Cycling,swimming. Brown
Labourer dec:(F) Home life,children        Blue
                                  No.   No.
REQ                 Melbourne State School
25-30               Protestant              5'4"-5'7"
I want to have children. Must be some one
willing to settle in Australia. Non dancer
prefered.Blonde prefered,but not red hair.
4357  4312  2663 .4503  .1789  4)5'1  5080
```

A thirty-two-year-old greaser in the Merchant Navy, Malcolm C's
laborer father and housewife mother had emigrated to Australia when
he was a child, probably soon after the First World War. Keen on
family life, he sought a blonde wife willing to settle in Australia, have
children and not want to go dancing. The interviewer classified him
as "Working Class" and immediately gave him introductions.

Doris G was earning a reasonable post-war salary working for the
Control Commission in Germany. At the age of thirty she was getting
too old to become a mother, and made it clear that a husband must
want children. He should also earn at least twice as much as she,
be of a similar religion, not more than ten years older, well made,
perhaps a business man living far away from depressing England.

```
5336
                                                    P.O.
30                    C.of. Scotland          5'7"
Slim                  £300p.a.               Scottish
Control Commission. Swimming,Riding,  Auburn
Commercial Agent(F)Dancing?Gardening.Brown
REQ: Glasgow High School   NO        None
30-40                 C.of.E. or C.of.S. over 5'9"
Well made             Over £600 p.a.      Immaterial
If possible I should like to meet a man who
has business abroad.Sth Africa,Sth America.
ect: He must want children as I intend to
have them.
1335 . 1784 .1445 .1829 .
```

" Have you by any chance a nice
coalman on your list? "

Unmarried herself, Dorothy Harbottle's
mission in life was to find husbands
and wives for others. Despite being an
incurable chain-smoker, she lived into her
eighties, remained unceasingly devoted
to the Marriage Bureau, and entertained
new secretaries and interviewers
with stories of her match-making.

Post-war shortages of fuel affected
rich and poor alike. Clients often
asked for a spouse in possession of
something they themselves lacked: a
house, furniture, a car, enough money.

"MARRIAGE BUREAU"

Established 1939

Proprietor
MARRIAGES LTD

124, NEW BOND STREET,
LONDON, W.1

Directors:
JENNER & OLIVER, LTD.

Telephone MAYfair 9634/5

Manager:
HEATHER JENNER

Office Hours: 10 a.m.–5 p.m.   Sat. 10 a.m.–12 noon

The purpose of the Marriage Bureau is to introduce, with a view to marriage persons who desire to find matrimonial partners. Applicants are required to give full particulars of themselves and those particulars are then placed on the register of the Bureau. These particulars are then compared and whenever an introduction between two persons appear to be suitable the Bureau sends particulars of a client to the applicant with a view to them communicating with each other. The more difficult the applicant's case, the more limited the introductions will naturally be. The Bureau cannot, of course, do more than effect introductions nor hold themselves responsible for results, and does not vouch for the correctness of particulars thus passed on. These particulars should be verified by you.

DESCRIPTION OF APPLICANT

Age   Height   Religion   .   Colour of Hair   Eyes

Figure   Income   Nationality

State Source of Income and Occupation

Interests and hobbies

If married before, give present status   Dependants, if any

Father's Profession   Where educated

Home address

Business address

Name in full

Through what source did you hear of us?

I HAVE READ AND UNDERSTOOD THE ABOVE CONDITIONS OF REGISTRATION; AND I CONFIRM THAT I DESIRE INTRODUCTIONS THROUGH THE MARRIAGE BUREAU FOR THE PURPOSE OF MATRIMONY. I HAVE WELL AND TRULY FILLED IN THE ABOVE PARTICULARS OF MYSELF.

(Signed)

Date of Registration

So that the Bureau may be guided in arranging introductions applicants are requested to give some indication of the sort of person with whom an introduction is desired, as follows:

Age   Religion   Height

Figure   Income   Nationality

Further particulars

Clients can be interviewed at their own homes if preferred for a further fee.

Passport to Matrimony?

The standard form. By the time Pam has completed it, Heather Jenner has a pretty shrewd notion what she is like and what sort of husband may suit her.

As advised by Counsel, the Bureau's registration form became more detailed and formal. The newly formed company "Marriages Ltd" was added. Applicants were asked to give their source of income, education and father's profession, and to sign a declaration. "Requirements" remained basic.

Leader Magazine, April 23, 1949

A Marriage Has Been Arranged

Heather Jenner

IN AN INTERVIEW

It seemed a wild idea, in 1939 of all years, to start a Marriage Bureau with a tiny staff and a small but expensive office in Bond Street. But now, ten years after, with over three thousand successful marriages to its credit, the mad idea seems sane enough to be worth examination

"BUT how does it work? I mean, how do people write to you, in the first place?" "We insist on a personal interview." "We" is Miss Heather Jenner (who is really Mrs. something else, very happily married herself, with two children). I can imagine, looking at her, that she is the perfect interviewer.

Stage One is the interview, a long and searching one. Stage Two is the First Matching Process, a comparison of files, to find the prospective husband or wife whose tastes match those of the new client most closely.

Here was the opportunity to put one of the most important questions in the world to

MARRIAGE
BUREAU
CONFIDENTIAL
HEATHER JENNER

MARRIAGE
BUREAU

FLOOR

Of course, I know lots of girls. I could marry any day I wanted to. I don't need help from so-called experts. Still . . . it might be interesting. Very interesting. Perhaps I'll just drop in . . .

someone well qualified to answer it.

"What is compatibility in marriage? What are the tastes which must be shared?"

There were so many things to remember, but in the end I managed to pare them down to a ten-point list, the essence of three thousand match-makings.

Here is the list of matching-point essentials in order of importance.

(1) Social position. (Includes upbringing, education, social ambitions or the lack of them. Women often show strong preference for certain professions—e.g. schoolmaster, doctor, business man, etc.)

(2) Income. (A close second.)

(3) Religion. (A bad third.)

(4) Nationality.

(5) Age. (From No. 5 onward, exceptions become more frequent. There are records on the books of exceptionally successful results where the man is considerably older than the woman. According to Miss Jenner, follow-up notes show that "the much older man should be either a very weak or a very strong character.")

(6) Type of personality. (Assessed at interview.)

(7) Health. (Outlook is unfavourable for two people who neither of them "enjoy very good health.")

(8) Interests. (Town v. country. Sport v. games. Social v. "liking to be alone." Outlook particularly bad if one client much more fond of going out and about than the other.)

(9) Choice of site of home.

(10) Readiness to accept the fact of a former marriage.

"And all these facts you get at your first interview?" I said. "Yes, but there is one danger, which only experience can overcome. The danger of the false answer."

"You mean clients don't tell the truth?"

"Far from it—but you will find that there are certain characteristics which not only my clients, but I myself, and you yourself, can never admit that we do not possess."

How You See Yourselves

Here was another list, more fascinating than the first.

The "what everyone believes themselves to be" list (in order of frequency).

Most people have an unshakeable conviction that they

(1) are capable of making a good husband or wife;

(2) are easy to get along with (companionable);

(3) are notable for their sense of humour;

(4) are willing to give and take;

(5) are home lovers;

(6) if not good looking have a certain charm, if somebody will take trouble to discover it;

(7) have a certain amount of culture;

(8) are broadminded, but . . . (object to women smoking in the street, etc.);

(9) are good mixers;

(10) are good hosts or hostesses;

(11) are industrious. (Women, even obviously lazy ones, believe this more firmly than men.)

After the matching processes, comes the meeting (the men are encouraged to make the appointment). During the walking-out period, there are follow-up interviews, for advice.

It is sometimes possible to suggest, for instance, to the lady client that the clothes she wears are not perhaps quite perfectly suited to this new step she is taking in her life. "Not quite that hat, perhaps." ("It is amazing what you can say, without offence, from behind a desk," says Miss Jenner.)

What Is The Need?

Clients usually find themselves suited, after meeting on an average three, or four, prospective opposite numbers.

And why is it so successful? Why should there be a need for this sort of thing in these modern, free and easy democratic days, when everybody meets everybody?

But do they? What are the chances, in modern life, of meeting the right person?

Where are those Edwardian days of large families, when each of the half dozen brothers had half a dozen friends for the sisters to meet? When the mothers spent three quarters of their lives in being marriage-bureau experts on their own account. When the weekly dance was a programme dance, and a girl was not stuck most of less to one dancing partner all the evening like a jujube, but had a chance, had the certainty, of being able to compare and contrast. It is because the business of "marrying is no longer organised at home that there is room for the professional marriage-maker."

"But you mean successful marriages can really be arranged in this rather cold-blooded way? Marriages are made in Heaven."

"Maybe, but the divorce rate of marriages made in Heaven happens at the moment to be one in eight. Marriages made at the bureau work out at one divorce per fifteen hundred weddings."

S.P.

In this 1949 magazine article Heather listed her ten "matching-point essentials," starting with: 1. Social position. (Includes upbringing, education, social ambitions or lack of them. Women often show strong preference for certain professions—e.g. schoolmaster, doctor, business man, etc.). 2. Income. (A close second.). 3. Religion. (A bad third.).

Passers-by in Bond Street could comfortably read the other signs at number 124 and slip up to the second floor without feeling conspicuous. A nervous person would quickly be reassured by the businesslike yet sympathetic manner of the interviewer. Here, Heather helps a tentative young woman fill in her registration form.

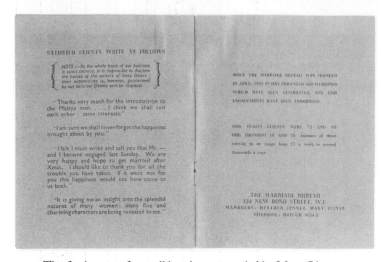

SATISFIED CLIENTS WRITE AS FOLLOWS

NOTE.—As the whole basis of our business is strict secrecy, it is impossible to disclose the names of the writers of these letters; their authenticity is, however, guaranteed by our solicitor (Name sent on request).

"Thanks very much for the introduction to the Malaya man, ... I think we shall suit each other; same interests."

"I am sure we shall never forget the happiness brought about by you."

"I felt I must write and tell you that Mr. — and I became engaged last Sunday. We are very happy and hope to get married after Xmas. I should like to thank you for all the trouble you have taken. If it were not for you this happiness would not have come to us both."

"It is giving me an insight into the splendid natures of many women; many fine and charming characters are being revealed to me."

SINCE THE MARRIAGE BUREAU WAS FOUNDED IN APRIL, 1939 IT HAS ARRANGED 600 WEDDINGS WHICH HAVE BEEN CELEBRATED, AND 1500 ENGAGEMENTS HAVE BEEN ANNOUNCED.

OUR OLDEST CLIENTS WERE 72 AND 65 OUR YOUNGEST 18 AND 20. Incomes of those writing to us range from £5 a week to several thousands a year.

THE MARRIAGE BUREAU
124 NEW BOND STREET, W.1
MANAGERS: HEATHER JENNER, MARY OLIVER
TELEPHONE: MAYFAIR 9654-5

The final pages of a small brochure compiled by Mary Oliver to explain the Marriage Bureau. The match-makers were always adamant that the Bureau's approach was practical but that "their" marriages were based not only on sound principles but also on love.

The Bureau's card indexes were a vital source of information. When a couple were suited, their cards were firmly stapled together and filed separately. They were "off" (though some returned after their Bureau husband or wife died).

de Pomfrets, kitted out in beads and feathers and bones and war paint, resisting my authority all the way. She made it abundantly clear that she would preside as chieftain in our not-so-native hut and I would be a useful slave—provided of course that I minded my Ps and Qs, and did not break any of her relics. I am a mild man, Miss Jenner, but not sufficiently meek to be Etheldreda's lackey."

Mary and Heather waited rather pessimistically for the Brigadier's reaction.

"Splendid female, Etheldreda!" he boomed, as if giving the order to charge into battle, his voice so loud that Heather feared the occupants of the waiting room would hear. "Seen her a few times, just had a couple of gins and a good talk with her, and come straight around to tell you. She hesitated a bit at first, she's accustomed to ordering her husbands around and she's had a lot of practice with the fellers, but she soon hoisted in the fact that I shall be in command. Got some spirit, though, and I like that in a woman, reminds me of my Aunt Hortensia, you could never put anything past her! Lot of damn objects around the place, some of 'em will have to go, I told her so. That damn Bruno will be first, it's hopping with fleas from the damn cat!"

The Brigadier paused, reaching up his hand to scratch the back of his neck. "Cat'll have to go too, can't abide feline creatures, told Etheldreda sharpish it's either Bruno and Felix or me. She looked a tad mutinous for a second or two, then she surrendered, said she'd part with 'em. Sensible little woman. I'm taking her up the aisle next month. So that's it. Most grateful to you two ladies. Here, brought you some gin." The Brigadier plonked a bottle down on the desk, clicked his heels, saluted, and marched down the stairs.

Astonished and relieved, Heather and Mary were reduced to whimpering with helpless laughter. Heather sloshed gin into two big glasses, while Mary leaned back in her chair, flung her arms wide, and cried out: "Another triumph! Quick, Heather, write and tell the Lady Chairman—no, don't write, she'll send us more Etheldredas. Have some more gin, but *don't write!*"

13

Other Agendas, Pastures New

The more word of the Marriage Bureau spread, the more the office became not only a honeypot for spouse-seekers (including men pressing their suit on Heather and Mary), but also a Mecca for salespeople: bridal car chauffeurs, makers of wedding dresses and trousseaux, proprietors of honeymoon hotels, hairdressers, fortune-tellers, caterers, photographers, manufacturers of babies' perambulators—anyone who saw in about-to-be brides and bridegrooms a ready market for their products and services.

"They descended on the office like vultures," Heather recalled, "without an appointment, very insistent. It was not always easy to get rid of them, even for me, and I had had a lot of practice in Indian bazaars. Some were pathetic, people who'd lost their job or their business in the Blitz and were desperate to turn an honest penny. Or servicemen who'd been badly wounded and so demobbed early, but couldn't get a proper job again in civvy street.

"I remember a doleful little chap, only about five foot one— the top of his head was level with my bosom. And it reached that far only because his hair stood up in an elaborate bird's nest of knitted or crocheted fuzz. I was quite mesmerized, staring down rather expecting to see a baby cuckoo or a squeaking little sparrow nestling in the middle of that extraordinary confection. It wasn't his own hair, he explained earnestly, as if I hadn't guessed, though it was made of real human hair, ingeniously woven into his own sparse thatch, and he was convinced that it made him look not only more hirsute but also taller. It didn't do the trick, rather the reverse, for it drew attention to the fact that he was almost completely bald and almost a dwarf. He pleaded with me to recommend his system to bald clients, who would surely be so transformed that they would attract a fleet of lovely ladies. I had to hedge, and accept his card, before he would leave."

Male clients were acutely self-conscious about baldness: "I have many interests," wrote a very presentable young man:

I play golf, dance (rather badly!), shoot, am very fond of an outdoor life, and have many other hobbies. I also possess a car, and am fond of foreign travel, when that is possible. All the above items sound quite good, but unfortunately I became bald at an early age, and I feel that I appear older than I am, and therefore no longer of interest to many girls.

A well-known scientist wrote: "I enclose a picture which makes me look perfectly repulsive, but in real life I look far worse, for I have no hair left." The photograph showed a perfectly pleasant face enlivened by an attractive smile, topped by a gleaming, hairless pate.

Unfortunately, female clients seldom wanted to meet a baldie. "No fat men, bald men, redheads, Welshmen or parsons," stipulated a young woman of thirty-two. An impoverished forty-eight-year-old widow, however, was happy to be introduced to any man, fat or thin, short or tall, hair or no hair, provided he was "a wealthy gentleman who will help me realize my ambitions. I do not want to be a domestic drudge." Heather thought she might like a very well-heeled and optimistic businessman, and be unconcerned by his admission that "my hair is thin at the back but will probably grow again."

Heather and Mary kept a sharp eye out for fortune-hunters of either sex. A key giveaway in a woman was a carefree unconcern about the age of a potential husband: if she was happy to accept someone twenty, thirty, or even forty years her senior, warning bells rang in the interviewer's ears. The client would be only too happy if her darling dropped dead soon after marriage, since her main interest was in the money he would leave her.

Both matchmakers became adept at asking innocent-sounding but searching questions to winkle out the truth from any client who made them feel uneasy, and developed a sixth sense for the outright lie: a man claiming to have an income of £5,000 who in reality had only £500, wanting to meet a woman with a matching £5,000. He would be vague about where he lived, muttering about being bombed out—ah, tragic!—and therefore living in his club, or with some relative, while in fact he lodged in a shoddy bed-sit. Very occasionally he would treat his intended victim to oysters and champagne at an expensive restaurant. As soon as he succeeded in ensnaring the hapless girl into matrimony, lunch out would be Spam or whale meat at a British Restaurant.

Some fortune-hunters were engagingly open: a beguilingly personable, intelligent and cultured Italian baron sent to the Bureau a cream-colored envelope containing photographs of his undeniably good-looking self and his exquisite pillared palazzo, together with glowing references. The accompanying letter, on thick, deeply embossed writing paper, described his wondrous garden: acres of terraced hillside planted with peach and lemon trees, perfumed by jonquils and jasmine running riot among secluded benches and antique marble statues, where the *Barone* and his *Baronessa* would stroll under pergolas dripping with blossoms, listening to the singing of birds, the humming and chirping of busy insects, and the melodious plashing of rills and fountains. With disingenuous honesty he wrote:

> I was brought up in England as my mother was English,
> so after the war I should like to have an English wife,
> a young woman who adores beauty, who is calm and
> brave, not like an Italian girl who is too temperamental
> and passionate. My bride will have money in order to

maintain my most beautiful palazzo and garden, and my family house in town. I should, of course, make her more ecstatically happy than any Englishman can.

"I have no doubt that he will lavish so much Continental charm on her that she will be captivated, positively euphoric," sniffed Heather. "All will be tickety-boo as long as she is too dazzled to perceive her flattering husband's priorities: himself and his palazzo joint *numero uno,* garden *numero due,* townhouse *numero tre,* wife around about *numero dieci,* after his mama, his mistress (you really can't believe that nonsense about temperament and passion), his car, his dogs, and a clutch of cousins. I shall write to him explaining that as our lady clients look for security in marriage, a husband must have a decent income, so we cannot assist."

"I suppose you're right," agreed Mary wistfully. "But it does sound so fantastically romantic, like a fragment of heaven that's come adrift from the celestial heights and hurtled down to this dark and savage world. I should adore to stand with the sun beating on my back, wearing a cotton frock and sandals, breathing in the scent of flowers, plucking a ripe peach from my very own tree, eating it, then dangling my sticky fingers in a cool fountain."

Shaking her head at Mary's flight of fancy, Heather turned to welcome a fabulously pretty twenty-five-year-old, Mrs. Rhoda Clarkson, who had divorced her fifty-year-old husband after only a few months of marriage.

"He'd always been generous to me before we were married,"

she hissed, her voice distorted by bitterness. "He gave me perfume and lovely dinners and a beautiful French silk negligée set, we went to swanky hotels and nightclubs, he paid me lavish compliments and sent huge bouquets. He had resolved to marry me, he wasn't going to take no for an answer. And I was an orphan, no family, and no job either because I'd been a high-class milliner, but ladies had no use for big hats when there were no garden parties or Ascot. I was nervous because he was so much older, and he'd been married twice, and divorced both times. But I needed money and somewhere to live; I only had a few savings. I quite liked him and he swore he adored me. And he was rich, that was the main thing. So I agreed.

"But after we were married he changed: he wasn't loving any more, he was like an animal. He wouldn't give me any money except after I'd slept with him. Then he'd sometimes give me two pounds, but sometimes only two shillings and sixpence, or even less. It varied according to how much he'd enjoyed himself. He used to give me marks out of ten. It was horrible, horrible.

"One day I couldn't bear it any more. I packed my suitcase and walked out. He stood in the hall sneering, and I shouted at him, 'Next time, marry a prostitute!' In fact, that's probably what he did. He let me divorce him, because he wanted his friends to think him a gay dog having an affair, rather than being walked out on by an attractive young wife. So he paid a glamorous tart to go to a hotel with him, and a photographer to take a snap of them in bed together. I got the divorce on grounds of his adultery. Can you find me a nice man, please? But with some money too."

Heather listened to Mrs. Clarkson's dismal tale and picked out a few men for her to meet. Privately, she pondered on how dangerous marrying for money could prove to be. She herself was being pursued by several men, one of them, like Mr. Clarkson, older, very rich, divorced, so persistent in his courtship that, far from responding, Heather was growing cooler and cooler.

Most of Heather's suitors were around forty, congenial, highly unlikely, she reflected, to behave like Mr. Clarkson, or like the ex-husbands or fiancés of various other distressed female clients. But having married very young, and divorced, Heather was wary of serious romantic involvement. In 1940 she had become engaged to a thirty-seven-year-old Welshman, Emlyn Griffiths, well-known in the West End as a top theatrical manager. He was good-looking, six foot three, loquacious, polished and popular, and he and Heather made a striking couple. But whether because she got cold feet, or because he was called up and became a captain in the army, or another reason, the engagement was called off.

By chance, at the party of a close friend, Heather answered a knock at the door to find a nice-looking man asking for the party at number four. Realizing that he was looking for number four in the street, not flat four in the building, she redirected him, but not before a lighthearted conversation during which he recognized her from a newspaper photograph. Mr Cox was delighted to make her acquaintance.

Heather thought no more of him, until a few days later a

note delivered to the Bureau invited her to a cocktail party given by Mr. Douglas Cox. Ignoring the bottle of champagne her upstairs admirer Hugo dangled optimistically outside her window, Heather dressed in a little black frock and a precious pair of prewar silk stockings, and took a taxi to Knightsbridge.

The cocktail party changed Heather's life. She met Douglas Cox's brother Michael, a landowner living in Scotland. Michael could not take his eyes off Heather and, in the following months, courted her single-mindedly.

Mary too was being wooed, but she was more interested in a new project than in any potential husband. When she contacted the press just before the opening of the Marriage Bureau in 1939, she had met Mary Benedetta, a journalist who wrote an entertaining article about the startling new venture.

Mary B. was a kindred spirit. Like Mary O., she had decided that she wanted to do something more with her life than leave school and marry. She worked as a secretary, first for a disorganized American woman, then for a scary Austrian count, a large industrial firm and a yacht dealer. She became governess to an obnoxious girl whose American mother had had her psychoanalyzed. She put a bold idea for publicity to an intrigued publisher, who hired her. She moved into journalism and films, writing about people with strange jobs, such as a man who constructed skeletons, and interviewing Marlene Dietrich, Marie Tempest, Boris Karloff, Alfred Hitchcock and Noël Coward. After writing books about London's street markets and her own experiences, she slid into script writing for the popular wireless program *In Town Tonight* and, in 1936, for one of the BBC's first television programs, *Picture Page*.

Mary B. and Mary O. rocked with laughter as they described their eccentric early jobs to each other. And Heather and Mary's audacious Marriage Bureau enterprise was right up Mary B.'s street, especially as she recalled another of her jobs, as a teacher of dancing. "The best pupils," she wrote,

> were young men home on leave from the colonies. They were pathetically anxious to get up to date. Nothing was too much trouble for them if we could save them from looking ridiculous. They worked conscientiously at every-thing we taught them, and though they were often very clumsy to begin with they usually learned in the end.
>
> Another pathetic thing about them was that, having had all these dancing lessons, they knew nobody to take out. London was just a cold-hearted stranger to them, and I think the leave they had looked forward to for years often fell rather flat. They sometimes asked us to go out dancing with them, but it was never allowed, and they had to go off hoping they would meet the girl of their dreams.

"How amazing!" exclaimed Mary O. "You know precisely the kind of men we set out to help! You can see exactly why we started the Marriage Bureau!"

The two Marys struck up such a rapport that soon they decided to write a book. *Marriage Bureau,* published in 1942, brought yet more clients to 124 New Bond Street.

Secretaries, receptionists and interviewers came and went. Some were too fearful to keep working in the ravaged West End; others were called up, or left to cope with family disasters. Administering the Bureau was a juggling act for Mary and Heather, who were run ragged. Mary had an added reason for feeling exhausted: she was working with the American Red Cross. In December 1941 Germany and Italy declared war on America, and thousands of U.S. servicemen and women were drafted and sent to England. In the same month the conscription of women became legal, and the first to be called up to do essential war work were single women aged twenty to thirty.

Perhaps the authorities considered the good work of the Bureau to count as a reserved occupation, exempting the matchmakers from joining up. Perhaps Mary felt she should also be doing something more obviously essential. Whatever the reason, she spent less and less time in the Bureau, and more and more helping to organize facilities for American troops in London.

Several American servicemen and women found their way to the Bureau. With regret, Mary and Heather had to turn away the girls, as the U.S. government would not permit servicewomen to be put in touch with strangers. The men were deemed able to protect themselves, if necessary, from strange women.

"Most of us have never been anywhere far from home,"

complained GI Brad, a melancholy young soldier who sat puffing his way through a packet of Lucky Strikes while Mary listened attentively. "We sure didn't want to go all the way to England and fight a war. The goddam war's got nothing to do with us. It's not our war."

Mary gave him her most winning smile, murmuring, "But we are so grateful to you Americans for coming to help us!"

"Good of you to say so, ma'am. Sure, we don't like this Hitler guy, and we're sorry you folks are having such a goddam awful time with the bombing and all. But when we arrived here there was a bunch of limeys waiting for us, smiling like crocodiles. They didn't directly say it was about time we showed up but boy, did we feel their resentment."

Brad leaned back in the chair, angrily stubbing out his cigarette as he relived his chilly welcome to cold, wet, ravaged England. Anxious to soothe him, Mary smiled as she inquired, "Do you know any English people at all?"

"No, ma'am, only you. It's lonesome here. All the people on the streets are kinda nervous-looking, not friendly. I want a girl. I had a sweetheart, Sue, back home. But my mom wrote me last week that Sue's got fed up waiting for me, so she's going with another guy. That's what's happened to a lot of us here. Even wives have gotten fed up. They think we're going to get ourselves killed so they'd best find another man."

"That's sad, I'm sorry. Well, let's fill in this form, and you can tell me more about the sort of English girl you'd like to meet."

Brad reflected, puffing thoughtfully on his third cigarette, before replying: "I've met a few English girls who liked me on account of they knew Americans can give them nice things like chocolate and nylons and cigarettes and food. I don't want a girl like that. I want a girl who wants me, not all the stuff I can get for her. Can you help me, ma'am? I'm a cheerful guy, but right now I'm real down."

Brad's life improved dramatically when Mary introduced him to some friendly, ungrasping girls who welcomed his frank and open approach. He often used to drop into the Bureau, giving Mary news of his progress and telling her about his life in America and in London.

Wanting to help people like Brad, Mary volunteered to work on the development of an American Red Cross club that opened in 1942, Rainbow Corner, in Soho. It rapidly became the London home-away-from-home for Americans, where they could jitterbug with volunteer hostesses, drink proper coffee, guzzle doughnuts in the basement Dunker's Den, get spruced up with a hot shower, a visit to the barber and the valet service, play pool, listen to bands and singers, or select their own favorites on the jukebox. They might bump into Irving Berlin, James Stewart and other famous visitors, even General Eisenhower. Homesick Americans were comforted that despite the sign over the reception desk, NEW YORK 3271 MILES, their homeland was not lost to them.

"It's a wonderful place!" Mary told Heather. "And it keeps the men off the streets, which is just as well because they're sex-starved and often very predatory. I've heard that rape is on the increase, and VD too—not all the fault of Americans, of course, but they're certainly not backward in coming forward!"

"Nor's them prostitutes neither!" broke in Special Constable and client Alf, who was paying one of his regular checkup visits to make sure "my marriage girls" were all right. "They don't half love that Rainbow Corner. I sees them tottering down Shaftesbury Avenue, two together for safety—but I reckon it's the Americans wot aren't safe with them tarts. One of their sergeants said to me, he said, it's suicide for a GI to go out in the evening, in the blackout, without a buddy. The girls are all over the place, outside the club is terrible, an' by the underground entrance they flash their torches on a Yankee soldier's ankles an' put their faces right up to 'is an' breathe at 'im, 'Hello, Yank, looking for a good time?'"

"Oh, Alf, you do see some life that we don't!" laughed Mary.

"I do an' all. Just you keep away from that Rainbow Corner, especially at night, Miss Mary, an' you too, Miss Jenner. Them girls know them Yanks want sex, an' they know they might catch some 'orrible disease, or be up the spout, but they're desperate for money, an' them Yanks are flush. That American sergeant, he told me even just a private gets three thousand dollars a year— that's about seven hundred and fifty pounds in our money—so he can lash out on a girl. But a poor ol' British private gets a hundred pounds. It ain't right. No wonder our lads 'ates the Yanks."

Mary heeded Alf's warning, but she was growing to like most of the Americans she came across enormously. Their positive attitude to life she found very refreshing, and in tune with her own. Being courted by more than one made her reflect on what her life would be after the war—whenever that might be.

She had deep discussions with Mary Benedetta, whose husband, unlike most married men, encouraged her to have a career, so that she was happily making documentary films for the Ministry of Information, the Ministry of Food and the British Council. From her own settled situation, Mary B. could see clearly that her conscientious and kindly friend was worn out by the effort of setting up and running the Bureau, working for the Americans, and living in the appalling conditions of war-stricken London. She understood that Mary needed a change.

The dilemma was resolved by the insistence of an American suitor bent on marrying Mary, combined with her longing for pastures new, particularly American pastures. She resolved to embark on a new adventure: living in America.

Heather was at first distraught at the likely effect of Mary's departure on the Bureau. But the whole situation had to be reappraised, for she too was on the verge of great change: she had accepted Michael Cox's proposal of marriage, and was going to live with him in Scotland.

So Mary and Heather sat down to plan the future, just as they had done when working out how to start the Marriage Bureau. Mary was helpful, but at the same time distant, her thoughts always drifting to the new life ahead. Three years with the Bureau had broken her previous pattern of change and uncertainty, when she had traveled, tried many jobs, and nearly married twice. Now she was ready once again for a new departure.

Heather was sure that with a responsible person in the office, keeping in constant touch with her in Scotland, the Bureau could continue to run efficiently. She had her eye on an interviewer she had just trained—but the girl was only twenty-eight, and was conscripted to join the WRNS.

Fortunately, Picot Schooling, a friend since Heather's brief flirtation with the film world, was at a loose end. Passionately fond of the theater, before the war Picot had acted in films and plays, and had been a casting director for a theatrical agency. But now that many theaters were closed, jobs were few and far between. Picot was over the calling-up age, a huge advantage for the Bureau, and she jumped at Heather's invitation.

Mary sold her shares in the Bureau to Heather and they took their farewell of each other, promising to keep in touch while knowing that at least until the war ended, communication between America and England would be difficult.

Picot came into the office to be shown the ropes.

"You need to keep a watch out for ear-nibblers," instructed Heather. "They can be quite harmless, but sometimes they turn out to be thoroughgoing wolves."

"How do I pick them out before they start nibbling?" inquired Picot, looking perplexed.

"Oh, it's almost impossible!" laughed Heather. "I thought I was rather good at spotting them, but I got caught once, by a suave client, Ralph, who complained that a gorgeous divorcée had turned him down, and that she and all the other girls I'd introduced him to were hard. Could I find him someone soft and feminine, if that kind still existed? And would I have dinner with him so he could explain better?

"I lunch with clients but rarely dine with them, but he was very persuasive, regretted he couldn't come into the office in the daytime because of his vital war work. So we had a very nice dinner in a quiet little restaurant. By then I'd heard from the divorcée, who didn't say much except that she found him rather forward. Well, over the oysters Ralph told me he had never in his life tried to kiss a girl unless she encouraged him. His handsome face and honest blue eyes, looking straight into mine, oozed sincerity. I partly believed him, and resolved that a sophisticated girl would be able to handle him.

"In the taxi going home I agreed to find him more introductions, but warned him firmly that if I had even one complaint he would have no more. He thanked me profusely and squeezed my hand gratefully—and then he pounced, grabbing my face and trying to give me a French kiss! I had to fight him off! When I managed to break free and sit back in the seat I was overcome by how funny it was, and was creased up with giggles—I snorted with laughter, I couldn't stop! Ralph was mortified, wounded in his manly pride, couldn't wait to dump me at my door and say a frosty good night! So there you are, Picot: you're an actress, you'll learn how to recognize the actors and play the right part yourself. Don't say you haven't been warned!"

14

Heather Chooses Mating over Chickens

For the next three years the Marriage Bureau prospered in spite of the total absence of Mary and the partial absence of Heather. Picot learned quickly, but as clients continued to flood in she needed help. She brought in two friends, both over calling-up age and overjoyed to be involved in such an original business. The new secretary worked quietly behind the scenes, answering the telephone, running errands, keeping the office supplied with essential writing paper, typewriter ribbons, registration forms and lightbulbs. Dorothy, whose surname Harbottle inevitably led to her being called Bottle, found her niche as a sympathetic interviewer. Her diminutive size, wavy gray-white hair, cozy presence and welcoming manner endeared her to the more tentative clients.

Picot kept in regular touch with Heather, who was leading a very different life in Scotland. On Michael Cox's farm, in the spectacular countryside of Angus on the east coast of Scotland, the air was pure, the view stupendous, the star-filled night sky a miraculous wonder, especially after the murk and gloom of London. Baaing, mooing, whinnying, barking, squawking, and birdsong replaced the wail of sirens, the scrunch of broken glass, the screams of terrified people, and the bloodcurdling whine and thud and crump and bang of bombs, anti-aircraft guns, airplanes, and crashing buildings. The farmyard smells were sweet compared to the noxious, putrid stench of blitzed London.

But gregarious Heather yearned for the city. She was nostalgic for parties, conversation, new friends and clients. "I am nosy, you see," she confessed. "I enjoy people, I like to find out how they tick; it entrances me." Heather blossomed in restaurants, offices, theaters, clubs, crowded streets, her beloved Marriage Bureau, whereas in Scotland, she recalled, "The only social event of the week was when I packed parcels for the Red Cross in Perth. Apart from all my office work, I did cooking and housekeeping which, before I went to live in Scotland, I had never attempted, and I found it all quite revolutionary. I wasn't too bad at some dishes, but never mastered pastry and was pretty heavy-handed at puddings. Things like making jams left me cold in spirit but not in everything else, and my language in the bottling season, when I could not get the jars to seal, left nothing to the imagination. I felt that in wartime it was part of a married woman's job to work in the house, but I had not been brought up to be a cook, char, or nursery maid, and I hated every minute when I had to be any of these things."

Heather spent a week a month in the Bureau. In between visits, she relished her telephone conversations and letters exchanged with Picot. Telephoning was difficult, as a trunk call had to be put through by the operator, who either took a long time to make a connection, or failed to make it at all. So Picot wrote daily, with news and queries:

Darling Heather

A girl who looks exactly like Greta Garbo has just come in. We have had a spate of pretty ones lately, one was more a Vivien Leigh type, too beautiful for words. I was staggered that she didn't have queues of young men after her, she'll surely be snapped up fast.

You asked me about Mr. James, who said he was completely bald because of an explosion. I tried to find out more, but he was very tight-lipped and would not enlarge, so I'm afraid I can't enlighten you.

I can't find your copy of registration cards for numbers 4079 and 4493. I've got our copy, so I'll make duplicates for you.

A shy young man, Peter Coles, came in yesterday, twenty-seven, working class, very pleasant, neat, polite, must be brave as he's a fireman. I'll send you a copy of his registration card. He says that as he's illegitimate he would like to meet a similar young woman. Can you think of anyone?

All love, Picot

Heather shut her eyes to the splendid Scottish view of open land and sky, to focus on searching her registration cards for a young woman to match with Peter Coles. She breathed a sigh of contentment as she picked out a card, took up her pen, and replied:

Dearest Picot

For your Peter Coles, I suggest Miss Daisy Sharp, a naïve little thing who has a six-month-old baby. She was conned by a smooth-talking cad into believing she wouldn't get pregnant if they did it standing up. Can you credit it? (No answer required!) She herself is not illegitimate, though she might as well be because her parents threw her out. She was taken in by a married friend who'd lost her own baby and whose husband was away fighting. But I seem to remember the husband was wounded so is due to come back home, and wouldn't take kindly to a stray girl-friend and her howling infant in the house.

Daisy wants a man who loves children and would be a good father to her baby. She calls herself "Mrs." and took the father's name by deed poll. He gives her about £2 per week (he's much more educated and richer than Daisy, but married, of course). She's only twenty and she'd like to have more children. I warned her that many young men will not meet an unmarried mother—or if they are willing they are unable because their parents raise a stink. I don't think you need to restrict yourself to illegitimate girls: your Peter probably means a girl who is in some way or another an outcast, maybe an orphan, or adopted.

There's also a girl who said she wanted to meet someone who has known loneliness. I can't at the moment remember her name or other details, but you'll probably think of some others.

Thanks for duplicate cards, they are a great help. Mr. James' explosion must remain a mystery!

I hope you are getting into the swim of the Bureau! Do tell me more about the very pretty girl. Have you got some good introductions in mind?

Love, Heather

Picot's reply came winging back, enclosing registration cards and more information:

Darling Heather

I asked the pretty girl, Dulcie Hope, why she was not hotly pursued, and she said that she doesn't get a great deal of time to meet people. She's a secretary in the office of a munitions factory, working from nine in the morning until six in the evening on weekdays, and till one o'clock on Saturdays. One evening a week she does First Aid, and another she sells Savings Certificates. Every other Saturday afternoon she helps in a Forces canteen. Every night she's an unofficial fire-watcher in the big house where she has a room. Last year she met a nice young man on the roof one night when they were both dousing incendiaries, he helped her when her stirrup pump got stuck, but then he rushed off. She almost wished there'd be more incendiaries so that she'd see him again! But I've introduced her to a very nice scientist, Clement Hill, who's doing some top secret research. He's stuck in a laboratory all day, and he too lives in digs and does lots of patriotic extras like fire-watching and emergency ambulance driving. He's a serious young man but with a lot of humour. He wrote on his form, "I'd like a young woman willing to place happiness and lots of fun before loads of wealth. Honesty and beauty combined." I'm really optimistic about these two, and I'll let you know how it goes.

Thanks for your suggestion of Daisy Sharp. I've put her in touch with Peter Coles, and I'll let you know.

You'll be glad to hear that that awful MP whom you married off to Lady M has got his heir: I saw the announcement of their son's birth in *The Times*. That was an excellent bit of mating! And Mr. and Mrs. Baldwin sent you a big bouquet of roses on their third wedding anniversary, with a sweet card saying "Thank you always. We continue very happy. We trust you now have a perfect secretary!" Shall I post it to you?

I am getting into the swim, thank you, but need your advice about some tricky ones. There's a retired stockbroker, Mr. Irving, said he's sixty but he's sixty-five if he's a day, very polished, said he was enquiring for a friend but that's a fib if ever I heard one. Claimed that he was a good husband but that his wife left him without reason, so he divorced her. The more I talked to him the less I liked him, he was creepy though I couldn't put my finger on it. He insisted on registering so I helped him fill in his form. He didn't put down much apart from the usual "Must be a lady." To my surprise he didn't want a young girl, he's not a dirty old man. But yesterday he sent a letter stating that he wants introductions to ladies who are strong and healthy, and willing to wear male attire in the house and in public. I am at a loss. Advice, please!

All love, Picot

P.S. Could you possibly bring down some potatoes and onions next time? One of the typewriters needs mending, and there's a little man who'll do it in return for some veg—it's so difficult to get anything fresh in London. We have to do either barter or the black market.

And if you could bring some bottled fruit too I could probably get you some real wax furniture polish.

Heather read this letter while standing in the huge farm kitchen, absentmindedly stirring an increasingly lumpy sauce. Slowly the spoon slid out of her hand and into the pan as she mulled over Mr. Irving's requirements. In the early days, she and Mary had been taken aback by clients with strange stipulations, but had learned to listen attentively while trying to elicit the reasons behind the words. She remembered recoiling from a man who had insisted that his bride should have only one leg—until he explained that his sister had lost a leg in a vicious bombing raid on Portsmouth. She had been sheltering in the cupboard under the stairs when the house was hit, and was lucky to survive. He looked after her, developing a huge sympathy with such victims, and wanted to help someone in similar distress.

Heather also cast her mind back to an immaculately dressed, wealthy man of fifty-five, Mr. Scott-Gilmour, who had drifted into the office one day and, in languid, high-pitched tones, apprised her of the fact that he had never married, but that his mama's dying wish had been that he should find a wife. He had already filled in the registration form, which he placed with a theatrical flourish on Heather's desk. Mama had just expired, so he was obeying her, his lifelong habit.

Expecting him to describe, as did most men of his age and class, a young woman in her twenties or thirties who would bear him an heir, Heather had been astonished to read that his chosen age range was fifty to sixty, and that she must be "a sports type, strong, active, preferring sensible clothes, tailor made, sweater, felt hats, flat-heeled walking shoes or brogues. Fair or dark hair, eyes blue, blue-grey or blue-green, hair bobbed square, forehead clear and open. Must be of good recognized family, top-drawer class."

"Of course!" Heather had suddenly realized. "He's queer—probably his father was too. He's lost without his mummy, and needs a replacement."

Abandoning the unappetizingly blobby sauce and the pan of anemic cauliflower that had been boiling for half an hour, Heather wrote immediately to Picot describing Mr. Scott-Gilmour and continuing:

And I am sure that your Mr. Irving is the same. They both lack a manly person in their life, telling them what to do. They would really like a man, but because of the law—which in my view is even more asinine about homosexuality than about most subjects—they have to find a woman in a man's clothing. Luckily there are several lady clients, especially over about forty-five, who would be very content in that role: bossing all day and being blessedly sex-free all night—their idea of heaven! I'll look through my cards and send you some suggestions; and you keep your eye out for a *Lady* or perhaps a *Lady For Here* + of the masculine type: brown felt hat stuck with partridge feathers, clumpy lace-up shoes, shiny face, pudding-basin haircut and so on. You're an actress, you know all about looks and style, I'm sure you will easily recognize the signs!

Heather was overjoyed by news of the MP's heir, only hoping that the baby was healthy, since the MP had been so overbearing and dictatorial that if his child was less than the perfection he demanded, he would take it out on his luckless wife, Lady M. She was even more pleased, and touched, that the Baldwins, the very nicest of clients, were happy and grateful, and wished she were back in the office to see their roses.

Before leaving London for Scotland, Heather had prepared for life on a farm by buying a mackintosh and a pair of stout sensible shoes. She had never lived in the country, which she found a strange and far from agreeable place. There was scarcely any petrol for personal use, so her car remained on blocks in the garage while she sailed around, an imposing figure sitting bolt upright on an antique bicycle, practically a penny-farthing. She also had a sturdy little Welsh pony called Gwendoline who used to pull her along the narrow bumpy roads in a cart, with her darling dog Cupid by her side. So she had transport, of a kind; but nowhere particular to go.

Heather tried to do her bit, but farming held no more appeal than cooking. A journalist and photographer from the *Tatler & Bystander,* producing a feature titled "Down on the Farm Up

North," photographed her engaged in utterly uncharacteristic activities: holding a squirming squealing piglet in each hand, she was captioned "Mrs. Michael Cox and Friends." Squatting in a cowpen to hold out a handful of hay to a dribbling calf, she was "Fattening up the Calf." Equally unconvincing to anyone who knew Heather were photographs of her hoeing the weeds between rows of vegetables, building stooks of corn, unloading unruly sheep from a filthy truck, digging potatoes, and controlling a tanklike tractor, all bearing out the text, which ran:

> It has been said that "farmers fatten most when famine reigns." Be that as it may, during four years of war, with possible starvation staring us in the face, it is largely due to the magnificent efforts of landowners and farmers in Great Britain that we still enjoy such a high standard of living. Mr. Michael Cox, laird of Easter Denoon, in Angus, works hard in the good cause, cultivating some 1,200 acres and raising a variety of livestock. Mrs. Cox, a daughter of Brig-Gen. C. A. Lyon, gives her husband some very valuable help.

Heather recalled her relief as the journalist and photographer departed, leaving her to unlace her muddy shoes, wipe the calf slobber from her jacket, flick bits of hay out of her hair, and look with distaste at her earth-stained hands and chipped scarlet nail polish: "The last straw was taking a photograph of me with the chickens. The photographer insisted I smile and scatter food for them. It was bad enough having to look after the smelly scruffy creatures every day: I loathed them and obviously the feeling was mutual as they always laid far fewer eggs when I was around than when I was away. But to be forced to smile at them was too much. I daresay that, stupid as they are, they could spot the malevolence in my forced grin, for I distinctly remember that they refused to lay a single egg the next day. Lord, how I needed a trip to London!"

Soon after, Heather made one of her monthly visitations to the Bureau. The train journey from Perth to Euston was long and tedious, but she was absorbed in her mating, and in anticipation of the buzz of the Bureau. On the luggage rack sat a suitcase full of account books and bills—for she continued to run the financial side of the Bureau—and a large holdall bulging with vegetables, meat and eggs for Picot's purposes.

Back at last in her office, Heather heaved a gusty sigh of happiness and took Picot out for a long, gossipy, updating lunch, leaving Dorothy Harbottle in charge.

About twice Mary Oliver's age, and very different in looks, Dorothy resembled her predecessor in the warmth of her sympathy, particularly for the less sophisticated and more troubled clients. Her deep concern for them produced such letters as:

> The minute I met Miss Harbottle I knew she would do all she could to help me. I felt as if she had wrapped me

in a big woolly blanket where I would be warm and safe
for ever. She made me feel like a much-loved puppy!

One of Dorothy's first clients was Cyril King, an RAF pilot
who had been hideously burned when his plane was shot down
early in the war. His face and much of his body had been partially
reconstructed with skin grafts in Stoke Mandeville Hospital, but
he did not look normal, and knew he never would. Undeterred,
he was tenaciously making the very best of the life that he considered himself fortunate still to possess.

RAF pilots were much in demand. In the matchmakers' experience, naval men were still very popular, but the air force had
gradually overtaken the navy in the search for desirable husbands.
Indeed, so many letters expressed a desire to meet an RAF man
that the matchmakers could not keep up with the demand. They
realized that pilots were so sought-after as husbands because
they had a highly developed sense of proportion: they knew what
truly mattered. Reported in the press, the Bureau's assessment
was: "You cannot fight 1941 air battles and have a mind for petty
quarrels and disturbances."

When Cyril came into the office Dorothy pushed her cigarettes to the back of her drawer, feeling that the smell of smoke
might unnerve him, despite his apparent confidence. Although
pilots were so popular, Dorothy knew that many young women
would be repelled by Cyril's appearance, so she wanted to find
one with great insight and understanding. He thought a girl in

the nursing profession might be sympathetic to his injuries. He also wanted her to be prepared to take the risk of going to a strange country and setting up a business of their own, as he hoped after the war to settle in one of the colonies, perhaps New Zealand, as he had friends there.

Dorothy assured him that quite a lot of young women were very keen on the idea of a new start, in a faraway place such as Australia, South Africa or Hong Kong. She understood his reasons for wanting a nurse, but thought there might well be girls of other professions who would suit. She asked him to tell her more and he continued, in his noticeably warm, humorous, well-modulated voice.

Cyril was an engineer, who before the war had worked in a steelworks in the Midlands. Then he got into what he really enjoyed: running a club for the Scottish lads employed in the factory, and who were a bit lost in a strange country, "and England is strange when you've been brought up in Scotland!" He learned to fly because he could see war coming; but he had hardly had a chance to fight before being shot down.

Cyril's main aim was to meet a girl who, like him, had had some trouble in her life. Together they could build something worthwhile, for he loved life, and was certain that, with the right woman, he could really live again.

Dorothy was determined to help, but she had not been in the Bureau long enough to think immediately of a suitable introduction. So when Cyril had left she lit a thought-aiding cigarette and decided to consult Heather, who breezed in full of joie de vivre after a deeply interesting discussion with Picot.

But Dorothy was forestalled, for hot on Heather's heels came a tall, uniformed man, radiating good health and high spirits, who grabbed Heather around the waist, spun her around, planted a smacking kiss on each of her cheeks, and whooped, "Hiya, honey! Great to see you! How're you doing?"

Startled but overjoyed, Heather greeted one of her all-time favorite clients, Hank, an American pilot who had married another of Heather's special protégés, a bewitching sweetheart of an actress currently serving in the Women's Auxiliary Air Force. "Hank the Yank" had become a friend and was always popping in to see Heather and give her bottles of perfume and bourbon whisky. Since she had gone to Scotland he had missed her, but had taken to bringing in packets of cigarettes for Dorothy, a heavy smoker for whom Lucky Strikes were manna from heaven. Everyone felt warmed and cheered by Hank's openheartedness and generosity.

"Picot told me you were coming, so I've got a special gift for you," Hank announced to Heather, picking up a large awkward-shaped object shrouded in brown paper, which he had dropped in order to kiss her. "Guess it's something you wouldn't ever have thought of. Here!"

Heather untied the string and pulled off the paper, which Dorothy picked up, unknotted, and smoothed out for future use.

There on Heather's desk sat a large, dented, dirty, bent bit of gray metal. Baffled, she walked around to look at the other side, where she was appalled to see an enormous painted swastika.

"What on earth?" she yelped. "What in heaven's name is this? Where did you get it?"

"Shot it down," said Hank. "Leastwise, my squadron shot it down. Got the bastards, thought we'd keep a few little souvenirs."

Heather was lost for words, but rapidly found some as she perceived that, for all his breeziness, Hank was in an emotional state, giving her a present of huge personal significance. She thanked him profusely, diverted him with tales of life on the farm, and kissed him a fond farewell. As he closed the door, she turned to Dorothy and Picot, laughing and frowning simultaneously. "Whatever are we going to do with it? It's a ghastly piece of junk—and it smells nasty too: some peculiar chemical, it must be the paint. We can't possibly have it in the office, and I'm certainly not carting it back to the farm on the train. I can't throw it away because Hank would be mortally offended. Any bright ideas welcomed!"

They puzzled and cogitated, until inspiration struck Dorothy: "Let's hang it out of the window! Maybe the smell will dissipate. Nobody looks up this high, and if they do, they'll just think it's a bit which fell off a German plane during the Blitz."

Heather sought help from Alf, who produced a length of strong wire, three stout nails and a hammer. Leaning out of the window he banged the nails into the wooden frame, ran one end of the wire tightly around the offending souvenir and the other around the nails, making a series of twists and turns of which any Boy Scout would have been inordinately proud.

Heather always meant to haul in the suspended token, to test the smell, but she never did. So there it remained, dangling above Bond Street for the rest of the war, noticed only by a triumphant Hank.

15

Picot and Dorothy Hold the Fort

Hundreds of miles away in Scotland, Heather listened anxiously to wireless broadcasts of renewed terror in London. In January 1944 the Luftwaffe launched a "Little Blitz" of air raids, followed by their most deadly new weapons: V1s and V2s. The macabre drone of these pilotless missiles, catapulted over the English Channel from Europe, caused extreme panic. But the silence when the sound suddenly cut out was even more dreaded, for it presaged a ton of high explosive plummeting to the ground.

Heather feared for the safety of her staff, the building, and her business. But surrounded by ever more unnerving death and destruction, Dorothy and Picot carried on, busily doing the mating, listening, advising, and making introductions, swinging from sorrow for the troubles of some clients to rapture when a happy couple announced their engagement.

Picot's correspondence with Heather continued briskly. She

stemmed her employer's anxiety by reassurances that, far from causing the Bureau to lose money, if anything the Luftwaffe had increased takings, which were in a healthy state:

Darling Heather

Back to a better week again. I wrote to you last week that the returns were £64 10s. I have not had a reply from you so I hope you got that letter. The postal service is not always reliable, hardly surprisingly! I am glad to say that takings this week are £94 3s! We are very busy.

There is a huge contingent of Americans in town. I do not like them much, though I know you are fond of them. But I must say that they are very good with people when the bombs drop, partly I think because they practically talk a foreign language. As I was walking to the office I heard one say to a very plain old woman who I should think had been a Wilton Road prostitute, "Say, lady, that's a lovely scrummie you've got!" He was referring to a very nasty cut on her forehead and cheek, but from her expression I think she thought he was paying her a compliment!

I went to see the new film *Love Story*, a romance, rather soppy and over-acted. Margaret Lockwood is a concert pianist who's dying of heart failure, and meets Stewart Granger, a former RAF pilot who's going blind. It reminded me of Bottle's latest coup, at least we all hope it's going to be a real coup. She's introduced that pilot with the horrible burns, Cyril King, to a lovely girl who was blind, Cora Church, you interviewed her so you may remember her.

This evening I am having dinner with my new friend Maurice and we shall reminisce about the theatre, which I always enjoy, I do so miss that life. I must get home in time to cook—Spam fritters and cabbage, not exactly a gourmet meal! So I must stop this and write out some more introductions.

All love, Picot

Cigarette in hand, for she was an incorrigible chain-smoker, Bottle had thought long and hard about Cyril, thoroughly examining the Black Book and the card indexes until she lighted upon Cora Church.

Cora was one of the most enchanting clients the Bureau had ever known. All the staff shared the view of a man to whom Heather had introduced her: "When Cora comes into the room, it's as if the sun has descended from the heavens and entered by her side. She radiates, she illuminates, she warms, she makes you feel glad to be alive, regardless of the bombs crashing outside."

Each and every man who had met Cora had become her friend, but she was still looking for the right one to marry. Her life had been fraught with tragedy, for she had been completely blind for ten years, until a revolutionary operation had largely restored her sight. It had been ten more years before she could see clearly, a decade of difficulty that Cora treated as lightly as if it had been an endless round of frivolity and amusement. At the interview she told Heather that at first she had been able to see only in a haze. One day she had walked with a friend to post a letter and, thinking she saw a pillar box, was puzzled that it seemed to be moving. So she walked closer and, as the red box remained stationary, she asked her friend to give her the letter to post.

"But that's not a pillar box!" exclaimed the friend.

"Oh, but it looks like one," said Cora. "If it's not a pillar box, what is it?"

"It's a Chelsea pensioner! Wearing his best scarlet uniform. He was walking ahead of us, but now he's sitting on a bench. He doesn't want a letter in his mouth, or even in his pocket, so let's keep walking!"

Cora delighted not only in her newfound sight but in life itself. Her sense of gratitude, her humor and her enthusiasm were boundless and infectious. But how might she react, wondered Bottle, to a man as disfigured as Cyril? She asked Cora to come into the office to discuss the possibility.

At first Cora was doubtful. After so many years of blackness, then grayness, before at last achieving clarity, she now took immense pleasure in being able to see beauty. She was fearful that she might shrink from a scarred and distorted face. But the more Bottle talked about Cyril, the more Cora warmed to the idea of meeting him. After all, she was committing herself to no more than an hour or two with a man who had given and lost so much, yet who was resolutely rising from the abyss to start again, as she had done. So she agreed to be introduced.

Cyril and Cora met in the huge foyer of the Cumberland Hotel in Marble Arch. As usual, Cora wore a brightly colored frock, for after so much time living in monochrome she relished colors. Cyril recognized her immediately, feeling the glow that seemed to emanate from her. Fearful that she might shy away in repugnance when she saw his face, he approached her boldly, holding out his hand as he announced: "I am Cyril King and you must be Miss Cora Church. I am very pleased to meet you. Would you like to go to a very amusing show at the Players' Theatre? We can get a taxicab and be there just in time, and we can eat during the performance. Have you ever been there? I think you will like it. Hattie Jacques is on tonight, a new star and extremely funny. It's Victorian music hall. What do you think? I've booked. Let's go!"

Startled by Cyril's masterful insistence, charmed by his melodious voice, and given no chance even to think, let alone refuse (as indeed Cyril had intended), Cora hardly noticed his damaged face, but accepted his arm as they left the hotel, laughing and talking like old friends.

The Players' Theatre, nestling in a basement in Albemarle Street, not far from the Bureau, was a revelation to Cora. Cyril cleared the way for her to get through the queue of people waiting on the street hoping to get in. Downstairs, in a haze of cigarette and cigar smoke, a potpourri of people, many in uniform, some in dinner jackets accompanied by bejeweled women, were laughing and joking as they jostled their way to their seats in the tiny auditorium. With great solicitude Cyril ensured that Cora was seated before going to the bar, returning with bowls of soup and glasses of wine balanced precariously on an old tin tray.

A pretty girl twitched the bustle of her long satin Victorian dress to one side as she sat down at the piano and began to play familiar old songs. Some of the audience joined in, others went on joshing and teasing, in high spirits. Suddenly, to huge applause, an imposing man in full evening dress, complete with gleaming black silk top hat, scarlet-lined opera cape, silver-topped walking cane, and red carnation in his buttonhole, swaggered onto the stage. He announced himself as the Chairman, lit the two candles standing on a small pink-velvet-covered table, banged his gavel, and proposed a loyal toast: "To Her Great and Glorious Majesty, Queen Victoria, God Bless Her!"

"Everything from now on happens in 1899," whispered Cyril to a bemused Cora, as the audience rose and drank the toast. Then the first artiste appeared, singing a tragicomic ballad that reduced her to tears of laughter. Act after act followed: singers, mimics, jugglers, dancers, tellers of far-fetched hilarious stories and dramatic monologues. The Chairman wisecracked with artistes and audience alike, calling out, "You, sir—yes, you," to a late arrival, a respectable-looking gentleman trying to shuffle in unobtrusively. "No luck in Shepherd Market?"

"More fun here!" riposted the gent.

Cora and Cyril joined the rest of the audience in singing

choruses, letting rip with "My old man said 'Follow the van!,'"
"Come into the garden, Maud," and a romantic ditty beginning,

> *I want to meet a good young man,*
> *A model young man, a proper young man,*
> *I want to meet a good young man,*
> *Who never goes on the spree.*

Cora became almost hysterical with laughter watching Hattie Jacques, constantly turning her radiant face to Cyril as she clapped and clapped.

At the end of the show, the audience stayed to drink and eat mushroom pie and dance on the stage. Cyril was a good dancer, guiding Cora with skill, quietly singing in her ear. She fell silent for the first time that evening, wondering if she was imagining things.

"It was wonderful!" cried Cora, as they emerged into the dark street. "I completely forgot about the war. I have never laughed so much for so long. Oh, please can we come again? We can, can't we?"

"Oh, I believe so," agreed Cyril gravely, taking her arm and trying to quell the feeling of hope that was rising in him. "It's a club, and I am a member, so although it is fantastically popular, if I book in advance we shall get in. It's a sort of home-from-home for me. And if we come on a bad night for bombs, they'll let us stay and sleep on the stage."

Both Cora and Cyril reported back positively to Bottle, who felt torn between excited optimism and gloomy fear that one lucky evening might never lead anywhere, that anything further would be an unmagical comedown. Sighing, Bottle turned to the problems of another young woman, Martha Webb.

Martha, the young woman who had been raped during an air raid and become pregnant, had been devastated by Mary Oliver's departure from the Marriage Bureau. Although Mary had not found her a possible husband, she had listened to the distraught young woman with great sympathy, and had even had conversations with Mr. and Mrs. Webb. As Martha had predicted, her parents were willing to help, but had not the remotest idea of what they could do. The prospect of their much-loved unmarried daughter having an illegitimate baby by an unknown father was shattering to the devoutly Roman Catholic couple. They could not pluck up the courage to talk to their priest, fearing that he would condemn Martha and forbid her to take communion, so talking to Mary brought them much relief.

Martha knew that as soon as her pregnancy became apparent she would have to give up her job as a postal censor. So she had insisted on carrying on with her ARP work; until one black night when she was four months pregnant, feeling her way along the murky street by the feeble light of a small torch, she bumped into a lamppost and fell clumsily to the ground. Poor Martha knew immediately that something was very wrong. A woman passing by tried to help but, lying on the cold pavement, deafened by the drone of the V2s overhead, Martha miscarried.

Nobody dared say that it was a blessing in heavy disguise.

Martha spent months in a state of profound shock, throwing herself into her work as if her life depended on it—as indeed her parents feared it might. But walking down New Bond Street one Saturday she passed number 124 and, without thinking twice, turned back, walked up the stairs, and was greeted by Bottle.

Bottle had just said goodbye to a potential client of forty-two who had waltzed in without an appointment, and been so pleased with himself, so confident that he was the catch of the season—"If not of the year or even of the decade," muttered Bottle tetchily to herself—that she had firmly put him right. He had told her that as he was very well dressed and good-looking he required his future wife to be equally attractive and polished, as well as domesticated, and fond of gardening and country life (though he admitted that he lived in an uninspiring suburb). Bottle asked him if he liked an occasional theater or dinner in London, but he said no, he worked in London and couldn't get out of the city fast enough. Every weekend, he said, he went sailing, and every evening too, when it was light enough, and invariably for holidays.

Puffing calmly on her cigarette Bottle heard him out, and as he paused for breath she announced, "I am afraid that the Bureau cannot be of service. It would appear that you are so set in your ways that a wife would be a mere appendage. You have not for one moment considered her desires or needs. I suggest that you go away and think more deeply, and perhaps come back later."

Stunned by this withering pronouncement by an apparently benign old lady, he gasped in shock and amazement, garbled an apology, and scuttled down the stairs like a rabbit fleeing from a fox.

Bottle had been told Martha's sad story, and turned welcomingly to the tense, strained-looking young woman. "Miss Webb! This is a pleasant surprise! Funnily enough, I was thinking about you earlier this morning. Do sit down. Would you like a cigarette?"

Martha refused the cigarette and sat, her shoulders tensed, gripping the edge of the desk, as she poured her hopes and fears into Bottle's receptive ear. She wanted to marry, she felt that Eustace, her dead fiancé, would have wanted her to find a husband, she longed to have a family; but would any good man consider her? She had been raped (she whispered the petrifying word), she had become pregnant and miscarried. Would not any decent man regard her as horribly damaged goods?

Bottle put down her cigarette, placed both her hands on top of Martha's bitten fingernails, and gave her a smile of such luminosity that the unhappy girl could not resist returning it with a tentative twitch of her lips as she blinked back tears.

"My dear," soothed Bottle, "any man who thinks a young woman who has been visited by such tragedy as you is 'damaged goods' is not worth tuppence. Not even a ha'penny. He is beneath contempt. He is to be avoided at all costs. Now tell me what sort of man you would like to meet."

Martha and Bottle went through the questions on the registration form. Martha's ideal husband was to be a Roman Catholic or, if Church of England, sympathetic to her religion and willing that any children be brought up as Catholics. He would be aged up to about forty-five, a bachelor or a widower, preferably living in London as traveling in wartime was difficult. He would not necessarily earn a great deal. He should allow his wife to have a job if she wanted, though she would be happy to stay at home and look after any children.

"If he were a widower and already had children, would you be prepared to take on the whole family?" queried Bottle.

Martha pondered only momentarily. "Yes, provided that he is not looking only for a mother for them rather than a wife for himself. And provided that he wants to have more children, and also that he is not still hopelessly devoted to his dead wife."

"And would you consider a man living abroad, say in South Africa, or Australia, or Singapore?"

Martha hesitated. "I'm not sure. I don't want to leave my parents: I am an only child and they are aging—the war is wearing them out, and my troubles are an added burden. But if there is a nice man working far away for only a limited time, and is coming back after the war, that would be different."

Bottle leaned back in her chair and blew a perfect smoke ring, which Martha's gaze followed as it drifted up to the ceiling. Bottle was visualizing a man she had never met, but whom she felt she knew well. Heather had often spoken about Frederick Joss, a client who had registered in May 1939, and Bottle had read the many letters he had subsequently written to the Bureau after his return to his Colonial Service job in Nigeria. He had met three young women before his home leave had ended, had liked them, but not enough for marriage. He had corresponded with another, and had written to Heather that he might meet her when he returned to England as he intended to do after the war. "I cannot envisage living permanently in Nigeria," wrote Frederick.

I came here with high hopes, and in theory the life of an Administrative Officer is worthwhile, interesting, and comfortable enough on account of plenty of servants. Certainly I don't have to do much toward running the household—or rather, shackhold!—though the cook is a rascal, feeds his family better than me, and pretends he can't understand me (but I've heard him gabbling away in pidgin English).

I am a Magistrate too (not properly qualified, but there was nobody else) and have to pass judgment on natives who simply don't think like us. Recently some villagers claimed they needed more land in a forest reserve for farming. In fact, food drops off the trees all around them and they don't know what poverty means; but they do know that the British government will not hesitate to send an expedition costing £50 to make sure that the poor darlings have enough to eat, and will almost certainly give them more land. So the District Officer ordered me to travel through the foulest bit of forest imaginable, nothing but damp and mud and swamp, in the heat of the day, to listen to their claims and complaints. I wanted to help them, but while I sat in their filthy village they told me lies, contradicted themselves, deliberately showed me the wrong boundary, and laughed up their sleeves at how they had previously tricked the Government into giving them extra land.

On the way back a labourer said quite casually that there was a body with a lot of flies just off the track, so I went to investigate, and, indeed, there lay some bleached bones, most of the flesh eaten away—the local vultures—and a great grey cloud of wrathful flies buzzing furiously around. A woman, I think, judging by a few scraps of fabric held together by a safety pin.

I cannot ask a wife to live in this baleful place, and above all I want to marry and have children. Please would you put me in touch with a girl who would be prepared to exchange letters until I come home? From all we hear here the war cannot last much longer, and I have written to various friends with a view to finding a job. I am a good administrator, with a Cambridge degree in Modern Languages, so I think that I shall find a place helping the country's reconstruction, which will surely start soon.

Frederick was not a Roman Catholic, but had described himself on his registration form as "Church of England—fairly high." He had also, unexpectedly, said that he would meet an unmarried mother, confiding to Heather at the interview that his very favorite aunt had given birth to a daughter while her fiancé was fighting in the Great War in 1917. He was an open-minded man with high ideals who had hoped to do good in Nigeria and was saddened by his disillusionment.

Bottle got out Frederick's details and showed Martha his photograph: a tall, spare, fair-haired man standing outside a straw-thatched hut, wearing baggy shorts and an open shirt, his eyes slightly narrowed as he smiled broadly into the African sun. "What do you think? Would you like me to put you in touch?"

Martha did not hesitate. She nodded, giving Bottle a real, heartfelt smile that transformed her taut face and rejoiced Bottle's heart. As soon as Martha had closed the office door behind her Bottle lit another cigarette, found a flimsy air letter form, and wrote to Frederick.

While Bottle was writing, Picot was ushering into the office an elderly policeman who had panted up the stairs. When he had lowered himself into the chair she leaned across the desk and, sensing that the potential client was not at ease, asked tactfully whether he had brought his registration form.

"Yes, Miss, I've got a form, but it's not the one you're meaning, I think. I've been married for forty years and I'm staying that way. I'm here on duty, and I've come about a man who isn't married, I don't think, and now he never will be. He's had a bit of bad luck, you might say."

The policeman paused and Picot inquired sympathetically: "Oh dear, what has happened to him?"

"He's dead, Miss. Murdered. Very nastily and all, shot in the knees and in the head, and hidden under a great heap of rubble."

"Oh, how horrible!" gasped Picot, shrinking back in her chair, horror-struck but also perplexed.

The policeman reached into one of his pockets. "And in his coat pocket he had a bit of paper with your address written on it—here, look." The policeman pushed across the desk a scrap apparently torn from a notebook. Sure enough, in scribbled but legible handwriting, was "Marriage Bureau, 124 New Bond Street."

"I can't imagine what this means!" exclaimed Picot in some distress. "Who is this man? What is his name?"

"We don't know, Miss. The murderer must've taken his watch and his wallet and his identity card—that's if he ever had a card, of course. There's a lot of foreigners around that don't have a proper card like they ought to. This man didn't look English, more Continental, if you know what I mean. Just middle-aged, shortish, dark hair. Do you get many foreigners coming along?"

"Yes, quite a few. I'll ask the secretary whether there have been any enquiries or appointments which might possibly fit, and I'll let you know."

"Thank you, Miss." The policeman lumbered off wearily. "We'll try to find the murderer, but I'm not hopeful. There's a terrible lot of wickedness about these days."

Picot rushed next door to tell Dorothy, who reached for another cigarette and gave one to Picot. "Well, Picot, you're always complaining that you miss the drama of the stage. But there's infinitely more drama in the Marriage Bureau than ever there was in the theatre!"

16

Peacetime Problems

124 New Bond Street
London WI
9 May 1945

Darling Heather

The crowds in the West End yesterday were huge,
everyone cheering, laughing, drinking, singing, dancing—
Americans doing the conga and cockneys the Lambeth
Walk—kissing, hugging, waving flags, bells ringing, some
loonies lighting a bonfire. We'll never forget VE Day. I
drove round after dinner to see the celebrations. But I felt
nostalgic and thankful rather than gay and triumphant.
The destruction is horrific. And a friend in Berlin tells
me that the Continent is crawling with displaced persons,

criminals, starving survivors, ex-POWs hunting their torturers—ghastly. Where on earth do we go from here?

There are plenty of clients, and plenty of problems I hope you can help with.

Problem 1: Reverend Hogg, remember him? A widower, sixty-six, we found him Mrs. Joy, a nice respectable lady, just the wife he wanted, to stop him being pestered by all the parish widows. Mrs. J. has been living in the rectory for over a year, and a friend of mine who lives in the next village says everyone calls her "Mrs. Hogg." They're obviously living in sin. But when I asked him for the After Marriage Fee he wrote back that she's "just my housekeeper." He must think I was born yesterday! What shall I do?

Problem 2: Miss Thora Palmer, twenty-seven, you interviewed her last year. She wants a gent but not a snob because "It is that kind with whom I have had so much trouble." What does she mean? Do you recall?

Problem 3: Philip Baird, a new client who has no hands, due to an accident in an aircraft factory in the war. He is very confident and independent, says he can manage everything himself. He's working class but superior, forty-four, tall and nice. Does anyone who could cope come to your mind?

Problem 4: another new one, Mrs. Lily Rose, forty, *Ladyish,* divorced because her husband got fed up with having her brother of forty-four and her elderly parents, now dead, in the house. The brother is mental but harmless, and useful in the bakery she inherited. She needs a man who'll be sympathetic and kind to him, not another stinker.

That's enough!

All love, Picot

Heather immediately replied:

Dearest Picot

1. Yes, I remember the Reverend Hogg. Of course he should pay the A.F.M., the dirty dog! He quite puts me off religion. I'm disappointed in Mrs. Joy, too, though perhaps she believes he's paid. I shall write to him myself, politely, and if that doesn't do the trick I shall tell him we must put the matter in other hands. He won't like the idea of solicitors (nor shall we, of course, as it'll cost us). I may know his Bishop, I'll check.

2. Miss Palmer: As I recall, she's a *Near Lady* we introduced to a *Gentish* chap. They got on famously, but her mother thought him not good enough for her darling daughter so, feebly, Miss P. gave him up. It was not the man but the mother, an almighty snob, who caused the trouble. Miss P. is completely under her thumb, can't say boo to a goose. Find her a nice *Near Gent*.

3. Is the answer in Problem 4? Mrs. Rose sounds like Mr. Baird's cup of tea, and she his. They both need an understanding spouse. Try it!

You and Dorothy are doing a wonderful job, thank you so much. I can't wait to be able to help you more.

I enclose a photograph of Stella, a pretty little thing who does not cry much, thank goodness.

Love, Heather

In 1944 Heather had had a daughter, Stella, and was now about to give birth to her son, but motherhood did not enthrall her so she relied heavily on a nanny. Perhaps echoing her own mother's unhappy experience of motherhood (following Heather, a second baby had died at a few days old), Heather did not take kindly to domesticity, and was far happier devoting herself to the Bureau.

Dorothy, always meticulous, hit problems when Picot was away on holiday. Puffing on cigarette after cigarette, she wrote anxiously to Heather:

Dear Mrs. Cox

I have been very unhappy and very uncomfortable. When Picot took her holiday she left me in charge. I asked her to give me the key of her writing table drawer, as I am sure you will agree that if one is responsible for any money one should be able to lock it up, but Picot told me I couldn't have it as it also locked something in her flat and she required it.

Picot told me to get a little book to keep a record of the takings and an account of the Petty Cash, as she didn't wish me to enter anything in the office books. As the various registrations came in I was most particular to enter them at once and then put the cheque or notes into the little box in the writing table drawer, but at the end of the week, when I counted the takings, to my horror they were £5. 5. 0. short. My receipts showed £58. 13. 0. and I only had £53. 8. 0.

I have searched every imaginable place but have failed to find the money.

I am afraid I cannot make it up in one lump sum, for as you know I only draw £3. 15. 0. each week. I felt I would rather write and tell you about this myself and ask you how you would like me to pay it back. I cannot tell you how upset I am, and it certainly is a mystery to me.

I do hope the new nanny is proving a success, it will be such a relief to you if she is.

Yours very sincerely
Dorothy Harbottle

Dorothy eventually discovered that a new secretary had refunded a client's registration fee and forgotten to enter it in the account book, but the incident added to Heather's craving to return to the Bureau, to be in charge again. Fortunately her husband, Michael, agreed that with the war over they should move from distant and lonely Scotland to Kent, from where Heather could commute to London. "Michael went ahead in the car, with a lot of the luggage, following the furniture van," Heather wrote later.

I left Perth by train with another mountain of suitcases, two children, a nanny, a nursery maid, my own maid and her husband, who was the farm mechanic and part-time chauffeur, their daughter and their niece. My little dog Cupid, one child and I shared a sleeper, nanny and the other child in an adjoining one. My maid, her husband, daughter and niece shared a four-berth compartment, and the nursery maid was in another, with the greyhound and two other passengers, who unfortunately had a cat. The greyhound was a well-known chaser of cats, so they all had a harassing night. I couldn't help, as the minute I even see a cat my face swells up like a balloon and my eyes become fountains. Added to this we were four hours late at Euston. But it is bliss to be back in civilization.

The new nanny was a success, so Heather started to spend three days a week in the Bureau. One of the first postwar clients left an indelible impression on her. She only caught a glimpse of John Paul when he came to be interviewed by Dorothy, but remembered "a very nice-looking, spruce type, not very tall but with an upright bearing. He turned out to be by far the most difficult customer we ever had to suit. He was the bane of our lives for four years, during which we introduced him to forty-eight young women."

Bottle had a particularly soft spot for widowers and was all sympathetic ears. In 1929, aged twenty-two, Mr. Paul had married Anne, whose parents were very old friends of his parents. Both families were delighted (though unsurprised) when they got engaged. They were well suited and had an easy, comfortable life together until the birth of their daughter, Viola, when Anne developed TB. Five years later war broke out and Anne died.

While Mr. Paul was soldiering in Italy he dreamed of the war ending and seeing his daughter again. He survived unscathed and was now back in civvy street, working as an advertising executive. Viola was living with an aunt and about to go to boarding school. Her father wanted a home for her, and a wife for himself.

One Sunday Mr. Paul, lunching with his sister, had glanced through a pile of her women's magazines, whose advertisements were of business interest to him. He noticed a piece about the Bond Street Marriage Bureau and the advantage of starting off without the usual illusions concerning one another. "That made a lot of sense to me," Mr. Paul confided to Bottle, "because I wanted companionship and a domesticated, adult type who, without being stodgy, was well over the starry-eyed stage."

He mentioned the Bureau to two colleagues. "Can't do that, old boy," harrumphed one of them. "Can't think of it. Can't buy romance like . . . like a new car or something!"

"Well, I don't know," pondered the other. "Matter of fact, we were talking about it the other day. Arranged marriages can be a good thing, don't you know. The chap doesn't feel he's being pushed into it, and the girl isn't marrying because she just has to."

The next day Mr. Paul walked down Bond Street, past the fashion shops and art galleries, and joined the queue by the sign marked MARRIAGE BUREAU. DIRECTOR, HEATHER JENNER. STRICTLY CONFIDENTIAL. SECOND FLOOR. Suddenly he realized that everybody was waiting not for the Marriage Bureau but for lunch at the Lyons Teashop on the ground floor. He scurried past the dumpy, sallow waitress, with a napkin over her arm, who was gazing at him through the glass of the teashop door, no doubt smirking at the idea of an old geezer trying to fix himself a marriage. At the top of the stairs he entered a little room filled with great vases of roses and lilies and carnations.

"What immediately caught my eye," recalled Mr. Paul, "hanging on the wall behind the door, was the usual Company Certificate such as one sees in any office. That reassured me, and I was wondering about the Articles governing a marriage bureau when a husky, gentle voice called out, 'Do come in—it's Mr. Paul, isn't it? How nice. I was expecting you.' And Miss Harbottle took me in hand like a spoiling aunt."

"Oh, I did like him," remembered Bottle. "He was a perfect pet! Definitely a *Gent For Here*. Such good manners, and he *listened.* Most men just talk at you, but he was interested in what *I* thought. He wanted to meet a young woman under thirty-five, not more than five foot three tall, single—not a widow, and certainly not an unmarried mother, nor a divorcee, not even a plaintiff, because although he himself was not very religious, his grandfather had been a bishop and his family did not hold with divorce. He preferred an upper- or upper-middle-class background, public school like himself, but said a penniless waif would do nicely! He had a private income and a high salary, and wasn't at all worried about the cost of keeping a wife. He didn't mind if she wanted to work after marriage, in any case he had a housekeeper, but his wife wouldn't need a job and he didn't imagine she would want one."

Bottle assessed Mr. Paul as a relaxed person who saw himself as cheerful and confident, easily able to establish good relations with all sorts of people. He admitted that he was inclined to manage, and to fuss about details that he felt only he could get right. But he insisted that he could laugh at himself, and that if Miss Harbottle could find him a young woman who was not "grand or elaborate," but honest, loyal, reliable, calm, with a sense of humor and fun, who liked a basically fairly simple life in town, enjoying parties and theaters and an occasional ball at the Savoy, they would all have a wonderful laugh together.

A stream of young women flooded into Bottle's mind. She felt confident that she would very quickly get him off. "But," she remembered wryly, "seldom have I been so wrong."

It was rapidly brought home to the matchmakers that

Mr. Paul did indeed desire to manage things. He was always writing to say that Miss Harbottle had got the wrong end of the stick: "No, I am sorry, dear lady—but she is not what I am looking for." He dismissed women in his own line of work as unattractive and hard-boiled even though lively and efficient. Others were too pitifully lonely, or excessively shy, or overeager and embarrassingly demonstrative. "Miss P. is too large and florid," he wrote about an adorably pretty, plump, milkmaid type of girl with pink cheeks and a dear little dimple; and about a clever girl: "Miss T. failed to stir my ossified emotions."

Miss D. was no beauty, but quite presentable, and Bottle knew that her superior manner and slightly affected voice grated less as you got to know her. So Mr. Paul's biting rejection—"She sent cold shudders down my back"—was so exaggerated and unfair that in an uncharacteristic rage Bottle vowed to cross him off the books. But, sensing that he had gone too far, Mr. Paul pressed the charm button and swept into the office bearing a bouquet of flowers and several packets of cigarettes, apologizing most humbly and smiling winningly until she could not resist, and was restored to her usual kindly and concerned self.

Mr. Paul's ideal woman was to be a lady of taste and refinement, yet also soft, and not pushy. Looks were very important. Of Miss H. he wrote:

She is most charming, but I do not think I shall ever feel matrimonially disposed towards her, though I hope to see her again, and I write this against my own feeling and only at your request—she is rather too tall, not pretty enough, rather too old in that she looks her age, walks badly, and her legs, though very passable, are not perfect. I know that this is a revolting physical catalogue, and mentally she is delightful. However, the physical is of vital importance also.

Bottle's irritation flared up again. "Blast the smug, conceited dolt!" she ranted, waving her cigarette wildly in the air. "Such odious, nauseating vanity!" Mr. Paul, however, remained calm, confident that, having been so blessed with his first wife, one day he would make another happy marriage.

When he met a girl Mr. Paul always gave her a double martini, to help break the ice. The ice invariably melted as the girl launched into the sea of her troubles. He wrote to Dorothy:

I should, if I may, advise any girl meeting a man with a view to marriage not to start off by telling him why she really must get married, for example because she can't stand living with the family any more, or doesn't get along with her mother or sister, or is too hard up, or dislikes her job. Whatever the reason, she should keep it to herself, at least for the time being, as it makes a bad impression on the man and makes him feel he may be used merely as an escape, which of course is only too often the case. Please pass this advice on to your clients, dear lady.

Bottle often relived her outraged reaction to this letter. "As if I didn't know my job!" she spluttered, grinding her cigarette ferociously into the ashtray while aiming a sharp kick at the much-dented desk. "If that blithering idiot hadn't generally been so pleasant and polite I would have struck him off then and there. He did at least behave well inasmuch as he met all the young women to whom I introduced him, so I never got 'He never contacted me' complaints. Nor did he make passes at them. On the other hand, he had the usual tedious, stupid, clodhopping male certainty that he would know at first sight if the girl was right for him or not, and if she wasn't, he immediately lost interest."

Bottle gritted her teeth as she scoured the records for a Mrs. Paul. Her delight when he met one girl three times was dissolved by the letter in all-too-familiar writing:

She announced that of course she could marry dozens of men; thirty were in love with her and wanted to become engaged. She started to string off a list of names and, to my horror, she ended up with my own name. "And now there's YOU!" she exclaimed triumphantly. That was the last she saw of me. So once more I am sorry, dear lady. Would you be so kind as to try again?

"You are a saint, dear Bottle," purred Heather. "I am sure you will get him off in the end."

The next few young women got in first and turned Mr. Paul down. One thought him too old—getting on for *forty*!—another that he was too highbrow. One very attractive and wealthy girl, living in a beautiful house off Park Lane, dined with him at his favorite little Continental restaurant in Soho, and reported, "Such a queer place he took me to, so different. Usually I dine at Claridge's."

Mr. Paul complicated Dorothy's job further by changing his mind: from girls under five foot three inches to tall ones; from no mention of languages to a demand that she speak Spanish and French; from only single girls to widows, though none with more than one child.

Luckily, several lovely young war widows were registering, among them Angela Smith. Heather cherished the memory of interviewing Angela:

She was awfully nice, an absolute poppet. Small and slim, pretty in an elfin way, with enormous blue eyes. Not a fashion plate but neatly dressed, in a red suit with a little hat just tipping over her fringe. A *Lady For Here*—probably would have become classic Home Counties if it hadn't been for the war. She was very concerned that a man should like her son, whom she doted on. She admitted that she used to think being tall, dark and handsome was everything in a man, but now didn't mind about his looks or his height, just wanted someone kind, reliable, good-tempered and trustworthy— and fun too. She rather liked the idea of a man who smoked a pipe.

After school Angela had taken a secretarial training. Her father thought it a waste of time and good money, but her mother persuaded him that modern girls should be trained, and able to do a job, because you never knew what might happen. Mrs. Smith had married at eighteen, and pensively envied her daughter's life outside the home, and the money she earned.

Angela thrived as a secretary in a big City trading company, so different from her all-girls' boarding school and secretarial college. She proved to be an asset as she could speak French (the family always summered in Nice). Her boss, Pierre, was half French, clever, tall and good-looking. They had a lot in common, laughed and talked away nonstop, and in 1935, when Angela was twenty-one, they were married. Company rules forbade her working in the same firm as him, but anyway she wanted to stay at home and look after the house and—three years later—their baby boy, Robert. They were very happy until the war, when Pierre joined the Resistance in France and was killed while blowing up a bridge.

Angela's parents begged their grieving daughter to come home and live with them, but she remained obdurate: she was an independent married woman, with her own house and child and a passionate resolve to combat Hitler. So her mother looked after Robert while Angela got a job in the War Office, working with some urbane and eligible men who often took her out, and became good friends. She enjoyed the camaraderie of the office, and felt that, despite the tragedy of losing her husband, her life had been a lot more interesting than her mother's. And she reveled in earning money.

When Robert was eight he went to boarding school, so Angela had time on her hands, and was clinging less fervently to Pierre's memory. A single girlfriend who wanted to join the Bureau, but was scared of doing so by herself, talked Angela into accompanying her to 124 New Bond Street.

Angela was greatly impressed by Heather, who pointed out in a matter-of-fact way that some men would shy away from a widow with a child, and might want to have children of their own. Angela responded that at thirty-five she was much too old for that, and didn't want to anyway, but she would happily take on an existing child. She didn't want to meet a Roman Catholic, because he might want to have children and because it would upset her father, who was convinced that the only church on God's earth was the Church of England.

Angela paid her registration fee and met a few pleasant men. But she was anxious, for she wanted to conceal what she was up to from her parents. They were pressing her to marry a family friend, James, whom Angela thought nice but dreadfully staid and boring. With some reluctance, she canceled further introductions and concentrated on work.

A year later, resisting heavy pressure from James, Angela telephoned the Bureau. A sympathetic Bottle said that her membership had lapsed, but she didn't consider Angela had had her money's worth and she would send an introduction.

Mr. Paul took one look at Angela, the forty-eighth young woman he'd met, and knew, definitely, assuredly, incontrovertibly and for ever, that she was the one. Angela reserved judgment a little longer, but was courted with such seductive conviction (not for nothing was Mr. Paul in advertising) that she was won over.

Mr. Paul sent Bottle the most enormous bouquet of her favorite carnations, and a gigantic box of cigarettes, with a letter that she clutched to her heart.

Dear Miss Harbottle

I feel that this letter written in great happiness will bring you real pleasure. I want you, dear lady, who have been so understanding, to be the first to know. Angela and I are engaged. She'll do!!

We grow more devoted every day, and after years of bitter disappointments and loneliness a new life has started at last, complete with a ready-made family. I think I must hold the record for your "difficult people," and at last I can join the satisfied men in that black box marked "MEN OFF" which I have so often envied.

Thank you again and again, and hang out the flags!

17

Loneliness and Heartbreak

Life in England in the aftermath of war was dreary. Despite high hopes of the new Labour government, which had ousted Churchill, rationing continued—indeed, in 1946 bread, available in wartime (though a nasty color and texture), became rationed. Housewives queued for hours outside shops that had very little to sell. Demobbed servicemen and POWs returned not to a heroes' welcome but to the indifference of bone-weary survivors in a haunted, pessimistic country. Families had changed beyond recognition: wives had developed a taste for independence; marriages were falling apart. Jobs were hard to find, housing was scarce, bitter loneliness prevailed. The war altered everything and everybody. But in 1947 the enchanting romance, engagement and marriage of Princess Elizabeth and Philip Mountbatten lifted people's spirits and prompted yet more to seek a spouse. The Bureau's stairs were rarely empty.

Some of the crowds of clients were heartbreakingly sad. Bottle sighed as she perused letters from women who, through no fault of their own, were in a desperate state. A widow of forty-four, whose husband had drowned when his ship was torpedoed by a U-boat, was being forced out of his house by the children of his first wife. Her only remedy was to marry again. The divorced wife of a fishmonger, who had beaten her black and blue when he discovered that she had spent two shillings on lipstick and face powder, now pathetically hoped for "a man with enough income not to notice a lot stolen from the housekeeping money." A schoolmistress who looked after her father, mentally unstable since the Great War, wanted "a husband who is home only for the holidays, e.g. Merchant Navy, Royal Navy or similar." A girl of thirty sought no more than a husband "who would not mind that I am not pretty, and who would not be too critical of my faults."

Sorrowfully, Bottle turned to letters from men, only to find more scarcely concealed sadness: an accountant demobbed from the army, whose job applications had all been rejected. He was living in a caravan on an isolated field, reliant on a small pension, theoretical compensation for a bad limp caused by bullets and barbed wire on the Normandy beaches. He needed a wife to help him build a house and start a fruit farm. Another letter came from an ex-POW who had returned to England full of optimism after four years languishing in a German camp, only to find his wife absorbed in the baby boy fathered by a German ex-POW who had been interned nearby. The resultant bitter fury, acrimony and violence had culminated in divorce.

Observing Bottle stubbing out cigarette after cigarette, growing more and more overwrought, Heather—who, while sympathetic, treated the horrors more dispassionately—set out to distract her invaluable but sometimes overemotional helper. "These stories are truly ghastly, dear Bottle. Picot's busy interviewing, and I need some help with my mating. Come and give me some advice. For a start, what about Miss Millicent Jessop? She is forty-two, *Ladyish*, never been married, frightfully neat and tidy. I remember her looking all scrubbed and shiny-faced and stiff, not a hair out of place, curiously lifeless. You could mistake her for a dummy in a shop window. She trained at Domestic Science College and teaches her subject at a girls' school. She wants a man who is 'particular about himself, looks as if he enjoys a daily bath.' Note the 'looks as if'—he doesn't have to have a bath a day as long as he *looks* clean! What do you think?"

"A man whose appearance is important to his daily life," reasoned Dorothy. "Perhaps a serviceman, or other uniformed chap: one who has to dress immaculately all the time. What about a footman? A very smart one came in recently: *Gentish*, highly presentable, lives up in Staffordshire, in a stately home. He has the advantage of good accommodation, which could be an attraction. No doubt it has a nice bathroom!"

"You're right, I remember him too. I'll look him out. And Miss Jessop is living in the school, but can't stay there if she marries, so the accom would be a definite plus. Thank you, dear Bottle. Now, what about Miss Agnes Johns? She's *Much Better Than Most*, only nineteen, but she's been set on marrying since her father ran off with her mother's best friend before the war. She's quite sweet but not very bright, works as a comptometer operator and is completely stuck on films. She wants a man with dark hair, she wrote, 'the Orson Welles, James Mason, Stewart Granger type.'"

"That's easy! I interviewed a young man yesterday, Henry Perkins. He's twenty-five, a film technician out at Pinewood, *Much Better Than Some.* He has almost black hair, slicked back and incredibly shiny, and looks like a film star. He wants a pretty, lively, affectionate girl."

"Splendid! Just one more: a countess, very impressive, a *Lady*, fifty-eight, widowed, no children, clever, did something high-powered in the war but couldn't say what, wants a man of similar standing, a governor or a mayor or a Lord Lieutenant."

"Difficult . . ." Dorothy blew smoke rings as she concentrated. "Would she consider a foreigner? There's that very clever and superior French baron, a publisher and writer, lives here and is completely anglicized."

"A brain wave! Thank you, dear Bottle!"

After her absence in Scotland, Heather was rapidly getting back into the swing of the Bureau. Picot, however, could not wait to return to the world of the theater, which she adored. But she had grown fascinated by the Bureau, so it was with some reluctance that she handed in her notice and departed, promising to come and see them often.

"Heather darling, you must tell me what becomes of Cyril

and Cora, I am positively itching to know. And that murdered man with our address in his pocket. And some of the ones I've interviewed. I'll never be a fabulous matchmaker like you or Dorothy, but I've got a taste for it now and I shall be practicing on all my friends! Good luck with all your plots, darlings. And Dorothy, I specially hope that you'll get that sweet little Ivy off happily. Goodbye, dear ones! Or rather, *au revoir!*"

Ivy was a client for whom Bottle felt an almost maternal, protective affection: a winsomely pretty, trim young woman with entrancingly vivid though sorrowful green eyes. Her parents, grandmother, sister and many friends had been wiped out in an air raid that ravaged the entire street while Ivy was at work. At the age of twenty-two she had been robbed of family, friends and possessions. She earned a pittance as a nurse in an East End hospital that was swamped with casualties and that, when Ivy lost her home, found her a small room—more of a large cupboard— just off the wards. Since she was always on the premises, and there were always crises, she was called upon night and day. At times she could scarcely squeeze another word or force another step from her exhausted body.

By the end of the war Ivy was physically and mentally dead beat, worn to a frazzle by the physical demands of the job, the pity she felt for the patients, who tugged at her heartstrings, and her terror of the strict nursing sisters and draconian matron. She exchanged the hospital for a menial but less taxing job fetching and carrying in a West End department store, Debenham & Freebody. By scrimping and scraping, she paid the rent of a room at the top of a semiderelict bombed house in Notting Hill.

Being efficient, honest, well-spoken and tastefully dressed, Ivy quickly rose to become a saleslady in the Ladies' Fashion department, where she flourished. But after work and at weekends she was paralyzingly lonely, spending most evenings in her cheerless room, eating tinned soup heated on an erratic gas ring. So when walking down Bond Street one Saturday she saw the Marriage Bureau's sign, like a homing pigeon she flew up the stairs into the metaphorical arms of Bottle, who took an instant liking to the lost soul she perceived, and resolved to help her at all costs.

Between 1945 and 1947 Bottle introduced Ivy to several young men, many of them recently demobbed from the army, navy or air force. Ivy did not jib at a man with some disability, for she had known plenty in the hospital who had been badly wounded, losing a leg, an eye, or part of their face, but who were still essentially themselves. Ivy's wounded heart had warmed to them, giving them comfort and hope; but they were patients, not potential husbands, any more than the wealthy escorts of the ladies to whom she now sold expensive dresses. Sometimes these well-tailored, well-fed men lounged outside the changing room while their wives tried on a succession of clothes. Occasionally one of them winked suggestively or even attempted to put his arm around Ivy's waist, which she had to endure with a tight, hollow smile while turning away.

Ivy quite liked "Bottle's Boys," though some she found rather forward, trying to kiss her when she scarcely knew them; and they reported to Bottle that Ivy was a bit shy, rather prim and proper, not much fun, not very modern. Ensconced in a double seat in the anonymous dark of the cinema they would put a hand on her knee, and were offended when she removed it and shrank back. Bottle listened to reports from Ivy and the men and scratched her white-haired head—until one day in 1947 Archibald inched his way up the stairs.

Archibald Bullin-Archer was so thin that he appeared taller than his five feet nine inches, dressed soberly in a quietly pin-striped suit, starched white shirt and somber tie, clutching a pipe in one long-fingered hand. Taking in his pale, fine-featured face, the tentative smile, the anxious little frown, the slight stoop and the light, hesitant voice, Bottle immediately heard "Ivy" in her head. She sat him down and talked calmly and comfortingly, gradually eliciting from him that he was thirty-eight, had gone from public school to university, and had a degree in his favorite subject, history, which he had taught at a boys' prep school in Hampshire until the outbreak of war. He had always been delicate, but was pronounced fit enough to join the army and be sent to India, where he had spent the war years in administrative jobs, organizing supplies of food to the troops. This had cut him off even more from his family, from whom he already felt separate: generations of well-off Surrey landowners and gentlemen farmers, the men tall, robust and noisy, the women hearty huntswomen and polished hostesses.

Archibald made it clear to Bottle that he was uncomfortable with his family and their friends. He had returned to England in a frail state, having contracted dysentery, which he had not managed to shake off fully, and he found the boisterous social bonhomie and physical activity—hunting, shooting, tennis—of weekends at his parents' home draining and alienating. He was not strong enough to return to teaching, but had a modest job subediting a history magazine, living in a small Bloomsbury flat that had been part of his mother's dowry. He was chronically, agonizingly lonely.

Archibald had virtually no experience of women, though he idolized them from afar. Cautiously he confessed to Bottle that he had had a crush on the matron at the prep school and, when rebuffed by her, had focused his dreams on the English mistress, who had promptly become engaged to the Scripture master. Archibald's heart had ached. In India, the few single English girls had been snowed under by the attentions of hordes of single soldiers, businessmen, tea planters, colonial servants, etc., all clamoring for a wife. Archibald hadn't stood a chance, and fled from the alternative of being inveigled into the bed of a predatory, disaffected wife. He would not have known what to do in bed anyway, suspected Bottle.

The longer she talked to Archibald, the more convinced Bottle grew that Ivy was the answer to his prayers. She categorized him as a *Gentleman For Here* or slightly lower who could meet a *Near Lady,* someone a bit lower class than him. He lacked the presence, the income, the poise, the tastes of a full-blown *GFH*—any *Lady For Here* would probably find him too shy, too lacking in ambition, living in too sparse a style in an unfashionable neighborhood. Ivy, a *Near Lady,* had all the qualities poor Archibald needed, and Bottle was full of optimism as she arranged for them to meet.

Bottle was right. The first reports from both Ivy and Archibald were touchingly grateful, for they found in each other a kindred spirit: modest, self-effacing, unassuming, and giddy with the desire to love and be loved. They met in the evenings, went to concerts and plays and talks, and on weekend outings. Ivy visited his flat, and sent Bottle a glowing description of its cleanliness and tidiness—Archibald was a fastidious man—and of the pictures on the walls, mostly of Princess Margaret and Princess Elizabeth with her dashing fiancé Philip, for Archibald worshipped the royal family as well as women. And the day before the sublime wedding of Elizabeth and Philip, Archibald fell to his knees and, stammering with emotion, asked Ivy to be his wife.

A lyrical letter from Ivy rejoiced Bottle's heart. But only a week later her joy was smashed to smithereens by a ten-page letter, the ink blotched by tears. Bottle picked up the first page:

Dear Miss Harbottle

Perhaps you have seen in the newspaper that Archie is dead. I cannot believe it but I saw him lying in the police station. I know he is dead but I do not feel he is. I do not know what to do. We were so happy. We went to see his parents. We went to tell them we were engaged. I dressed ever so nicely, I wore a new suit, emerald-green because Archie says that matches my eyes, simple but nice, and a hat and gloves to match. And Archie always looks nice but he looked extra handsome in a new white shirt and a dark red tie and I bought a red carnation for his button-hole, and we took some cheese sandwiches and a Thermos of tea in the car. It was a cold day being as it's November and Archie tucked me up in a big car-rug. He is always so kind and thoughtful to me. We stopped and had a picnic about half way, and talked about our wedding and where we would live afterwards. We just want a small wedding, in a Register Office. My parents wouldn't have liked it, they always wanted me to have a proper church wedding. But they're dead and it doesn't matter to Archie and me. He wants to marry me and I want to marry him, that's all. He's dead now but he isn't really you know.

Bottle paused, wiped away the tears beginning to trickle down her face, and picked up the next pages.

We got to his parents' house, through some great black gates and then down a long drive. The house is very big and grand and four huge dogs came rushing out barking their heads off and nearly knocked Archie and me down the front steps. Archie's mother and father were having tea in an enormous room full of furniture and paintings and photographs and big silver cups. Mrs. Bullin-Archer is taller than Archie and she was wearing a pair of riding trousers and a tweed jacket. She was warm but I was cold, it was freezing in the room with only one log fire.

Archie's father doesn't look anything like Archie, he's big and heavy and his face is red and he has great bushy eyebrows and a curly moustache though he's bald. In fact I didn't see how he could be Archie's father. Archie was getting very nervous, I could tell. His parents didn't smile at us, they just said, "Good afternoon," and, "Well?" and they didn't say anything when Archie said, "This is Ivy." He went on, "Ivy and I are engaged," but they still didn't say anything, just shrugged their shoulders as if they were impatient, so he stopped. He hoped they would be pleased. But Mrs. Bullin-Archer looked at Archie, very coldly. She didn't look at me. And she said, in a very crushing voice, "And who IS Ivy?" Well I could feel Archie getting more and more nervous, so I said, very quietly, "I am Ivy." Then Mrs. Bullin-Archer turned and gave me such a terrible look, her mouth all pinched and her eyes half-closed, and she hissed like a snake, "My dear girl, I can see that. But who are you? Who are your parents? Where did you go to school? How much money do you have? I want to know WHO YOU ARE!"

Appalled, Bottle fumbled with her cigarette packet but abandoned it as, transfixed with horror, she read on.

Archie was white and stammering and he could hardly get the words out but he did: "Ivy is Ivy Bailey and her parents are dead and we love each other and

we're engaged and we're going to get married, and ..."
He couldn't go on because his father barged in in a
big loud voice like a foghorn at the seaside: "No. Your
mother is right, we want to know who this young lady is.
Now tell us. Or she can tell us."

He turned to me and stuck his head forward like a
turkey cock and raised his great eyebrows and gave me
such a scornful look. I said: "My name is Ivy Bailey and
I live in London and I work in Debenham and Freebody
and ..." I couldn't go on because Mrs. Bullin-Archer interrupted in a voice as chilly as the room: "You work in
a department store? Do you mean you are a salesgirl?"
"Yes, she is," said Archie, "and a very good one too." "It
is immaterial whether she is good at her job or bad,"
snapped Mrs. Bullin-Archer, "it is quite impossible that
a Bullin-Archer should marry a salesgirl. Now take her
away, Archibald, and let us have no more of this nonsense."
"Your mother is right," Mr. Bullin-Archer boomed, in a
terrible exploding voice. "The idea is ludicrous. I am sure
that Miss Bailey will see sense, will you not, Miss Bailey?"
He took a step toward me and I almost feared he would
hit me. "As your mother says," he carried on to Archie,
"take her away and keep out of our sight until you have
got over this stupid nonsense. Goodbye."

Archie was white as a sheet and I thought he might
faint. He stood still, in silence, like a statue, then he
grabbed my hand and we walked out. We drove back to

London and he didn't say a word all the way. I got out at my door and he still said nothing. He's dead but he was alive then and he was in hell. I was too.

Unable to control her tears, Bottle put the pages down, pulled her handkerchief out of her pocket to rub her eyes, tugged a cigarette from the packet and lit it with trembling hands.

I cried all night and at six o'clock in the morning my landlady banged on my door and said irritably, "It's the police for you." I put on my dressing gown and went downstairs and a young constable was there with an envelope with writing on it. I recognized the writing, it was Archie's, it said "Miss Ivy Bailey is my love. PARK 4589 is her telephone number." The constable asked, "Are you Miss Ivy Bailey?" and of course I said yes, and he asked if I knew who had written my name on the envelope and I said "Archie," and he said very kindly, "I'm very sorry, Miss, I'm afraid Archie is dead."

They had found him in the dark little alley next to his flat, hanging from a lamp-post. He had strangled himself with his new white shirt. He had cut it into strips, I saw it at the police station. It was beside his body. He looked calm and peaceful and he was dead. He is dead.

He did it because he knew I was his only hope of a happy life. He knew that if he disobeyed his parents they would destroy us, him and me too. He told me they had always terrified him, he told me that when he was alive. He told me when he told me about being strangled at school. The boys were only seven but they were all at a boarding school. He told me the parents didn't love their children so they sent them away. The boys were very cruel to each other and they had games to prove that they could stand up to things, only they weren't games. In one of them a new boy had to cut up his shirt and join the strips into a sort of rope, and the others wound it around his neck and pulled the ends hard until he almost choked to death. Then he had to pretend to the matron that he had eaten something nasty which made him feel sick, and he had to pretend that he'd somehow lost his shirt, and so he had to pay a fine for being careless.

Bottle's hands were quivering so violently that she dropped her cigarette into the ashtray. Half-blinded by tears, she lifted the remaining pages nearer her face.

Archie is dead so I can tell you. He hated his parents but he had to pretend to love them. And he hated his prep school and he hated his public school. At that school he told me he was a "fag," a sort of servant of an older boy. He had to clean this boy's shoes and make him toast and run errands for him and do whatever the boy asked. And one day the boy asked him to touch his private parts and when Archie refused the boy beat him.

And he hated India, the heat and the flies and the sickness and the smells, and he hated the Army too. In the Army there was a young subaltern who was under Archie. They both slept in a big tent which was divided by a partition. Archie slept on one side and the subaltern the other. The subaltern wanted to get promoted, so he asked Archie to recommend him, but Archie didn't think he was good enough so he said no. And in the middle of the night, when it was very hot, and Archie had only just got to sleep, he thought he heard a bump. He didn't do anything as there were always a lot of funny noises outside the tents. In the morning he called the subaltern, as usual, but there was no answer. So he pulled back the partition and saw the young man hanging from a high cross pole supporting the tent. He was dead. He had cut a shirt into strips and hanged himself.

My parents are dead, my sister and my granny are dead, most of my friends are dead, the subaltern's dead and Archie's dead. In the envelope in his pocket there was a bit of paper with "Sorry" in his writing; and a beautiful little gold ring with an emerald. He always says my eyes are green like emeralds.

Bottle could bear no more. She dropped her head into her hands and howled. The cigarette smoldered, flickered, faltered and went out.

18

Mr. Hedgehog, Journalists, a Tiny Baptist and Lies

As postwar supplies of paper gradually improved, and newspapers had more pages to fill, the press grew increasingly interested in the Marriage Bureau. Journalists reported Heather's succinct, authoritative views on the marital chances of ex-servicewomen, the cost of weddings and the foolishness of old men seeking young brides. Heather and her Marriage Bureau developed into a goldmine from which newspapers could always extract a shiny nugget on the importance of family life and babies, the demands for equality of women who had done men's jobs in wartime, on loneliness, divorce, and personal problems of all kinds.

The *Daily Express* published Heather's assessment of the postwar marriage market:

Things have changed entirely since VE Day. Until then, most of the younger women who came to me wanted anything but English husbands. They favoured Americans particularly—seemed to think that if they got to America they would all live like Hedy Lamarr. Now, suddenly, they are clamouring for Englishmen again. Women aged between thirty-five and forty-two are the most difficult to get fixed up. They try to be too coy and young. After about forty-two the job gets easier—I can get women of fifty-five off like shelling peas.

One pea who was not shelled with such confident ease was Miss Doris Burton. She had registered soon after the Bureau opened in 1939, saying that she was thirty-nine, though Mary Oliver had been convinced she was nearer forty-nine, and quite possibly a lesbian. Over the next few years Miss Burton had been introduced to several men but with no success, for they all found her off-puttingly businesslike, severe in her attitudes and in her somewhat mannish looks: "I felt as if I was summoned to my bank manager to explain why I had exceeded my overdraft, and she disapproved of my jacket too," was a typical reaction.

Miss Burton had canceled her membership in the Bureau when she took up with a smooth talker who came into her tobacconist's shop in search of cigarettes. Mr. Smooth was addicted to smoking but earned little from his intermittent job as a cosmetics salesman, and with cigarettes in very short supply he sometimes had to resort to the extortionate black market. He had immediately sensed Miss Burton's loneliness, and put himself out to be so irresistibly agreeable that she, unaccustomed to male admiration, sold him a packet she had kept under the counter for a favorite customer. Emboldened by this stroke of luck, Mr. Smooth had ratcheted up the compliments, flattering Miss Burton so fulsomely that one thing rapidly led to another and, shortly, to him moving into her small flat above the shop.

Convinced he had fallen on his feet, with no rent to pay and an unfailing supply of his favorite Players cigarettes to hand, Mr. Smooth grew careless, helping himself to too many packets from Miss Burton's secreted hoard. She soon found him out, wrathfully brushed his compliments and pleadings aside, kicked him out, licked her wounds, and devoted herself to her shop. Until one gloomy rainy day she thought again of the Bureau.

Heather calculated that, as Mary had judged Miss Burton to be nearly fifty, she must now be not far off sixty. She still wanted the same solid type, a man with no encumbrances such as children or dependent parents, and enough money for a home. However, since her unfortunate experience with Mr. Smooth, and some other dishonest customers, she had grown disenchanted with running her tobacconist's, and resolved to leave town and live in the country. As a competent businesswoman she visualized herself helping her husband in some small enterprise. Having originally said a categorical *no* to any pets, she now fondly imagined the pleasure of owning a dog, cat, or other animals.

"It is only a pity," reflected Heather, "that Miss Burton is no more attractive a proposition than she was when younger. She still smokes like a chimney, which makes her skin so leathery—apologies, dear Bottle. But you seem to be lucky, all your smoking doesn't seem to affect your complexion!"

"Pure luck," smiled Bottle, who knew very well that Heather abhorred her smoking, but tolerated it. "What about Sidney Headley for Miss Burton? He's embarrassed about still being a bachelor so he says he's fifty, but I'm sure he's older. You can't tell properly because you can't see much of his face except his eyes, he's got such thick hair, and great bristly sideboards too, as well as a scrubby beard and a rather moth-eaten mustache. Hair everywhere, even sprouting from his ears! And he snuffles. I felt as if I was interviewing an oversized hedgehog blowing its nose on a rather smelly handkerchief—it smelled of petrol."

Mr. Hedgehog was *Better Than Some*, had never married but lived with his parents on a decaying smallholding in Northamptonshire. Their death from pneumonia in their vast moldering bed at last set him free to find a wife, but the few local girls had long since got married, or moved to a town to get a job during the war and not returned. He wanted an honest, practical-minded woman who would interest herself in his home, his work and his person: although not bad-looking he was scruffy, his jacket patched, his shoes scuffed, his teeth heavily tobacco-stained (though partially concealed by his mustache). He was a decent, steady type, a gauche "set bachelor," as the Bureau termed such men. His conversation about his three cows and twenty chickens was stilted, but a torrent of words spilled out on the glorious subject of his petrol pump.

Mr. Hedgehog's petrol pump was his pride and joy. After

his parents died he had heaved the mildewed mattress off their bed to burn it, along with the filthy, torn, worn bedclothes, and had been flabbergasted to discover £1,000 tucked into the bedsprings. Poor downtrodden Mr. H. had never been allowed to go anywhere without his domineering mother's permission, nor to spend anything unless his magpie father agreed. So with this miraculous windfall he splashed out on the object he had long craved: a shiny silver petrol pump. He had shrewdly realized, even during the war, that more and more people would buy cars, and the cars would need petrol. His cows and chickens produced a modest income, but he lived on a small country road that was due to be widened, traffic would increase, so surely a petrol pump would make the Headley fortune.

Heather summed up: "The future Mrs. Hedgehog should be prepared to live on a busy country road, serving petrol and taking an interest in Buttercup, Daisy, Clover, and chickens. How can anyone be interested in chickens? They are loathsome creatures, I detested mine (and they returned the sentiment). But now she's disposed toward animals, perhaps feathered clucking creatures will be just up Miss Burton's street!"

"You may not be able to understand how she can be interested in chickens, Heather," commented Bottle, "but she would be baffled by your interest in clothes. She favors the simple look: plain, austere, somber—though impeccably clean. I am sure she will have a beneficial effect on Mr. Hedgehog."

Bottle introduced Mr. Hedgehog and Miss Burton. Several weeks later a knock on the office door preceded an unrecognizable

Mr. Hedgehog who, seeing the bewildered look on Bottle's face, burst out, "Mr. Headley, Sidney Headley. I've come to thank you."

In a flash Bottle took in the transformation. Gone were the brown stains on his teeth, the sideboards, the patched jacket and scuffed shoes. Mr. Hedgehog was dressed in a smart gray suit, polished black shoes, blindingly white shirt, pristine navy handkerchief (for show only), and navy-and-white-striped tie. The shaggy tangle of hair was reduced to a short, Brylcreemed back 'n' sides, the mustache to a close-clipped line, the beard to a neat equilateral triangle which lent him a jaunty, vaguely Continental air. His ears were hair-free. He looked dapper and only faintly self-conscious as Bottle, beaming in anticipation of the announcement of his engagement to Miss Burton, held out a congratulatory hand. "Oh, Mr. Headley! You look wonderful! Congra—"

She got no further as Mr. Hedgehog interrupted. "Thank you for sending me Miss Burton. She did me a power of good—cleaned me up a treat, she did. When I went into the garage in Kettering to look at their petrol pumps, the nice lady in the office, who's often talked to me, couldn't believe I was so different. We chatted as usual, and she showed me their new pumps, and I took her to the pictures, and we've been out dancing and now—you won't believe it, Miss Harbottle, but we're engaged!"

Poor Bottle struggled to look delighted as her heart sank under pity for Miss Burton, mingled with dismay at the fearsome prospect of trying once again to marry her off. Heather was annoyed at so narrowly missing an After Marriage Fee.

While Bottle disconsolately resorted to the records, Heather was ensconced with a journalist. She had long since lost her anxiety about the press: now she basked in their attention, as they featured not only her opinions but also her appearance: THOUSANDS WANT PARTNERS, proclaimed the *Star*.

> Stately, 6 feet tall, Miss Heather Jenner, who has been responsible for hundreds of happy marriages, left London Airport today to spend a fortnight's holiday in Portugal. Miss Jenner wore a flowered hat with a casual veil on top of her head, a two-piece grey suit and a smart Russian enamelled brooch as she waited to board her plane. She told me that she had the names of seven or eight thousand people on her books who were looking for life partners.

Many of the thousands of clients married: in December 1946 Heather announced that the Bureau had made nearly 2,000 marriages, an astonishing figure that eighteen months later rose to nearly 3,000. Many couples married within a few months, even a few weeks, of meeting; yet, despite this haste, Heather knew of only two couples who had "come unstuck."

Many non-Bureau marriages did, however, flounder and fail, as spouses tried to readjust to married life after separation in wartime. One proposed remedy was that not only transport, major industries and medicine should be nationalized, but also marriage bureaus. Heather's scathing rejection was reported in the press:

> If a Bureau is to function satisfactorily, it needs to be organized on a fairly large scale, so that for each client there is a wide choice of "possibles". But Heaven forbid that it should be on a State scale with all that that implies, with all the unmarrieds tabulated and card-indexed and brought together on a national footing, rather like a national stud.
>
> *Hitler organized something on similar lines not many years ago. And if a nationalised Marriage Bureau came to Britain we should know that totalitarianism was really upon us.*

The humorous writer Patrick Campbell, who stuttered incurably, tested the Bureau. In the *Sunday Dispatch* he described how, posing as "Sir Hubert," he inquired on behalf of an invented friend, "George McKechnie," who was, he insisted, too shy to appear himself but happy that his trusty emissary would find out all the necessary facts.

The interviewer smelled a possible rat, but comported herself as if the client were genuine, politely asking him to fill in a registration form on behalf of his bashful pal. "Sir Hubert" filled in the details of "George McKechnie": "a chromium bathroom fitting salesman, earning £4 a week, aged forty-two, a Baptist,

5 feet 3 inches tall, slender, with reddish hair, living with his mother, sister and brother, interested in botany and club cycling." The interviewer did not turn a hair at this improbable description, for she had seen many details that beggared belief but were in fact entirely true. Politely she requested information about Mr. McKechnie's requirements in a wife, adding that she supposed Sir Hubert knew what kind of person that would be?

"Certainly I kn-kn-know," protested "Sir Hubert," bridling at the faint implication that the interviewer suspected deceit. His friend, he asserted, was in search of "a fellow Baptist, 5 feet 1 inches tall, with a private income of £250 a year, of a quiet and studious disposition, interested in botany and cycling." "Sir Hubert" leaned back in his chair and focused a challenging smile on the interviewer: "Look, I kn-kn-kno-know this may be irregular, b-b-but I don't b-b-believe you've got a lady B-B-B-Baptist on your b-b-books, f-f-five feet high, who can ride a b-b-b-bicycle."

The interviewer's eyes narrowed and glinted as she rose to the challenge: "I can't tell you offhand, but I'm quite, quite sure we have."

"Show me. Have a look through the f-f-files. Show me one tiny f-f-female B-B-Baptist on a b-b-b-bicycle."

The interviewer's eyes contracted again until they were little more than arrow slits, through which she fired quivering visual darts at "Sir Hubert." "Very well. But you must realize that our business is entirely confidential. I must conceal the name on the card. But I will show you the rest of it." Whereupon she pressed the bell on her desk, summoning the receptionist, to whom she handed "Mr. McKechnie's" registration form and whispered a few words that "Sir Hubert," engrossed in smug satisfaction at the prospect of wrong-footing her, failed to hear.

For the next five minutes the interviewer busied herself with forms on her desk while her self-congratulating client lolled comfortably, humming "Daisy, Daisy, Give me your answer do" as he conjured up a mental picture of "George" and his bride freewheeling into a roseate sunset on a dwarf-sized honeymoon tandem.

The receptionist glided silently back in and, without a word, put a small pink card into her client's hand. His ebullient triumphalism quickly collapsed as he read the details of a "Baptist, 5 foot 2 inches, school teacher, serious-minded, interested in classical music, children, dogs, cycling & botany." The name of this wonderwoman was masked by a strip of paper pasted over it.

With shaking fingers "Sir Hubert" passed the card back to the interviewer, whose overly bright, quelling smile stopped far short of her hooded eyes.

"Thank you," he mumbled unconvincingly. "I shall t-t-t-tell George that there is hope for him in your esteemed B-B-B-Bureau. I trust that he will f-f-f-find the courage to overcome his shyness sufficiently to v-v-v-visit you." He slunk off, deeply impressed but chastened and discomfited, consoled only by the knowledge that he could now abandon "Sir Hubert," breathe freely, and write up his adventure.

· · ·

Patrick Campbell's article about his lighthearted deception gave Heather, Dorothy, the interviewers, and the receptionist a good laugh (and brought in new clients). But graver deceit caused anger and pain. Looking back, Heather considered that the war had increased dishonesty, with desperate people turning to crime—forging coupons for extra rations of food, petrol and clothes, looting bombed properties, selling stolen goods on the black market, making false declarations to avoid conscription, drawing rations for dead people. More mountainous bureaucracy added to the problem, wrote Heather:

> The forms that the government made us fill in increased, for private people as well as for businesses. They became more and more complicated, so that more people had to go to already overworked accountants and pay enormous fees to have what should be a simple matter sorted out. Together with the effects of the war, which made us into a paternalistic state, this undermined people's feelings of responsibility and honesty. In the Bureau we find that our clients are much more dishonest about paying their After Marriage Fees than they used to be, and this applies often to people with plenty of money rather than those with less.

Heather uncovered one of the most blatant examples of dishonesty when a woman rang up, spluttering with fury: "How dare you introduce my son to a girl without him knowing she was a divorcee? We have never had any divorce in our family, but now he's married her, it's too late. How DARE you!"

"Would you be so kind as to tell me the names of your son and daughter-in-law?" asked Heather, shaken by the venom in the woman's voice but maintaining a glacial control.

The woman spat out two names, neither of which Heather recognized.

"Thank you," she replied, icily polite. "I shall check our files, and shall telephone you in half an hour. Would you be so kind as to give me your telephone number?"

"It is Welbeck 3267." The woman banged the telephone down.

"Phew!" breathed Heather as Dorothy raised her eyebrows in inquiring sympathy. "She is really spitting tacks! I don't know every single client's name, but it is beyond doubt that I would recollect a recent marriage. Help me, please, dear Dorothy. We must check every possible record."

Heather and Dorothy searched the registration forms, the record cards, the ledgers of new registrations, the accounts, the letters, the boxes of clients "off" for one reason or another (courting, or ill, or going abroad, or just wanting a pause). They questioned the receptionist and the interviewers, all to no avail. Neither name was anywhere to be found.

Heather braced herself and telephoned the woman. "I regret to inform you that we have no record of either your son or your daughter-in-law. Would you be so kind as to tell me when your son registered, and whether he paid his registration fee by check?

And exactly when did he marry and pay his After Marriage Fee, and was that by check?"

There was a long pause. Heather could hear the woman's mind churning. "I gave him the money to join your Bureau in cash, and the same for the After Marriage Fee. It was such a sudden marriage, too."

The unfilial son had never been a client, but had found a devious and dishonest way of laying his hands on a quick bit of cash. He had probably met his divorcee before he accepted his mother's kindly given money for the Bureau's fees, and had spent both payments on a more lavish honeymoon than he could otherwise have afforded.

As the inescapable truth dawned on her, the wounded mother started to sob, first quietly then noisily. For once at a loss for words, Heather visualized the woman's face crumpling, the tears furrowing her makeup, her bosom heaving, her heart breaking.

"Oh the poor, poor woman," sighed Dorothy, anger rising in her usually calm breast. "What a wicked, cynical, cruel, unforgivable thing to do. I should like to thrash that evil son. He's an even more poisonous toad than the Reverend Hogg!"

For years that reverend clergyman had been living in sin with Mrs. Joy, whom he had met through the Bureau, but was still maintaining that she was merely his housekeeper. He had failed to reply to Heather's latest letter, and she had failed to establish any connection with his bishop or other churchman of influence. However, the resourceful matchmaker persuaded a theatrical friend of Picot's, who lived in the next village, to attend matins in the Reverend Hogg's church.

The cooperative friend duly shook the Rector's hand as she walked out of the church and complimented him on his sermon, enthusing until there was a small queue of villagers behind her. Then she announced in clear, carrying tones: "I am so pleased to meet you as I believe we have a mutual friend, Miss Heather Jenner of the Marriage Bureau in New Bond Street. Isn't she marvelous? She has made so many wonderful marriages—her couples are always so happy and grateful. She has a God-given gift, don't you think?"

The Rector blanched and turned rapidly to greet the next person in the queue. Mrs. Joy, at his side, seized the friend's hand and, on the pretext of urgently needing to show her the ancient lych-gate, steered her firmly away from the crowd. Two days later, an envelope enclosing a check for two After Marriage Fees was delivered to the Bureau. The check was signed by the Reverend Hogg. There was no letter.

Heather did not reveal such unpleasant episodes to the press. The Bureau remained a source of positive, entertaining, helpful stories, headed eye-catchingly:

MIND OVER MARRIAGE

300 EX-SERVICEMEN SEEKING BRIDES

ARE YOU HAPPY?

BOGUS BLONDES NO MORE

MATRIMONY WITHOUT TEARS

700,000 WOMEN WANT A MIDDLE-AGED MAN!

The more the press wrote about her, both in the United Kingdom and in America, the more in demand Heather became. Much though she loved doing the mating and organizing the Bureau, she was ready and thrilled to spread her wings, and eagerly accepted an invitation to sit with a psychiatrist, an MP and the Governor of Holloway Jail on a public brain trust discussing marriage and divorce. The *News Chronicle* photograph showed Heather, beautifully dressed in a chic dark suit, seated with her elegant legs demurely crossed, looking thoughtful. Next she joined the Principal of Westfield College, film producer Herbert Wilcox, film star Anna Neagle, the President of the National Federation of Business and Professional Women's Clubs, two MPs, and an Auxiliary Territorial Service Senior Commander, to advise on career opportunities for girls demobbed from the Services or the Women's Land Army.

A newly acquired journalist friend, Eve Brent, backed Heather in another new venture: a Tell Us Your Troubles bureau. TUYT was open to inquiries by post or telephone, to be answered for five shillings by the Misses Jenner and Brent, aided by an advisory panel consisting of a solicitor, doctor, midwife, and experts on dress, travel, beauty, hairdressing and cookery. A psychiatrist and adviser on domestic problems would be added.

TUYT rapidly led on to Heather's own advisory column:

"Tell Heather Jenner Your Troubles" in the *Metropolitan Times*, which ran the preface:

> We have much pleasure in introducing to our readers a columnist who is understanding and helpful with regard to all questions on marriage. Miss Heather Jenner is an authority on the subject and yet sophisticated.

The first letter sought help for a common postwar dilemma. Many men separated from their wives for years, in a foreign country, had inevitably found solace with another woman. Similarly, wives, left to fend for themselves in the harsh and lonely conditions of wartime Great Britain, had lapped up the attention of foreign servicemen, especially Americans, and those prisoners of war who were allowed to help with such jobs as farmwork (Italians were particularly popular POWs, considered more romantic than other nationalities, and better at singing). The letter ran:

Serviceman Returns

When I was in Italy during the war I had an affair with a girl who really meant nothing to me. Now that I am back in England I am engaged to a girl with whom I am very much in love and whom I have known since she was a child. She is a good deal younger than I am and very unsophisticated. Should I tell her about the girl in Italy?

Heather's solution was characteristically realistic and practical:

Miss Jenner Answers . . .

I don't think that it is necessary to tell her specifically about this girl. If she is young and unsophisticated she might be made unnecessarily unhappy. If the subject is mentioned at all I should explain tactfully that you are older than she and were living under different conditions owing to the war, but that nothing that you may have done in the past could in any way affect your love for her.

All letters were to be addressed not to the *Metropolitan Times* but to Heather Jenner at The Marriage Bureau, 124 New Bond Street, London WI. In yet another way, the press was putting the fascinating Heather Jenner and her marvelous Marriage Bureau ever more prominently on the map.

19

A Chapter of Accidents and Designs

In late 1940s Great Britain, austerity held crushing sway. In 1946 the meager sweet ration was halved. Canned and dried fruit, chocolate biscuits, treacle, syrup, jellies and mincemeat remained rationed until 1950, tea until 1952. Petrol coupons allowed only ninety miles a month; clothes were limited to one new set per year. The ferocious winter of 1946–47 froze bodies and spirits. The National Health Service promised change but was in its infancy. The 1948 London Olympics raised morale, but only briefly.

No wonder that many dreamed of a new life in a sunnier, more optimistic continent. Europe was a disaster area, the Far East too far, the Middle East and most of Africa too alien. Female clients wanted a man living in Australia, New Zealand, South Africa or Canada, foreign but blessedly English-speaking, and home to troops who had helped us during the war. Sun, fun, food and security beckoned beguilingly.

In March 1949 an article in *Queen* magazine about why people want to get married concluded that in the current austere post-victory days people did not like living alone, but that "with an agreeable companion even *snoek* may appear to be palatable." However, for women the writer identified a more compelling reason than improving the taste of an unpleasantly oily and bony fish:

Women, of course, as the more practical sex, look upon a man as security. That is quite natural, because not only do most women suffer from an inferiority complex, but they are well aware that though they may work as efficiently as two men, they'll be lucky to get the price of one. Besides, what happens when a woman gets old? Unless somebody leaves her legacies she must go on toiling until some kindly slave-driver of an employer advises her to seek refuge in the workhouse.

Many female clients of the Bureau felt as this one:

I would like a man from South Africa, or perhaps Australia, or other warm climate. Not necessarily anyone English, although myself I am proud to be. He must have a comfortable income and a good job, to look after me.

Conveniently, plenty of men living abroad wanted an English wife. Heather and Dorothy put them in touch with women with whom they corresponded until they could meet. After exchanging several letters and photographs, one girl bought her ticket, sailed out to Kenya, met her correspondent on the dock, fell in instant, mutual love, and married two months later. Another girl allowed a generous American businessman, Austin, to foot the bill for her fare to New York and a hotel there. Hours after her feet touched American tarmac she met and soon married one of his friends, but did not suggest paying back any of the money. "She had a great vacation," a considerably resentful Austin wrote to Heather,

> and now she's gotten a great future, at my expense. And she pinched my best friend into the bargain. She could at least offer me some return. I reckon she's a tough cookie, and I'm best off without her—but gee am I sore!

Heather sympathized and immediately put Austin in touch with Mrs. Phyllis Duke, the unmaterialistic young widow of Reginald, a returned POW.

Reginald's death had stunned and grieved Heather, since she had happy memories of introducing Phyllis and her army officer husband in 1943, and receiving euphoric reports of their whirl-wind courtship. They had been model clients. Reginald had been bowled over by Phyllis, an alluring twenty-year-old art student, and had wanted to marry immediately, fearing that some honey-tongued American would sweep her away if he didn't pin her down fast. Phyllis was delighted to flirt with her many American suitors but adored Reginald, and one cold February day in 1944 they married in St. Mary le Strand, followed by a reception in the nearby Savoy Hotel. Two weeks after the wedding Phyllis brought minuscule slices of wedding cake into the Bureau, and told Heather and Dorothy the story.

Reginald had chosen London as the most convenient place for people with no petrol to get to the church by train, and there was a lull in the bombing. But the night before, V2 rockets suddenly renewed their deadly attacks. His deaf mother, reading stories to the four-year-old pageboy and bridesmaid in a hotel on the Strand, was blissfully unaware, and the children were happily excited by the din. But the rest of the party feared that neither the church nor they themselves might be standing the next day.

In fact, the only no-show was the organist, whose railway line was bombed, but fortunately Phyllis's former music teacher stepped in, managing the unfamiliar instrument with only a few false notes. Reginald's dispatch riders collected the cake from a Knightsbridge friend, whose well-connected cook had resourcefully located the ingredients, and a bouquet of freesias was conjured up by the florists Moyses Stevens. The bride enchanted the congregation in her grandmother's wedding dress, which fit after she took out the bones in the bodice—even so, like her grandmother, she had to be laced into corsets underneath. A front panel of embroidered sateen was badly worn and couldn't be replaced, so Phyllis had bought some net, which did not need coupons, and fellow students at her art college stitched it invisibly into place.

Snow was falling heavily as the wedding party walked from the church to the Savoy. The sodden wedding dress wilted and clung to Phyllis's slight frame; Reginald's mother slipped and dropped her big black box of a hearing aid, which squeaked and died; the pageboy hurled a snowball at the bridesmaid, who burst into unquenchable tears. But in the hotel joy erupted like a genie from its bottle, and hours later Reginald and Phyllis, standing squashed together in a train crowded with troops, on their way to their honeymoon, were dizzy with delight.

A week later, Reginald was posted to Burma.

After his departure, Phyllis dropped into the Bureau occasionally, once accompanying her younger sister, whom she encouraged to register. But since the end of the war she had not appeared, so Heather was taken aback when one day in 1949 Phyllis poked her head nervously around the door, inched her way to Heather's desk, and sat in the chair as if on a bed of nails. Gone was the pretty, smiling girl. Phyllis was unrecognizable: her clothes hanging from her bones, wan-faced, as if she had been dropped in a tub of bleach.

Haltingly, she explained. "Reggie's dead. But he wasn't Reggie any more. I'll never know exactly what happened to him in Burma. He was captured the minute he got there, and put in some ghastly camp. The colonel who visited me when Reggie came home after the war said he'd been tortured, beaten, starved, forced to do heavy laboring work in blazing sunshine. The prisoners regularly fell ill and were left to die. By the end of the war his mind was eaten away, the same as his body—he was a walking skeleton. He'd look at food, but he couldn't eat more than a morsel. Yet if I left anything on my plate, or put a bone with a bit of gristle into the bin, he'd fly into a fury and fish it out, wave it in my face, and shriek, 'Don't waste! *Don't waste*, do you hear?' Once there was a caterpillar in the salad so I pushed it to the side of my plate, and he went berserk, howling that I must cook it and eat it. He was shouting and sobbing all at the same time. I was terrified.

"He'd been home a year, but he was still crying and yelling in his sleep, twisting and jerking and thrashing his arms, suddenly sitting up and staring pop-eyed at me as if he'd seen the devil himself. He flinched if I reached out to touch him. I tried to talk to him about our wedding, and our home, but he just looked blank, then sprang up as if he'd been electrocuted and staggered out of the room, slamming the door so viciously the shelves all shook. He cursed and swore, couldn't bear to be indoors, so he used to go striding off. I never knew where he went or when he'd be back."

One day in October Reggie hadn't come home. Nor the next day. Phyllis went to the police, who searched and searched in vain. People kept ringing up and telling her they'd seen him in the local town, or catching a bus, or waiting on the station platform. But they were all wrong, because in March, a man walking his dog in a field only a mile away found Reggie's body. He'd fallen into a deep ditch, and leaves and then snow and water had hidden him. The police estimated he'd been there for about six months, and that almost certainly he had died quickly. That was some relief to Phyllis, and would have been to his mother too, but she was so deaf she couldn't understand what her daughter-in-law was saying, and she'd lost most of her sight, so it wasn't any good writing down the fearful news.

Phyllis's sympathetic sister, now married to another of the Bureau's clients, had taken her into her new home and wrapped her in loving-kindness until she revived, got a job as an art teacher, and felt able to go in quest of a future.

In 1949 Heather introduced Phyllis to some pleasant, untraumatized men who aided the revivifying process. When she started to correspond with Austin, she was almost back to her former happy self. Austin's letters were refreshingly straightforward and lively, and when he came over to London to do some business deals Phyllis felt she already knew and almost loved him. The day before Austin returned to New York, Phyllis stretched out her left hand to show the jubilant matchmakers her sparkling sapphire and diamond engagement ring, while Austin thanked them for "the best goddam deal I ever did!"

Being so often in the news, the Marriage Bureau inevitably inspired imitators, more and less scrupulous, giving the press a new storyline: "WOMEN BEWARE! These Friendship Clubs can snare the lonely." Undercover reporters investigated agencies that refused to reveal their fees, assessed a client's wealth and charged the maximum they could extract, made totally unsuitable introductions, or were even—a *Sunday Pictorial* reporter asserted—"thinly veiled adjuncts to the vice trade."

Such reports stirred public anxiety and indignation. The Marriage Guidance Council weighed in. Meetings were held with the three most reputable bureaus, two run by ex-army officers who wanted to establish a Marriage Agents Association. They proposed a code of conduct, one committee to settle disputes and another to decide the principles on which bureaus should operate, together with their policy in relation to new social trends. The colonels also sought a confidential blacklist of "undesirables and moral perverts, who might seek to use a marriage bureau for improper purposes."

"Good Lord!" groaned Heather, "there'll be no time to run the Bureau. We'll spend all day in blasted committees! And those high-minded but hidebound colonels won't let us bend a single rule—everything will conform to some sacred article in the holy Code of Conduct. We'll have solemn powwows about social trends, as if we're all earnest do-gooders, which I most certainly am not! And we'll be banned from taking on any moral perverts, who are much the most interesting of all the clients. I do so love a cozy little conflab with a nice moral pervert after a morning of melancholy moral high-grounders. Moral perverts have such an unusual take on life, so different from one's own dear family and friends!"

"Come now, Heather," tut-tutted Dorothy, shocked even though she rather agreed with Heather's flippant views. "The colonels mean very well, and it would certainly benefit us to stand out from the dubious agencies that are giving everybody a bad name."

Despite the worthiness of the cause and the insistence of the colonels, the Marriage Agents Association never materialized. Before it foundered completely Heather pulled out, disagreeing with the recommended fee structure. The Bureau had always charged a modest registration fee, so that everybody could have a chance, and an After Marriage Fee payable only by those who were successful. Both Heather and Humphrey the solicitor thought this "payment by results" structure much fairer than a flat fee for a number of introductions. It also gave the Bureau a strong incentive to find good matches, rather than dish out only superficially suitable introductions. Once again the press reported Heather's opinion:

I am in complete agreement with the idea that a control of the undesirables is fundamentally sound, but I do not consider the proposed association is going the right way about it.

Simply stated, my view is that essentially it should be to the advantage of a bureau to get people married rather than to benefit by merely introducing men to women. Disagreement on that point led to my withdrawal from the proposed association, but I wish them every success so long as they do not claim a monopoly of respectability.

Outside the association there will be one bureau which for over ten years has employed "methods and principles of the highest possible level" and provided for the public a bureau "to which they can go without fear of embarrassment or exploitation."

• • •

A project that did come to fruition was a play, *Marriage Playground*, produced in London's Q Theatre. It had been conceived in 1944 by Picot's friends, playwrights Simon Wardell and Kieran Tunney. While working at the Bureau, Picot had written to Heather in Scotland:

29 May 1944

Darling Heather

Simon and Kieran, the Boys who are writing "our" play, have just left, and I think their idea is quite good. One set and eleven characters, tentative title *It Started in Bond Street* (mine. If you can think of a better one let us have it.)

Action takes place at the country house of Chichi Templeton who runs the Bureau, and who invites the clients for the weekend when things have gone well with them.

Characters: (This may not be quite accurate as it was told me over dinner and I did not make notes but the Boys are going to discuss it with me all the time.)

—A friend of Chichi's just back from America

—A glamour deb, based on Amelia Hutton

—An Irish girl who has come into a little money and wants to "better" herself

—A Russian (based on your Princess Poppy who is a great friend of the Boys. For your ear alone she isn't and never has been a princess!)

—Chichi's housekeeper

—A South American who is rich and wants to marry a society girl and finally marries the housekeeper

—An American based on a man they know

—An intellectual (ditto)

I can't remember the other two.

The final curtain is Chichi's American friend saying he had no idea what a grand job she is doing, he would like to come on the books, and she having been vague and gay during the play suddenly becomes very official and says, "Well, we give you a form to fill up," etc!

I think it might work out quite well, and they will get it done in two months, and Bill Linnet has promised to read it and Peter Danbery has asked for first refusal of the Boys' next play (which is this one) and Binkie is interested to read it, so if it is good it should get taken, and they are setting out to write an amusing play, but to stress that the Bureau is of social value, so I do hope it will come off. It should be done in time for a birthday treat for your son and heir!

I wish you were here to help.

All love, Picot

Marriage Playground was not performed until September 1948, and only after a legal dispute. Always ferociously protective of her Bureau's reputation, Heather objected to some scenes in the chirpy little comedy, and to the name of the fictitious bureau: she took action to prevent production unless *New Bond-Street Marriage Bureau* was changed to *Mayfair Marriage Bureau*. Recognizing that Heather was far too redoubtable to fight, Kieran Tunney and Simon Wardell yielded to her demands and made her requested alterations. Peace was declared, and Heather attended the first night accompanied by fifty of the married couples she had introduced.

The play was, wrote one critic, "written in a vein of bright banter and youthful cynicism," and was remarkable only for some excellent performances, principally by Irene Handl, whose "raucously overacted lady of uncouth mind and utterance reduced the rest of the company to dim helplessness whenever she appeared." It rapidly vanished from the theatrical repertoire; but the Bureau's name had appeared yet again in the press, together with photographs of Heather, elegant as ever, pictured laughing as she dispensed advice to an actress at rehearsal.

Heather was further pleased by the publicity attracted to the Bureau by a film first shown in 1949. *Marry Me!*, produced by Betty E. Box, frolicked merrily through the adventures of four couples matched by two elderly spinsters running an eccentric but ethical marriage bureau.

When planning the Marriage Bureau in 1939, neither Heather nor Mary had had much idea of what making introductions would entail, and never imagined that they would be constantly called on for guidance. But the clients had soon disabused them of this fond ignorance: they regarded the matchmakers as founts of wisdom and knowledge on how to assist their courtship. They telephoned and wrote letters, or even turned up in person in search of help. In her book *Marriage Is My Business* Heather cast her mind back to those early days:

> In private life I am a coward. If I am asked to praise a new hat, I will rave about it even if I think it hideous. In my office, securely behind my desk and having heard from Mr. X that he likes Miss Z but thinks that she is overdressed, I will look Miss Z straight in the eye and tell her to wear one less brooch, no flowers, and no eye-veil, if she is going to wear a flowered dress, fur, choker necklace and long earrings. I will also tell Mr. A that none of our clients like him because his manners are gauche, and suggest that he takes off his hat at the proper times and lets the lady through doors first, even holding them open for her rather than letting them swing back in her face. And when Miss A comes in to ask why she has heard no more from Mr. Z, she can't understand it, she liked him so much and it was the same thing with Messrs U, V & W, what can the matter be?—then I have to tell her, because we have had similar reports of her from all the men she met, yes, they liked her, but she chases them up too hard. She frightens them to death.

Some clients were skillfully deflected from unrealistic aspirations. Heather's book again:

Although I never attempt to tell a client what I think would be the right kind of person for him, a little toning down or some good sound commonsense remarks may be necessary sometimes. One young man who had a salary of six hundred a year told me that he wanted to meet a girl who looked and dressed like Betty Grable. As in her last film she had worn little but a raffia skirt, I asked him to be more explicit, and also pointed out that it might be somewhat difficult to look like any film-star on his salary. We had a long talk and I told him I thought that it had better be Betty Grable or nobody for him at the moment, and a few months later he came back and said he'd be happy if he could meet a girl with a good skin and complexion and shapely legs.

And when another young man described his preference for "a very sophisticated, much-travelled, elegantly dressed kind of woman," I had to point out that she might not fit into his life as a clerk in an office in Worthing. He said, "Perhaps you are right," and married a very pleasant, if less spectacular, girl working in a bank in Brighton.

Dorothy too developed her innate knack for dealing with clients' problems and impossible ideals. Looking after her aging parents had kept Dorothy at home, so she had never married, but her heart and soul were in marrying off others. Heather disliked Dorothy's chain-smoking, and worried about her hacking, bronchial cough, but she greatly admired her beautiful manners and her astuteness. Dorothy was cheerful and sympathetic without being sentimental, and if she thought that a client was asking for too much she would tell them so, kindly but insistently.

One day a woman came in who had divorced her husband after he ran off with his secretary. She was full of self-pity and had obviously let herself go, putting on weight, which made her clothes—which needed a good brush—too tight. She had decided that the world was against her and become a thorough misery. Dorothy gave her a good talking-to. Other people's husbands had left them, she admonished, and anyway who would want to marry her, looking as she did now? Before the Bureau would take her on she must pull herself together. The woman took the advice to heart and did just that.

Dorothy was exceptionally conscientious. Calling into the office one day just before going on holiday Heather found her sneezing and wheezing like a grampus. She waved a letter at Heather, looking anguished. "Oh, Miss Jenner, I do hope I'm not going to have flu—and just while you're away too! What shall I do with this letter—it's from a man who's impotent and wants to join?"

"Tell him to come in for an interview. Then you'll find out if he's just trying to shock us. If he really is impotent, maybe he'll suit Miss Burton: she's got hardly a female bone in her body."

"All right," snuffled Dorothy. "And how shall I reply to this woman?" She handed Heather another letter.

Miss Jenner seemed bored when I told her about my holiday in Wales. This disappointed me, as I had an hour to spare before I caught my train, and I came in to the Bureau simply to have a cosy chat, nothing to do with business. Next time I would like to talk to Miss Harbottle.

"I am spared! Thank the Lord!" hooted Heather. "I remember her maundering on and on about Wales—she extolled its virtues as if it were paradise. She even told me how much she loves leeks, and how to cook that insipid veg—you can imagine how that went down with me! You have a cozy chat with her, dear Bottle, and find her an excruciatingly dull Welshman who adores leek soup. So sorry to leave you with impotents and dullards, but I know you'll do beautifully, you always do. So over to you—I'm off! Toodle pip!"

20

Thanks to Uncle George

CUPID'S FRIEND HAS BIRTHDAY headlined the *Evening Standard*, above the information that "The most deliberate client took very nearly the ten years' existence of Marriage Bureau to make up his mind, the quickest decided in two months."

"Not true!" exclaimed Heather. "Far more than one couple took far less than two months. The quickest decided the very first time they met, and one of the speediest sent us a telegram: 'MET AT LUNCH STOP ENGAGED AT DINNER STOP THANK YOU.'"

Heather and Dorothy decided to give a party to celebrate the Bureau's tenth birthday. Since opening day, April 17, 1939, Great Britain had undergone startling changes, beginning with the war. A decade later, the demoralizing shortages of food, housing, money, petrol, jobs and gaiety were diminishing. The NHS was established, self-service stores appeared on the high street, the first West Indians trail-blazed into London. The Kinsey Report exposed the country's buried sex life, the first Motor Show since the war pulled in thousands, and women were entranced by the full-skirted, feminine New Look, a sensational contrast to utility clothing.

In this atmosphere of burgeoning optimism, Heather and Dorothy reveled in planning their party. They conferred at length about the invitation list. They omitted various difficult or unpleasant clients, including the Reverend Hogg, who had done his unchristian best to withhold the After Marriage Fee, and the critical MP, a very early client whom girls had greatly disliked for his arrogance and coldness. They also blacklisted the thrice-engaged Miss Jenkins, who had foolishly ignored Heather's strictures about having affairs and talking about them, and had embarked on a torrid liaison with a well-known married man. Others with a black mark were the Sheikh, from whom they had heard, blessedly, nothing since throwing him out, together with Mrs. Dale-Pratt who, despite being splenetic about the Sheikh, still plagued the Bureau with incessant telephone calls pleading for an introduction.

They invited some clients whom they would dearly have loved to see, but who were too far away. Fred Adams, now married to Nancy, sister of his childhood sweetheart Elsie, whom she closely resembled, was back in Australia. John Parker and his wife, Ada, had left London as soon as the war ended, to set up a cabinetmaking business in Cornwall. Myrtle and Rory seldom crossed the Irish Sea, but sent still-glowing letters telling of Myrtle's skill at singing and dancing, and enclosing snapshots from which it was impossible to judge the color of her hair.

Air letters sent to Mary Oliver in America had not been answered since soon after the end of the war, so Heather did not know what had become of her friend. She posted an invitation to the party, but sadly, no reply came.

As they wrote in and crossed out names on the party list, Heather and Dorothy fell to reminiscing about some of the strange and wonderful clients who had walked up the Bureau's stairs.

"Do you remember that American, quite out of his depth in London, who never met the girl we introduced him to?"

"Oh yes, I didn't meet him, but Picot wrote to me about him when I was in Scotland. Picot wasn't particularly fond of Americans, I really can't imagine why, and she was very scathing, said he was completely humorless, the girl had told him he would recognize her because she would be carrying a penguin. He complained to Picot, said he was baffled, was this some goddamn British custom? Did the girl have a zoo? What did Picot mean, a penguin was a book?"

"Yes," reflected Dorothy, "he did make rather a song and dance of it, and Picot was a bit crisp—but I think she had been very fond of an American actor who didn't reciprocate, that was the problem."

"Ah, that would explain it. I remember some really funny ones: that trapeze artist who needed a woman to be both wife and partner in his act. I told him that if I were to ask a young woman if she would be prepared to wear scanty satin knickers and two stars on her nipples, and swing on a little bar from the top of a circus tent, she would probably walk straight out. Luckily, my reservations filled him with such indignation that *he* walked straight out! And almost immediately a very ordinary-looking suburban girl sidled in and announced that she was set on marrying a gypsy and going a-roaming with the Romanies. She hadn't told her parents, she explained with great seriousness, because she thought they might not like the idea: they wanted her to marry a nice solicitor from Surbiton. I told her the nearest thing to a gypsy we might have had on the books was the trapeze artist, but he hadn't registered. She looked glum and wandered out, so that was two impossible clients in succession!"

Once they got going, Heather and Dorothy spent an hour capping each other's stories. Dorothy described in dramatic detail the young man who flung into the office announcing that he would shoot himself unless the Bureau found him a wife, but who did not stay to find out whether such a lifesaver could be found, turning abruptly to dive back down the stairs.

Heather particularly cherished the memory of a paralytically shy young woman, who had sat in the interview room blushing furiously, twisting her handkerchief, curling her legs under the chair, staring down at the desk, only just managing to stammer, scarcely audibly, that she wanted to meet a quiet, steady young man. Nobody party-loving or flash or noisy. Unhelpfully, in the presence of any male at all Miss Shy was so overcome that she could scarcely utter a word. So she took herself off to be treated by a psychologist, and returned to the Bureau released from all inhibitions and demanding a husband with an exciting, adventurous job. The Bureau accordingly introduced her to a robust and intrepid explorer, who the next day appeared in the office a nervous wreck. Miss Shy-No-More had run him ragged with nonstop scintillating talk, wild dancing, and traipsing from nightclub to nightclub. She had outraged him with suggestions verging on the lewd, and it had taken all Heather's diplomacy to soothe him, assuring him that Miss S-N-M was not typical of the Bureau's female clients.

Heather subjected the bruised explorer to her entire battery of cajolery and persuasion, until he agreed not to broadcast his unhappy experience, and to meet the adventurous but demure young lady she proposed. At last he departed, leaving her exhausted. Some weeks later she read with relief a letter from Miss Shy-No-More canceling her registration since in a nudist camp she had met a Czechoslovakian doctor as uninhibited as she, and was now rapturously, nakedly, married.

"Miss Shy-No-More would certainly make the party go," judged Heather, "but she would be quite capable of turning up in the buff, and very likely with her Czech husband in tow, and equally stark-staring. We shall not invite them."

On the Bureau's tenth birthday the office walls were covered in congratulatory telegrams, and great vases of flowers teetered on every horizontal surface, as crowds of well-wishers crammed the stairs and squeezed into the small rooms where Heather and Dorothy presided benignly.

"Remarkable, quite remarkable!" thundered Colonel Champion as he steered his bride of nine years, the former Miss Easter, toward Heather.

"We are so happy, and eternally grateful to you," echoed Mrs. Champion. "You gave me not only a wonderful husband but also a beloved daughter. She is twenty-four now and quite the career girl, but if she is not married soon I shall send her to you!"

"Our two children are still too young, aren't they, darling?" joined in Angela Paul, smiling up at John Paul, who had chosen her after years of introductions. "And they get on so well, John's daughter and my son, that I sometimes wonder if they might marry each other—it would be entirely legal."

"Our baby is of such a beauty she vill always find men who luff her!" proclaimed Polish Teddy, his aquamarine eyes blazing with uncontainable pride. He was less skeletal than when he had come to the Bureau eight years previously, no longer haunted by the horrors he had suffered, but radiating contentment with his newborn daughter and his heart's delight, Gertrude, recovered from the trauma of Nazi Germany.

Standing regally in the middle of the interview room, whose desks had been evacuated to the furrier's shop downstairs, Heather welcomed clients from the very early days of the Bureau. Commanding monarch of her little kingdom, she accepted a huge bouquet of red roses from Mr. and Mrs. Baldwin—"in memory of that diabolical secretary of yours!" winked Mr. B. She greeted Percival and Florence, who had traveled from Coventry for the occasion, with real pleasure, remembering the complicated journey she had made to the war-ravaged city to advise Percival on furnishings for his new bride. She accepted their earnest invitation to come and see that her designs were still in place. Behind them she spotted Winifred and Gyles, who reduced her to sobs of laughter as they relived their wedding, at which Heather had saved the day by diplomatically taking an elderly drunken guest in hand.

Dorothy held court to the affectionately grateful clients who flocked to her side. "Dorothy regards each and every client as her special charge," Heather later wrote in her book *Marriage Is My Business:*

> and to her, getting people married is a mission in life, and she even spends her days off visiting the couples she has introduced and are now wed. They write to her on their honeymoons, she acts as godmother to their babies, and never tires of listening to their problems. She is, indeed, the clients' confidante and fairy godmother. I am not like Dorothy. I regard my matchmaking as my job and my profession, while to her it is a vocation.

Dorothy was so lacking in inches that she was always lost in a crowd, so was receiving admirers from a tall chair. She was thrilled to talk to Cora and Cyril King, who had married a few months earlier. Skillful treatment was slowly restoring Cyril's scarily scarred face, which Cora could see almost 100 percent clearly with her near-perfect eyes, now filled with tears as she thanked Dorothy for the nth time for bringing them together. Dorothy too was filled with emotion by the incandescent happiness that illuminated the couple, and mentally blessed her own good fortune in having come to work in the Bureau. The bitter loneliness after her mother died had made her able almost to smell the sadness in others; she had sometimes felt drawn to sorrow as a hound to the scent of a fox. There was no dearth of sadness among the clients, and when a successful introduction brought joy, Dorothy too rejoiced.

" 'Ere, come on, chin up!" chuckled a familiar voice. Alf tapped Dorothy on the shoulder. "I thought you was going to turn on the waterworks!"

"Oh, no, dear Alf. It's just that I'm so happy! And I hope you are too?"

Alf had registered with the Bureau in 1939, and though he had had little success in finding a wife, he had adopted Heather, Mary, Picot, Dorothy, and every other interviewer, receptionist, and secretary, calling in frequently to check on "my marriage girls" as he went on his Special-Constable rounds. Alf was always ready with a joke and a practical solution to niggling problems: he mended the swivel chairs when they refused to turn, the filing cabinet drawer that stuck, the unstable coat stand, the faltering electric fire. He was now caretaker in a block of Mayfair flats, where every day he chatted with a spirited cockney, Doris Hudson, who came in to "do" for a wealthy resident.

"I'll bring Doris in to see you one fine day, Miss Harbottle," promised Alf. "We got an understanding, if you know wot I mean. She's a very independent kind of a woman is Doris, but I'm working on 'er an' I'll wear 'er down soon. Now there's a whole lot more people wanting ter talk ter you, so I'll say cheerio!"

Alf made way for Ivy Bailey. After the shattering suicide of her soulmate, Archie, she had clung to the ever-responsive Dorothy, whose maternal heart bled for the stricken girl. They had spent many evenings away from the Bureau, Dorothy listening while artfully easing the pain of Ivy's past by dropping the merest of hints about a future. She discovered that Ivy loved music, took her to some concerts, and surreptitiously inveigled her into joining a local choir. Nudged by Dorothy, Ivy moved from the bleak, decaying house where she knew nobody to a room in a girls' hostel, where she made friends with whom she went to the theater, high up in the cheap seats in the gods. At a tortoise pace Ivy crawled toward stability, until one day she flung her arms around Dorothy.

"Oh Miss Harbottle! Oh! Oh! Such a nice man, a departmental manager in the store, has asked me to go out with him! He wants to take me to an opera—not Covent Garden, I mean, it's an opera he's singing in himself! He's called Harold Winter and I've often noticed him in the store, and talked to him a bit, and thought he was ever so pleasant. Oh, Miss Harbottle, whatever shall I wear?"

Swelling the party numbers were friendly journalists who had followed the Bureau's prodigious progress and were sharpening their pencils for the next installment. Heather's theatrical friend Picot, who had helped to keep the Bureau alive in the worst of the war, visualized the dramatic scene as glamorous Rhoda Clarkson retold the story of how she had come to the Bureau after walking out on her loathsome husband. Picot then had her ear bent by Miss Burton, who had been both indignant and inconsolable when Mr. Headley, whom she had transformed from a rustic ragamuffin into a presentable suitor, had gone off with a woman who shared his interest in petrol pumps. Petrol pumps!

Miss Blunt, the Bureau's ultra-efficient secretary until she was called up, was recognized with pleasure by Mr. Gentle, the matchmakers' splendidly helpful bank manager. Together they toasted the Bureau, he silently congratulating himself on not having been shocked by the eccentricity of the project laid before him a decade previously, when Heather had wandered casually into his bank and emptied out a brown paper bag of takings in front of the incredulous cashier. Another early stalwart, Heather's solicitor chum Humphrey, stood chatting to Miss Plunkett, who had "married out" to an old boyfriend but had remained a great admirer of the Bureau despite the shock of her first introduction to the obnoxious Cedric Thistleton.

Heather and Dorothy often wondered fearfully what had become of Cedric and his decisive bride, the Honourable Grizelda, and to her father, Lord W., and his new wife. They had sailed off to Malaya just as war broke out, and only two years later the Japanese had invaded and ravaged the state. It was highly likely that the quartet had been interned, in damnable conditions. Heather had tried to discover what had befallen them, but their fate remained a mystery. She could no more invite them than she could Martha Webb, who had met Frederick Joss when he returned from Nigeria after the war, had become engaged, moved with him "to Ireland," she said—and disappeared off the face of the earth. Letters sent to her parents' home were returned marked "Not known at this address," and inquiries about Frederick at the Colonial Office, for which he had worked in Nigeria, were politely rebuffed.

So to Dorothy's grief and anxiety, for she had taken the gravely damaged girl to her expansive heart, Martha and Frederick, together with Mr. and the Honourable Mrs. Thistleton, and Lord and Lady W., were consigned to the Bureau's "Mystery" file. In it lay also Picot's account of her dealings with the police about the murdered man who had the Bureau's name and address in his pocket. The weary policeman had sweated up the stairs to question Picot a second time, but since no inquirer of the Bureau seemed to fit the case, and nobody had reported such a person as missing, the victim's identity remained tantalizingly shrouded, and the verdict had been "unlawful killing by person or persons unknown."

Out of the corner of her eye Heather glimpsed a mountainous silver fox fur slinking its way toward her through the throng. Cocooned inside was the Lady Chairman of the baby show Heather and Mary Oliver had judged ten years previously.

"Did you not invite my dear friend Etheldreda?" inquired the

Lady Chairman in ringing tones, as if giving a speech to a deaf audience in a packed hall.

"But of course," purred Heather. "But I believe she and the Brigadier had a previous engagement, so regrettably they cannot give us the pleasure of their company."

Heather smiled to herself as she told this glib lie. She had indeed invited the former Mrs. de Pomfret and her Brigadier but, though very happy with her fourth husband, Etheldreda could not bring herself to accept the manner in which she had met him. Introductions through a marriage bureau, like interviews, she considered fit only for servants. Heather doubted that the Brigadier would share this view and suspected that, although he believed himself in command, his formidable wife had kept the invitation card out of his sight.

As the last guests were leaving, and Alf was preparing to restore the furniture to the office, a boisterous "Hiya, honey!" resounded up the stairs.

"Hank!" shouted Heather, clapping her hands and rushing to hug the tall American striding through the door.

"Hank the Yank!" echoed Dorothy, immediately remembering the favorite client whom Heather had married off during the war, and who had always kept in touch. "You're the man who gave Heather that piece of a German plane!"

"That's right, ma'am," acknowledged Hank.

"It was me wot 'ung it outside the window," interpolated Alf. "I fixed it good an' strong, but it rusted a bit, an' every now an' again I seed it was a bit smaller. An' one day I seed it wasn't there no more, so I reckon that like them Nazis it just give up. I should—"

Alf was interrupted by an eerily sepulchral sound that seemed to be echoing up the stairs, growing gradually louder.

"Twit, twoo! Twit, twoo!"

Heather's face lit up. "It's Miss Owl! Wonders never cease!"

The office door was pushed open to reveal a pretty, laughing young woman who rushed into Heather's welcoming arms. Operator Wireless and Line Margaret Fox, trained in the war to send and receive Morse Code and to operate wireless sets, field telephones and switchboards, had become a Bureau favorite. She had been plucked out of the Women's Land Army, where her technical ability was wasted, and blossomed into a highly skilled OWL, working such long hours that she had no time to find a husband. So immediately after the war she had registered with the Bureau, and in 1947 had married Patrick Badger, provoking innumerable jokes about animals scenting one another.

Patrick, a lawyer, worked in Germany on the grisly job of trying Nazi war criminals, and Heather had heard very little since their honeymoon, graphically described by Margaret. In the Dolomites, just north of Lake Como, her new husband had woken her every day at 4 A.M. to don her shorts and Land Girl shoes (all she had) and climb a mountain. They took salami, some hard gray bread and a bottle of strong red wine, and had to reach the top by midday in order to get back down before all-obliterating darkness fell. With luck, they returned to their primitive hut,

more bread and sausage, and a more or less sleepful night huddled on the unyielding wooden slats of their bunk beds.

Margaret dined out on her Horror Honeymoon, gaily blam-
ing it all on Heather. Now she was back in England, waiting for
Patrick to join her. The couple had been invited to the party but
the invitation had not reached them, so she had simply taken a
chance on turning up at the Bureau.

"What a coincidence!" Heather rejoiced. "You couldn't have
picked a better moment!"

"Lucky for me," rejoined Margaret. "Another lucky day, like
the one when I came here in 1945, and was introduced to Patrick. You really did start something, Heather, all those years ago.
You've made so many people wonderfully happy!"

"Hear, hear!" said Hank, "I'm another lucky one."

"And so am I!" came a small but firm voice.

Heather, Hank, Alf and Margaret all turned to look at Dorothy, who returned their gaze as she went on, "It's the staff too. I
don't know what on earth would have become of me if I hadn't
had the luck to find the Bureau. It saved my life, and I love it."

Heather's customary coolness was vanishing. She raised her
glass, her voice faltering slightly as she addressed her small audience: "The Bureau was not my idea. It came from Mary Oliver,
my first partner, who was given it by her Uncle George. I've never
met Uncle George, but we are all indebted to him. So on this
auspicious occasion I give you a toast: Uncle George, thank you!"

"*Uncle George!*"

ACKNOWLEDGMENTS

Heather Jenner always wanted to write: "in my teens, rather as some people become compulsive drinkers, I became a compulsive writer. First I wrote short stories that nobody wanted, and then a novel that nobody wanted either. The literary agent I sent the novel to did say in a polite note that, although he had been unable to place it, the dialogue was good and I should keep on trying. I didn't keep on trying because I started the Marriage Bureau."

Fortunately, Heather's compulsion was not quenched: her reminiscences and views became the basis of her first book, *Marriage Is My Business* (1953), and of her decades-long flow of articles. I am hugely indebted to Heather's daughter, Stella Sykes, for preserving her mother's copious archive, and for stories galore, and contacts, especially with Heather's goddaughter, Sarah Hamilton.

Heather's later books, *Men and Marriage* and *Marriages Are Made on Earth*, were invaluable, as was the vivid 1942 account of the Bureau's first two years in *Marriage Bureau*, by Mary Oliver and Mary Benedetta. The latter's *A Girl in Print: Experiences as a Journalist* (1937) was also informative. Further contemporary detail came from my inspiring aunt, Jean Reddaway, and equally redoubtable Patricia Dean, together with archives, principally Westminster's *West End at War*, the BBC's *WW2 People's War*, the *American War Brides Experience*, the *Lady*'s incomparable store, Companies House, the British Newspaper Archive, and the letters, diaries, and photographs of friends and relations. Visual sources included films, particularly *Perfect Strangers, Marry Me!* (thanks to Steve Tollervey of the British Film Institute), and footage of the Bureau made by British Pathé.

Key to the existence of this book are Jane Bidder and Beverly Davies, organizers of the Freelance Media Group, where I heard Tara Cook speak. I am most grateful, since Tara's enthusiasm for the story of the Marriage Bureau set in train the events that, aided and abetted by Katie James (Heather's stepgranddaughter, publicist at Pan Macmillan, and friend), resulted in the book which I have long wanted to write. The idea was born years ago in conjunction with Anne Moir, who with other friends informed, questioned, advised, and heartened: my thanks to Peter Ellis, Thomas Gibson, Denise Goss, Xandria Horton, Prue Keely Davies, Pat Morgan, Linda Newbigging, John Parsons, Joy Parsons, Andrew Roberts, Ed Rubin, Howard Slatter, Gillian Spickernell, Kathy Stimson and Maureen Watson. Lynette Ellis patiently researched obscure American newspapers; Anna Raeburn brought vivacity through her reading. Throughout, Bill has encouraged, strengthened, and mastered the technology: a human rock, backed up by the indispensable Lorraine Laguerre.

Professional confidence and competence completed the picture: advice from the Society of Authors, positive action from my agent, Clare Alexander, and terrific input from my publisher, George Morley who, with editing from Graham Coster and Laura Carr, has shaped the book. For her enthusiasm and skill in realizing this American edition, I am gratefully indebted to Lucia Macro.

A comprehensive *thank you* to one and all.

PICTURE ACKNOWLEDGMENTS

All photographs are courtesy of the author, with the exception of the following:

Page 1 top courtesy of the estate of Daphne Wace

Page 1 bottom, page 3 top and bottom, page 6 bottom footage supplied by British Pathé

Page 6 top, page 7 top, page 8 and page 16 bottom courtesy of Stella Sykes

Page 12 top and page 15 bottom © Daniel Farson/Picture Post/ Getty Images

Page 15 top © Daniel Farson/Stringer

About the author

About the book

Insights,
Interviews
& More . . .

Meet Penrose Halson

WHEN PENROSE was twenty-five and still unmarried, her mother sent her to the Katharine Allen Marriage & Advice Bureau. Twenty years later, after a career in teaching, writing and editing, she and her management consultant husband Bill bought the Bureau. They also acquired The Marriage Bureau, which had been set up in 1939 by two twenty-four-year-olds. As Bill had predicted, matchmaking suited Penrose down to the ground, and they remain happily in touch with many former clients who visit them in London. ❧

www.penrosehalson.com

Requirements of Female Clients
1939–circa 1949

- A real pal and friend, who is willing to share the good and evil of life with equal cheerfulness.
- Australian, New Zealander or Canadian with job abroad or in country (not Australia). Not too serious as I am shallow emotionally.
- Broad-minded. Should drink, smoke and be capable of swearing.
- Serviceman, but must have a commission.
- Dark, not very good-looking. <u>Large</u> poultry farmer, accountant, civil engineer, solicitor or other good profession.
- Someone interested in doing good in the world. Connected with church, schools, children etc.
- Nobody who wants me to help him in his business.
- Someone who loves children and would be a good father to my baby. I took the name of my baby's father by D.P. [Deed Poll] I will provide for my baby's education etc. Her father allows me £2 per week at present.
- A bon viveur who likes his coffee and liqueur, give me a man, a connoisseur, then he should be alright. NICE HANDS rather important.
- Dutch or Dutch interests or partly Dutch.
- A homely man with just a theatre or cinema now and again.
- Clean living, fastidious but not faddy. Not a schoolmaster, clerk or parson.
- Must not be deaf.
- Someone interlectual [*sic*].
- Sensible but not stodgy. Not living in or near Southport.
- Must be a gent, never let you down.
- With creative talent, who understands something of art; a well-stocked mind and charming personality rather than just good looks.
- No working man or shopkeeper.
- Only tender-hearted.
- Full understanding of world problems.
- An idealist. Someone with vision. I have £1,000 capital and will inherit a third of my father-in-law's business at his death. *(She aged 34.)* ▶

Requirements of Female Clients 1939–circa 1949 *(continued)*

- I don't mind how ugly.
- Not working class. Not one who works with his hands, as I like well-kept hands because I have been a film artist.
- Must be a gentleman by birth, preferably a clergyman (if broad-minded) or at any rate a believing Christian, not too worldly.
- Introductions in Johannesburg or as near as possible.
- Straight and honourable.
- If in politics, must be "progressive." An unsociable man slightly preferred.
- If age is nearly forty, his figure must be well preserved and independent.
- Fresh and good to look at.
- A gentleman of respectability as I am very lonely.
- Not too portly, not helpless, not a recluse.
- Gently bred.
- Educated. Good looking. Self-assured. Mechanically minded. Handy around the house. Must have wavy hair.
- Engineers preferred but any really well-educated man except actors or theologists.
- Interested in travel and post-war reconstruction.
- Don't mind where I settle, preferably British Empire. I don't want a "good time" but I do want a really nice home and to be able to give any children I might have every possible chance in life.
- Wanting a companionable wife rather than a super-domesticated one. Able to appreciate the artistic temperament and an original turn of mind.
- Not a Communist or Socialist.
- Someone who has known loneliness.
- In the Army or RAF from overseas. I would be content with usual allowance during war.
- Above all, a man who will talk to me.
- He must have enough income to make a settlement of about £400, and be able to keep me in comfort and perhaps travel after the war.
- I am secretary to a Duke. Any man must be of my own standing.
- Someone with a title who has travelled and likes sport.
- No racial hatred.

- One who has or would adopt a child. I will inherit £400–£600 per annum in a few years.
- Refinement essential. My late husband was secretary (F.I.S.A.) of a public company.
- Would like to meet just an ordinary man.
- A Roman Catholic or willing to become Roman Catholic.
- No-one with false teeth.
- If a civil servant, must not have an official mind. Minimum wage £6 per week.
- No dropped "H"s, please.
- If possible I would like a man in a reserved trade. If not, I do not mind a sailor or a Canadian soldier.
- Who looks on marriage as a serious partnership.
- Brainy. Nice teeth. Interested in housely hobbies more than dances etc. Civilian preferred.
- Someone who wants looking after, either in England or abroad.
- Man of character. I do not mind if he is a war wreck.
- Not the rough common type.
- I have an open mind. Would like to meet different types of professional men: artisans, missionaries, tea planters, business-men etc.
- If in Forces, not Bomber Command.
- Ambitious man (medical or missionary).
- Not amorous.
- Preferably heavy, 15 stone or over. *(She only 5 feet 5 inches.)*
- Not the boisterous type.
- One who believes marriage is not all give.
- A divorced man if it was not his fault.
- A nice type of person, a Freemason or golf enthusiast.
- If Englishman must not be prejudiced against Irish.
- Not bald. Must have savoir faire, not mind girl who smokes, likes a drink and wants a motorcycle.
- I am an ex-WAAF. If possible, a man interested in cars and car mechanism.
- Who speaks the King's English.
- Someone born in February or May. ▶

Requirements of Female Clients 1939–circa 1949 *(continued)*

- A man whose early life was not too easy, but who has overcome such difficulties. Not a mother's boy or anyone with artistic temperament.
- Someone who is wounded and alone would do, or someone over 60. *(She is 48.)*
- With knowledge of building repair, fruit growing and poultry.
- Someone willing to marry an unmarried mother.
- If a widower, definitely no children though I do not dislike children.
- I do not like anyone called Longstaff.
- No trace of neurotic trouble.
- Not an ardent member of any political party.
- Prefer with a Welsh background, lawyer or in a clerical position providing he has a sound religious basis, with knowledge of Welsh life and a country house.
- Not too corpulent. Well mannered, not conceited. Bonhomie essential.
- Someone who will be a pal in every sense of the word.
- I would not object to a disabled man.
- Dominant but not dominating.
- Must have sense of humour but I hate "life and soul of the party" types. Must have good skin. He must not marry just to get a housekeeper.
- Man who will cherish a large woman.
- A publican in a small business or a working man who would be interested in the business of a publican.
- Just a friendly sort of person.
- Not a gambler (to a great degree).
- Not a Red or Labour. Believe in God and go to church sometimes.
- Any professional and well-educated man whose interests are connected with the Colonies—Africa, the East, West Indies, not Australia.
- Personal cleanliness important.
- No encumbrances, fine character, no doctors.
- Not too sophisticated but not too dumb. Fond of country but also fond of comfort.
- Good prospects after the war.

- Someone in Sussex who is not too keen on dancing as I am not very keen.
- Man in a safe position—schoolmaster, bank clerk, police officer, accountant or medical profession.
- Gent or behaving like one.
- Alone in the world or with not many relations.
- Someone in the Services, say Navy, without home or roots, who will be retiring in a few years and appreciative of a comfortable home and easy to live with partner. *(She is 44.)*
- My husband was killed serving as captain in the Royal Artillery in North Africa. Would like another.
- Not hearty, perhaps absent-minded, fond of fishing or quiet pastimes.
- Patient, not more selfish than most men.
- I am rather shy so not anyone too gay or too energetic. Preferably good looks, golden hair and blue eyes. If not available, any decent type will do.
- One who would appreciate a nice comfortable home, which I possess, and have refinement.
- Progressive, socialistic in outlook.
- A Naval Officer, Clergyman (C. of E.), Doctor, Barrister or a (Westminster) Bank man or Schoolmaster who is fond of the sea.
- Not above 65. *(She is 24.)*
- Must be a Socialist and supporter of present Labour government.
- Man who was disabled through war injuries and needs some care and help.
- I divorced my husband who was a teacher. Not another teacher.
- Who will have an established position in peacetime.
- Anything but Chapel.
- Since my husband's death I have had P.G.s [Paying Guests] and would be willing to continue and glad of help on the business side.
- Similar to Church of England. If you had a Catholic Apostolic Church member we should have I think much in common. Preferably not R.C.
- Tolerant outlook toward other people and their affairs, keen on his work, more than two weeks' leave annually, know his way about town, in peacetime run a car. ▶

Requirements of Female Clients 1939–circa 1949 *(continued)*

- I like a man who is somebody, works hard and doesn't lead a monotonous life.
- Do not mind divorced but the widowers I have met have an ideal it is difficult to come up to.
- Don't mind anyone slightly solitary. Cannot bear "good mixers."
- Interested in ballet or opera or both but not the Bloomsbury type that haunts both. Not a clergyman or Conscientious Objector.
- No man who has been in India for long.
- Able to manage income tax papers etc. but not too clever.
- A sportsman and not unfamiliar with trouble.
- Not a Welshman or anyone with a Northern Accent except Scottish.
- Not a marriage in the ordinary sense, but purely for social reasons & to ward off well-meaning matchmakers.
- A gentleman by birth or has acquired these instincts.
- Character more than looks, a Sahib.
- Physical attraction in some small degree.
- Widower, a man you can lean on.
- A normal human being who believes in the Golden Rule no matter what his religion may be.
- Averse to intoxicants, moral.
- I am not a very strict Catholic but I would prefer a Catholic, otherwise I'm usually very easy to please.
- No bridge, pub crawling, golf, passion for The Club, or Americans.
- A car if possible because I can help him pay for it. If in business it doesn't matter.
- Preference for a member of the Metropolitan Police force, if you have one with similar ideas (interest in literature, philosophy & psychology).
- Not resident in Kensington as I know so many people there.
- I like a quiet man, especially a sailor. Providing he has enough for the necessities of life with a little over for a few luxuries I should be satisfied.
- Preferably an admirer of routine and orderliness.
- Not too gay as I am quiet.
- Man who desires children and can hope to employ domestic help.
- Religion immaterial, but a sense of honour or duty required.

- Above all clean & wholesome in appearance, fairly fastidious but not fussy.
- Someone interested in progressive farming and who would allow me to remain at business because of supporting my mother who is all I have.
- Someone untidy, careless, with sense of humour, keen on moving around.
- Up to date in all ways.
- My boy was killed during the war. If I can find through you someone like or as near as possible to what he was I should be very grateful.
- Pref. one who can darn his own socks.
- Must not expect me to sit in a pub. I drink but not like the English. *(She is half French.)*
- Without too great an interest in money and without a talent for accuracy. People of Irish blood are always acceptable.
- Not anyone who thinks that quiet shades of brown & grey are worn by respectable women as I love colour.
- Someone liking a "good time" & the artificial things of life.
- With cheer, courage and tact. ∾

Requirements of Male Clients 1939–circa 1949

- Prepared to accept my sons and treat them kindly.
- Someone who could stand loneliness and be able to make her own pleasures. *(Colonial servant, Nigeria.)*
- Must be pretty or attractive facially and the only essential qualification: must have only one leg.
- No clinging vines.
- Looks and voice of a Shakespearean heroine.
- Not a nurse or woman doctor. Not vulgar.
- I would like to meet with a wealthy ambitious lady, who apreciates [*sic*] my attainments and will help me to the top. A titled lady or American. *(Consulting physician, age 45.)*
- Beautiful girl with a big breast and lovely legs. Not had any men friends, not been married before.
- Prefer a widow without relations.
- Some nice girl who would be willing to come over and marry me. *(New Yorker, 5 feet 2 inches.)*
- Would like a wife to go to Australia by liner and meet me there. *(Captain, Merchant Navy.)*
- Attractive and chaste.
- Tall with excellent legs & feet & attractive bust. Colouring immaterial but must be feminine & virile.
- Perhaps one like myself who has lived in digs.
- Willing if passage is paid to join me here for the purpose of matrimony, and to make S. Rhodesia her permanent home.
- Not a large nose nor flat chest or too talkative.
- Must be prepared to spend considerable time in British Colonies, probably Gambia, which is the favourite colony in Brit. West Africa.
- She must have a good income as I would wish her to be attractively dressed.
- I would consider it my duty to support the person I married but should she wish to continue earning her own living and was happy in her job I would not interfere in this or any other matter.
- Someone who has not a large number of relations.

- Not a "fast type."
- Waitress, usherette, factory worker—nice looking. Someone who has helped old age pensioners or the sick.
- In these days of lack of help for domestic purposes an introduction is desired to some person who is very active both in the house and outside & fond of outdoor pursuits. I have no house and no desire to remain in Birmingham. *(Solicitor, 62, wants woman, 35–40.)*
- A nice stylish girl, not too brainy, with the appearance of a West End mannequin. No objection to a rich widow. Someone who likes living and is human.
- Greer Garson type as opposed to Ginger Rogers type.
- Must not chew gum.
- Just so long as not too common I would prefer a girl in domestic service although this isn't important.
- Income not critical providing it is not high enough to overshadow mine.
- A good churchwoman preferably with a home of her own within 100 miles of Charing Cross. *(Retired clergyman.)*
- A slim figure—by slim I mean not fat.
- She must be a plain working-class girl.
- Good cook and homely (I am only home on Sunday).
- Keen on golf would be a great asset. No one of higher social standing. *(Clerk earning £450 p.a.)*
- Prefer spinster without encumbrances. *(i.e. without children, dependent parents etc.)*
- A nice quiet girl who likes music and doesn't dance a lot as I can't dance.
- I am serving another three years, then hope to retire into business. I had in mind marrying someone who is in business or with a little capital with similar ideas. I have registered with a licensed house in the West Country. *(Army officer.)*
- Respectable person.
- Dancing partner only (divorce not started yet).
- One who wants to be a schoolmaster's wife and can act the part.
- Young playmate would be pleasant.
- Necessary wife have some private income as my income from dairy farm is settled on daughter and stepson.
- No dancing or jazz or racing or cards. Not T.T. [teetotal], prefer single but consider widow or plaintiff. ▶

Requirements of Male Clients 1939–circa 1949 *(continued)*

- Preferably English, stage or model, and who realizes I am in the Navy until 1954.
- No hysteria, no gold diggers; like mountaineering.
- Non-smoker, little make-up, tidy appearance, prefer non-driver.
- Who plays tennis as a game.
- Constance Spry touch with flowers.
- Able to play a portable instrument (string or woodwind) well. Rather a prairie than a hothouse flower.
- Reserved rather than forward disposition. Not too expensive tastes.
- Domesticated. Have had bad experiences with gold diggers, am very credulous.
- Neither working class nor hard-boiled night clubber. Who would like me and marry me for myself not for my income.
- Someone not dependent on externals for happiness.
- Keen on public affairs e.g. local government, housing. Not sophisticated or "county" or merely dull.
- Must be interested in sex.
- Keenly interested in land work as I am endeavouring to start a small farm.
- Not a film actress.
- My reasons for wishing a wife are to get a home of my own. I am in lodgings at the moment.
- Someone willing to have children, a theatrical girl if possible. I would not mind an unmarried mother.
- Christian real faith but not R.C., not American.
- Must be domesticated and full of exuberance.
- Fond of home life—Army life has made me appreciate such.
- I require primarily a mother for my children & therefore a genuine fondness and sympathy with the young is essential. No one used to or wishing for the gaieties of town life.
- I don't like them made up to hell.
- Preferably working on her own account, who would like to continue after marriage as I think this makes for better relationship than when one of the partners is confined to the home with no career.
- Bright, good sport, will take the bad with the good. Above all, faithful.

- A girl who knows her way about as after four years in the East I feel out of things.
- Not lazy or bored, near to Epsom if possible.
- Being illegitimate I would like to meet someone who is the same.
- Charm, sound sense of the absurd. I emphatically have no money. *(Economist, 28, earning £1,000 p.a. c.1943.)*
- Someone of my own class, the working class, who would be content with the simple things of life and who cares for children.
- Someone who doesn't expect too much.
- A dainty girl. I do not mind if she has earned her own living.
- Not a glamour girl, just someone to help an ex POW settle down to a quiet life. *(Carpenter age 26.)*
- I like Germans, Austrians and French.
- Wide interests, not bounded by local cinema and dance hall.
- I am a slight diabetic, a nurse might be suitable, a good companion who will be kind and considerate and look after me. Prefer someone in the North. *(He died shortly after, aged 54.)*
- Genuine, sincere type of girl, willing to wait until I return from overseas. This will not be for two years. On this account we can only become acquainted through correspondence. *(Regular in RAF, 1949.)*
- Not ultra–New Look type, or widow or divorcee.
- I should prefer a Jewish girl but if no-one suitable any other will do.
- Average-plumpish preferred. One who speaks the "Mother" tongue.
- Cool temperament, radiant disposition.
- Pref. not in services, but if so, pref. Land Army. With science degree if possible.
- South Welsh (not North Welsh, not avowed intellectual or frequenter of art schools and communist parties).
- Not particularly prudish.
- Better to be fond of music, there will be much made here. *(Music master.)*
- NOT bossy, impatient or Socialist, NO bridge players. I hate "rows" and sarcasm.
- Genuine lady prepared to take her place as mistress of fairly large country house.
- In a position to put me in touch with suitable employment. ▶

Requirements of Male Clients 1939–circa 1949 *(continued)*

- Must have sex appeal.
- Sound girl with capital and ability—I want a farm.
- Passionate and loving nature.
- No objection to blood test or medical exam—also applies to myself.
- Go to church now and again.
- No children but if really very nice, a child overlooked.
- Her income not important, the larger the better.
- Good teeth essential.
- Not masculine, dominating or slovenly.
- Knowledge of King's English.
- Nobody who has been left on the shelf.
- Any reasonable young woman.
- Person who has lost her husband would be suitable.
- I am hoping to have a commission in future, would like someone who can conduct herself with reasonable assurance with other officers' wives.
- Someone who, like myself, comes from the East End of London, who is "down to earth" and has no "airs or graces."
- Woman capable of bossing and showing authority.
- Similar family background (my grandparents doctor and parson), not too athletic or mannish.
- She <u>must</u> have a little girl (about six). No spinsters.
- I have suffered serious losses and would like someone with private means.
- Willing to go in for poultry farming on smallholding.
- Not Christian Scientist.
- Divorcee if innocent party.
- Child no bar but cannot be educated in Curaçao.
- Someone with furniture would be an advantage.
- She must live on gravel. *(He has arthritis, wears surgical collar.)*
- May wear glasses or be lame rather than the butterfly type.
- A kind hearter, not too modern.
- Not too old, not too fat.
- Agreeable to my continuing to fly after the war.
- Well educated and suitable to be hostess at political gatherings etc. *(He is an MP.)*

- Her belief in the Christian God must be the predominant feature in her life. Willing to help me along the road to recovery.
- Must be willing to finance building or buying of modest home in or near Glasgow.
- Not frightened of becoming a mother.
- Proud of her figure and legs and likes wearing high-heeled shoes.
- Not thick ankles or short podgy fingers.
- Blonde (not essential [*sic*]), no prejudice against debutantes.
- A working-class girl of refinement.
- Servant or nanny type.
- Matter-of-fact, not slushy or sentimental. Names disliked: Gertrude, Emily, Lucy, Eleanor. Names liked: Mary, Elizabeth, Anne, Jean, Jane, Sheila.
- Not German, Australian, South African, Japanese or Italian but otherwise any nationality.
- Intelligent but uninformed in national affairs, must have beautiful hands.
- Congenial companion, would be an asset to promotion. Income not essential but would help to increase wife's comfort.
- Fairly sentimental and if possible a brunette.
- Natural, willing to pose occasionally. Can be invited to a Public Dance. *(Artist.)*
- No objection to painted finger nails, scent or a dowry.
- Not an only child unless an orphan.
- Ordinary working-class lady, fairly tall, slim with fair or light brown hair. Nothing else matters.
- Ready to make a home for my father as well.
- Dark, not bossy or Irish.
- Able to drive Talbot car.
- She must have something out of the ordinary—money or a title.
- Prefer her to be of the "Business Girl" type, one who is unassuming, moderate in habits, and to whom the hectic life favoured by so many does not appeal.
- If possible, not liable for war service.
- Must be good cook, able to make jam, dress poultry and rabbits. Must reside Yorkshire. ▶

Requirements of Male Clients 1939–circa 1949 *(continued)*

- I should prefer a War Widow.
- Right disposition and character, affectionate nature, not only to men but to the world at large, cripples, animals, etc.
- Younger the better. Modern to a limit.
- Able to run six- or seven-roomed house, good plain cook.
- A home-loving girl who does not want to go out every evening but would enjoy a theatre trip and picture show weekly.
- Must not frequent public houses.
- No freckles.
- Neat breasts. Up to £400 p.a. Of gentlefolk.
- Peace and happiness main things.
- No permed hair.
- Able to take things on the chin in rough times.
- Able to stand my hours of railway duties.
- Ability to type and take shorthand an advantage and willingness to learn a language—Esperanto.
- Able to entertain and impress people.
- Suitable to be a Headmaster's wife.
- No objection to glasses as I wear them myself.
- With sufficient character to stand up to the vicissitudes of the RAF & acceptable in an officers' mess.
- Medium slim with good bust. Honesty and beauty combined.
- Refined and well educated, of what is called the "upper middle class." *(1950.)*
- No sulking. Living near Wembley or Pinner.
- Girl without parents or who has been in trouble not objected to, provided she is sincere about this.
- Marilyn Monroe with homely ways.
- Gentle birth, flair for dress, no illusions about life in wide open spaces.
- Not Irish, Scotch or a civil servant.
- Not snobbish as I do not believe in class distinction too much. With job of some sort. Of middle-class family.
- British or French. Some intellectual interests and no aversion to a prospect of a life of perpetual poverty. *(Lecturer, £500 p.a., 1948.)*
- I don't mind a little make-up but not a painted doll.
- Someone I can fall in love with. I am very lonely.

- Able to keep and look after a working man.
- Someone with a loving and understanding nature, fond of children, who trusts and believes in human nature and the fundamental goodness of life. In other words someone with a Hedonist outlook tempered with a Christian philosophy and who is well disposed toward her fellow creatures.
- Her parents must be happily married.
- Dolicocephalic [having a relatively long skull, typically with the breadth less than 75 or 80 percent of the length] small nose tip-tilted or straight, small teeth. Qualities in order of importance: figure and nose; femininity and brain. Vivien Leigh, Jessica Tandy for figure and nose, Rebecca West for femininity and brain.
- I like a person with a pleasing personality, kind (I am very kind myself), not jealous.
- A wealthy lady preferred.
- Someone I can trust.
- Preferably officer in ATS, WRNS or WAAFS.
- Warmly affectionate and desiring full reciprocation and understanding to the extent of idolisation.
- I am desirous of settling down with a hope of a child or children. Waste to introduce me to elderly ladies. *(Schoolmaster, aged 52, wants woman, 20–30.)*
- Pref. Italian. I spent the greater part of the war in Italy and have become very fond of the country and its people.
- Evident good birth and family (fewer the better). Disciplined upbringing.
- If she is respectable and healthy I am not particular.
- An equal who can share thoughts, problems, pleasures and difficulties.
- Must be able to live in a hot climate. *(Zanzibar.)*
- Not frigid.
- Nobody called Florence.
- Not a member of the Society of Friends or Peace Pledge Union.
- God-loving, placid, possessive but not unreasonably jealous; fond of curry and other rich or savoury food, able and willing to bear and rear at least two children. ▶

Requirements of Male Clients 1939–circa 1949 *(continued)*

- She must be prepared for possible moves from one part of the Empire to another during marriage.
- Preference for blue eyes.
- A fair type with some philosophical bias.
- My wife will have to spend a large part of her life in Africa and must be perpared [*sic*] to mix with Africans of all classes.
- Providing she has a good heart and is sincere I don't care if she comes from the slums of London, New York or Bombay.
- Must be able to produce a doctor's cetificate [*sic*] of good health and preferably have been to a finishing school.
- Capable of driving or learning to drive a car, no Communist connection (I work on official secrets), well read (not a black and white personality), not too witty, able to increase one's morale.
- I do not like Lady Teachers or Nurses either in active service or retired.
- She will be required to live in East Africa, but in one of the best climates in the world. Not too brainy, but intelligent, who does not mind a fairly lonely life with all modern conveniences but who can enjoy dancing etc. when available.
- Independent means or dowry.
- Not a "yes" woman.
- Somebody who would like my baby so I can give him a good home he is 5 months old. *(Father, 31.)*
- Essentially out of top drawer, sound in wind & limb, fairly easy on the eye, willing to produce a family of non-Catholics.
- Interested in outside things but not necessarily a gadabout.
- I most admire wit and a generous outlook toward others.
- If the person is a widow, no male children, and if there is a girl she must be at least 8 years old.
- Not a member of the Forces.
- Widow of pharmacist particularly suitable.
- Lady interested in a business e.g. poultry farming.
- Best summed up in Lancashire expression [*sic*] as "Januk."
- Must be non-smoker, non-drinker and non-dancer, also must not use cosmetics. *(He 32, an "amusement worker" in a seaside resort.)*
- Above all, a real pal with a beautiful soul.
- I would like to meet someone with a few hundred pounds likely to become interested in farming.

- A girl who is serving with HM Forces or engaged in War Work (eg Land Army, Munitions).
- I do like to feel that other people (men) look enviously.
- Unselfish yet not saintly.
- Unoccupied daughter of well-to-do parents.
- A clean appearance.
- Able to save money.
- An asset if she can drive.
- Should be able to cook and mend.
- Voice is most important physical factor—standard Southern English with trace of Scots or Irish preferable.
- Attitude toward physical relationship in marriage natural as well as idealistic.
- Able to fit into naval society which is somewhat "public school."
- Orphan preferred.
- Attractive and chaste.
- Prefer emigrant or D.P. [Displaced Person] or orphan. Need have very little education but be kind and gentle.
- Small feet and ankles.
- Lady who is sophisticated and matured. Perhaps someone who has been married before and able to understand the difficulties of married life when one was younger and whose past experience would be beneficial at the present.
- The lady should have some interest in other people's welfare but may be quite unorthodox in religion or politics.
- Either a sophisticated bohemian sort preferably with some secretarial experience in literary work, or else a country girl, good at baking.
- Someone who can be an equal and share thoughts, problems, pleasures and difficulties, if any. No nurses. *(He cancelled registration, decided not to marry after all.)*
- Sufficiently educated to make a fair success of a Times crossword puzzle.
- I am not particular if she is respectable and healthy.
- Young lady possessing considerable capital or property, willing to assist re-establish pre-war business (Furniture Manufacture). ∽

Interviewers' Comments
1939–circa 1949

MEN
- Very Irish and definitely Working Class.
- Talk a donkey's hind legs off.
- Nice smile, like Laurence Olivier.
- Fine big man, well turned out, might have touch of tar brush.
- *Gentish*, rather big red nose, beard but sweet.
- Rather an old woman. Thick glasses.
- Absolute poppet, lovely country voice.
- Not bad-looking but no Adonis.
- Not a gent. Common, noisy.
- Scar on face.
- Nice little man, v. sensitive about being bald.
- Gent. Lovely hands.
- A gent but very superior.
- Like John Mills.
- Terrible head of hair.
- POW, lost a leg.
- Dear old boy, looks so clean.
- Gent, mad, amiable rotter, beard.
- Looks older than he says, awful voice, very rich.
- Nice manners but deaf and a few teeth missing. BTS. *(Better Than Some.)*
- Stupid and slow.
- Always mention crippled leg on intro.
- Common little man. Has paralysed hand.
- Full of his own importance.
- Slightly lame owing to war wound. Sounds better on phone than on paper.
- In a hurry. Returning Nigeria 10 July.
- Nr Gent. Lost an eye.
- Belgian. Awful.
- *Gentish*, quite mad, out for money.
- Working class. Very quiet. Seems a bit dotty.

- Lost an eye and arm.
- Dull. Likes young girls.
- Gent. Charming but impotent. *(Age 33.)*
- Very nice honest-to-goodness superior working class.
- Not a gent, v. nice, has artificial leg.
- Not a gent (thinks he is), quite nice. Be careful.
- Dear little man. Working class, v. blue eyes. Saved up to come here.
- Very difficult and fussy, well dressed, Hitler moustache.
- Terrible. Mad stare. Looks like hell.
- Scarecrow, spectre, long thin face and body, glasses. But pleasant.
- Very hirsute.
- Sheer hell. Quite batty. Goggling eyes. Smells.
- Very nice man, diabetic.
- Typically business man. No fool.
- Sticking-out ears. <u>So</u> dull. Verbose.
- Shy, untidy hair, boffin type, nice boy, ambitious.
- White eyelashes.
- Has lost both hands but can do everything for himself.
- Nice hearing aid but v. deaf.
- Bestially stupid, didactic, drums fingers on desk, quite good-looking, v. lower middle class.
- Nice, Gent (not *Debrett*), inoffensive-looking, well dressed.
- Cheque bounced.
- Scruffy, smells, full of self-pity. <u>Might</u> be made into something.
- Died. *(Aged 32, been registered two months.)*
- Nice-looking. Speaks English well. *(Polish man.)*

WOMEN
- Rather superior but thaws out in time.
- Usual old body. *(Woman, age 41.)*
- Mother is pure suburban.
- Dainty, well dressed, dyed hair, not like a teacher.
- Could be nice looking, hair wants perming.
- Ladylike, soignée, infuriating.
- Rather lumpy, not bad looking, Manchester accent.
- Better than usual but oh, so fat, bad legs, dark fuzzy hair. Pleasant, plain.
- Lady, v. nice, cast in left eye otherwise not bad looking. ▶

- Long face, better without hat.
- Dreary, usual, very "prism."
- Lady, not top drawer, arthritis.
- Good looking, gushing, genteel.
- Paralysed—goitre, bad breath, terrible.
- Can't read. Print address.
- Frightful false teeth.
- Very dirty (tatty).
- Illiterate.
- Good eyes, a lot of teeth & moustache. *(Woman.)*
- Duck's bottom, divided teeth, not bad looking, unpleasing.
- Dotty!!
- Common, barmaid type.
- Long horse's face. Loves herself.
- Typical spinster.
- Shy mouse, pretty in elfin way, lives SW3, likes men from the North.
- Came with one daughter, v. well behaved. Pink cheeks, awfully nice, short hair, rather tearful.
- Plumpish, red outfit, glasses (false eye hardly shows), *MBTM + (Much Better Than Most +, i.e. almost VMBTM—Very Much Better Than Most.)*
- Pretty little girl, v. neatly dressed, v. nice speaking voice, is Dutch— obviously Sinhalese.
- Leopardskin hat and scarf. Rather toothy. Sweet and friendly.
- Awful cheap scent.
- Lady, v. nice, plain.
- Tiresome bitch.
- Full of her own importance and breeding.
- Lovely eyes. Liked a Jamaican.
- Rather like a ferret, though friends of the Coxes.
- Plain, shows all her gums.
- Usual. Says she's sex-starved.
- Spotty & awful.
- Pleasant, faded.
- Not bad. Legs badly burned in Blitz.

- Typical country parson's daughter.
- Intelligent—too bloody bright.
- CAREFUL MISS J'S FRIEND.
- Silly neurotic little thing, no chin.
- Ordinary, faded, only child of old parents. *(Girl, 26.)*
- Better education than most but seems an ass.
- Scotch and rather nice-looking but bad false teeth. *(Girl, 30.)*
- No lady—but a snob! Smells like a polecat. Says she has £5,000 p.a.
- Very refeened [*sic*]. Rabbit teeth.
- Large, fat, cheerful, quite hideous.
- Nice child. Quiet. Had nervous breakdown.
- Dumpy. Plain. Nice. Dull. Neat. Plum-bottling type.
- BTM *(Better Than Most)*. Could meet better. Nice little thing, pretty (chocolate-box type).
- Shows her underteeth. Ugly, pleasant.
- Touch of the tar brush.
- BATS!
- Says she's v. highly educated, seems stupid.
- Unattractive but superior.
- V. direct. Has had insides out.
- Was staying at Claridge's with her boy-friend—likes racy!
- Lovely hair, real little cockney.
- Droop eye. Fat. Lady.
- Protruding teeth. Rather intense.
- Enormous ears. Common. Pleasant enough.
- Looks like the back of a cab.
- Dull. Goody-goody. Ordinary.
- Has her own grand piano, will inherit £40,000 when her parents die. *(She is 34.)*
- Filthy hands and badly made-up mouth.
- Paid only £1. 1s. HELL!
- Rather like Nellie Wallace. Very Baptist.
- Like a caricature of Bea Lillie.
- Scotch. Intelligent, quite attractive, not top drawer, introduced by May Carr (bitch).

Interviewers' Comments 1939–circa 1949 *(continued)*

- Lady. V. nice, rather nut-crackery, fine eyes.
- Completely early Victorian.
- At school with Heather. Like a horse.
- Was in a convent for 28 years.
- Very nice type. Had child (dead) by POW who walked out on her.
- All correspondence to be sent to Mr. W. B. *(father of 31-year-old client).*
- Coat and skirt type. Ladyish. ∾

Reading Group Questions

1. Audrey Mary Parsons changed her name to Mary Oliver and claimed to have been the debutante daughter of a parson. What might have been the reasons for her to go to such lengths to conceal her true identity?

2. A fundamental criterion of the Marriage Bureau for matching two clients was class. During World War II Great Britain's rigid class system started to crumble, largely due to the profound changes in the lives of women: they served in the armed forces, went out to work, moved away from their family homes, raised children on their own, earned money, experienced independence. How have such changes developed since the war?

3. In 1939–49 clients' requirements of their spouse were usually practical and simple, and frequently associated with money, property and reliability. Adjectives that are commonly used today, such as *attractive*, were rare. Many couples, satisfied by basic requirements, married only a few months after being introduced. Were such marriages likely to be strong?

4. Information about Mary Oliver after she left the Marriage Bureau is sparse. At some point she went to the United States, had two American husbands but no children, and died there. Heather was a very businesslike and practical person; Mary was imaginative and romantic. Given the differences in personality, what might have contributed to Mary's leaving the Bureau?

5. The Bureau always sent a letter giving brief details of a man to a woman, and only if she said she would like to meet him were her details sent to him. This procedure maintained confidentiality and privacy. Would it work today? (A propos, the names of clients in the book were changed to ensure that they would not be recognized.)

6. The Bureau operated a kind of "payment by results" scheme: a registration fee for all clients and an "After Marriage Fee" for those who married through an introduction. Most of those who married paid the AFM. Is this a good system, and could it work today?